Text Structures

Teaching Patterns in Reading and Writing

Dianne Dillabough

Education Resource Center
University of Delaware
Newark, DE 19716-2940

Text Structures

Teaching Patterns in Reading and Writing

Dianne Dillabough

Reviewers
James Coulter, Assessment Consultant
Kathleen Doyle, Advisor/Consultant
Joan Irwin, Professional Development Consultant

THOMSON
NELSON

Australia   Canada   Mexico   Singapore   Spain   United Kingdom   United States

With love to my mom and dad who have always

and continue to model life-long learning.

~ Dianne

THOMSON
NELSON

Text Structures
Teaching Patterns in Reading and Writing

by Dianne Dillabough

Director of Publishing
Kevin Martindale

General Manager, Professional Learning and Assessment
Deborah Millard

Publisher, Professional Learning and Assessment
Audrey Wearn

Executive Managing Editor, Development
Cheryl Turner

Product Manager
Jennifer White

Program Manager
Caron MacMenamin

Director of Research and Teacher In-Service
Jeanette McKenzie

Developmental Editor
Jeff Siamon

Editorial Assistant
Kirin Wright

Executive Director, Content and Media Production
Renate McCloy

Director, Content and Media Production
Lisa Dimson

Content Production Editor
Karri Yano

Copy Editor
Susan McNish

Proofreader
Monty Kersell

Production Manager
Helen Locsin

Production Coordinator
Kathrine Pummell

Design Director
Ken Phipps

Art Management
Suzanne Peden

Interior Design
Peter Papayanakis

Cover Design
Ken Phipps

Cover Image
Jasenka Lukša / iStockphoto

Compositor
Carol Magee

Printer
Webcom

Library and Archives Canada Cataloguing in Publication

Dillabough, Dianne

Text structures : teaching patterns in reading and writing / authored by Dianne Dillabough; edited by Jeff Siamon; program manager, Caron MacMenamin.

Includes bibliographical references and index.
ISBN 978-0-17-633734-6

1. English language—Study and teaching (Elementary)
2. Exposition (Rhetoric)—Study and teaching (Elementary)
3. Narration (Rhetoric)—Study and teaching (Elementary)
I. Siamon, Jeff   II. Title.

LB1576.D554 2007   372.62'3044
C2007-903764-X

TABLE OF CONTENTS

ACKNOWLEDGMENTS

The author wishes to thank the following people for their help with this book:

To the many teachers and students in the Peel District School Board who allowed me to try out my ideas in their classrooms and so willingly shared their writing samples with me.

To my **grade 4** students at Kindree Public School who enthusiastically participated in the text structure lessons and tried out the activities for the "Alternative Activities sections." Special thanks to Abbigail Butler, Sadaf Bajwa, and Maher Akhtar for allowing me to use their work.

To Jeff Simon, my editor, a special thank you for answering my many questions and patiently guiding me through each step in the creation of this book.

To my friend, Mary Wallace, for all the brainstorming sessions around her dining room table or down on the dock.

To my family for their encouragement and support.

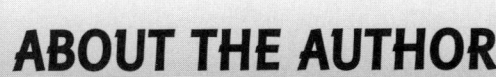

ABOUT THE AUTHOR

Dianne was born in the Northwestern Ontario town of Dryden and spent most of her childhood in Kenora, Ontario. She attended McMaster University and then went to Queen's University for her teacher's training. In her thirty years of teaching, Dianne has taught kindergarten to grade ten but finds the junior grades the most rewarding. She has taught in Ottawa, Moosonee, and Terrace, British Columbia and presently teaches for the Peel District School Board in Mississauga, Ontario.

It was while Dianne was completing her Master of Education degree at the University of Toronto that she started to research why students have difficulty with nonfiction texts and created lessons to help students understand the nonfiction text structures. Dianne has done many workshops in Ontario on the topic of Teaching Expository Text Structures to Junior and Intermediate Students and has also done workshops in other parts of Canada. Dianne received the Prime Minister's Award of Teaching Excellence – Certificate of Achievement for her work in this area. She believes strongly in offering teachers practical ideas for helping their students read and write more effectively.

Dianne presently lives in Georgetown, Ontario with her husband Steve, and daughter Karen.

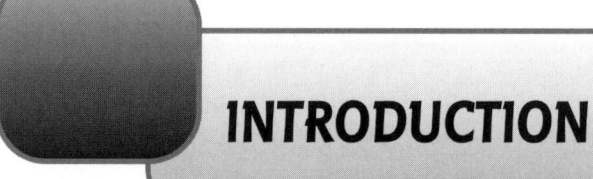

INTRODUCTION

I have found that most teachers of **grades 4 to 8** have experienced the frustration of teaching their students research skills and receiving student projects that were plagiarized versions of the books they used and that showed little or no understanding of the concepts involved. Why is this?

Englert and Hiebert (1984) and more recently Griffin & Tulbert (1995) discovered that students have much more competency with narrative text than they do with expository text. It is thought that most students possess a schema for narrative text because they have been exposed to it from a young age. This schema development may have started as early as their first year of life if the children's parents spent time reading to them. It has many opportunities to develop further in the primary grades as they listen to and learn to read stories in narrative form. In contrast, very few students seem to have a schema for expository text structure. This may be due to limited exposure to this kind of text, to the fact that expository text usually contains new and unfamiliar concepts, and to the fact that "students can't see the basic structure of the text" (Dymock 2005, 177). Simply stated, students have difficulty seeing the big picture. They read the text as a set of separate sentences and cannot see the relationships between the ideas and/or judge the importance of the ideas. Lucy McCormick Calkins (2001, 455) states it well: "Many researchers stress that in teaching children to read nonfiction, we need to help them learn to distinguish between more and less important ideas. The challenge to 'determine what is important' is also about 'determining what is unimportant.' This challenge also involves coming to understand how ideas are related to each other and how a text structures and presents ideas."

For students to become effective readers and writers, it is important that they understand that narrative and nonfiction texts have different purposes. The main purpose of narrative text is to tell a story, while nonfiction text is intended to inform, describe, or report (Moss 2004, 712). When we teach students about narrative reading and writing, we discuss the parts of the story such as the setting, characters, conflict, plot, climax, and resolution. We have students work with these concepts until they are able to apply them to the different fiction stories that they read and write. We must do the *same* for nonfiction material. We must teach students the patterns that authors use to represent ideas and information. The greater children's awareness of nonfiction text structures and organizational patterns, the better they can follow the author's message. Several researchers (Dymock and Nicholson 1999, Pearson and Duke 2002) have shown that "teaching expository [nonfiction] text structure awareness has a positive effect on reading comprehension" (Dymock 2005, 178). Dymock goes on to say that "having a clear understanding of how the text is structured will help the reader build a coherent model of the text" (ibid.).

It is important here to differentiate between **text structures** and **text features**. Both are extremely important for students to learn as they are both critical for the understanding of informational text—but they are not the same.

Text structures (or text patterns as they are sometimes called) refer to how a text is organized and the specific patterns of organization that authors use to inform, describe, and explain. *Sequence* and *compare and contrast* are two examples of text structures.

Text features, on the other hand, refer to the features that help a reader navigate through a book to locate specific information. They include

- **organizational features** such as titles, table of contents, glossary, headings, and subheadings
- **visual features** such as labels, captions, illustrations, diagrams, graphs, tables, maps, and timelines
- **graphic features** such as bold and italic words

THE EMERGENT READER

The importance of children being exposed to and working with informational text at an early age cannot be overstated. However, by **grade 4**, students are expected to be able to read informational text, even though many have not had enough exposure to it in the previous grades to be competent readers. This results in what some educators call the "fourth-grade slump" (Chall 1983, Chall, Jacobs, and Baldwin 1990). Yopp (2000, 2) states clearly that "early classroom experiences with informational texts help children build the background knowledge they would need in order to experience success with future reading materials." Until recently, it was felt that primary children could not handle such texts. However, Duke and Kays (1998) and Kamil and Lane (1997) disagree and provide evidence that young children are capable of interacting with informational text and, with opportunities presented to them, improve in their ability to interact with the text.

In the past, many primary students were only exposed to narrative text. The comprehension strategies they learned were appropriate for fiction (i.e., **character, plot, setting, etc.**). However, they were often of little use in understanding non fiction books and textbooks.

I agree with Nell Duke (2004), who believes that children should be exposed to informational text in the primary grades. She makes four recommendations.

"Teachers should:

- increase students' access to informational text
- increase the time students spend working with informational text in instructional activities
- explicitly teach comprehension strategies
- create opportunities for students to use informational text for authentic purposes" (p. 40)

One of the comprehension strategies Duke recommends is "attending to and uncovering text structure." She believes that "explicit teaching should include information about what the strategy is, when it is used, and why it is worth using" (ibid.).

I have taught sequence, enumerative, and compare and contrast text structures to **grade 3** students. After only two hours of instruction, most of the students were able to identify the structure and write a paragraph using correct signal words and format. What's more, they appeared to enjoy working with these structures.

A **grade 1** teacher at our school very successfully teaches text structure to her students. She uses graphic organizers with pictures to help students understand the signal words and does a great deal of "authentic writing." For example, when there was an unwanted mouse running free in her classroom, she had her students write a sequence paragraph about how to build a mousetrap. The students were totally engaged and did amazing work!

If children are exposed to informational text at a young age, they will be much better prepared for the material they will encounter at **grades 4 to 6**. As Duke says, "Incorporating informational text in the curriculum in the early years of school has the potential to increase student motivation, build important comprehension skills, and lay the groundwork for students to grow into confident, purposeful readers" (ibid.).

UNDERSTANDING NONFICTION TEXT

A text structure is only one element in nonfiction text. Students need to understand all of the common features of exposition in order to understand what they are reading or to clearly express what they are writing. I have found that teaching nonfiction text involves three steps; only the last is teaching text structures.

- First, I actively engage students in the use of format cues such as headings and subheadings.
- Second, I introduce the use of graphic organizers.
- Last, I teach students the different text structures with the aid of the graphic organizers.

Format Cues

I was once under the misconception that students in **grades 4 to 8** knew the reason for headings and subheadings, but when I asked two classes of **grade 6** students why the author used headings, only one student knew that headings state the main idea. Most students thought the heading was simply decorative, and some had no idea!

It became obvious to me that teaching students to obtain information from headings and subheadings would be time well spent, and I developed a very simple lesson plan:

- I put a four-paragraph report on an overhead transparency and asked students to give me the main idea of each paragraph. They struggled with this task.
- I then gave students the same paragraphs, but now they contained headings and subheadings. Again I asked them for the main idea of each paragraph. This time they quickly realized that the main idea was stated in the heading of each paragraph.
- Finally, I asked students to use what they had learned to skim through the chapters of library books and textbooks to find the main ideas using the headings as a guide.

Using Graphic Organizers

I have found in my own classroom research (Dillabough 1996) that **grades 4 to 6** and **grades 7 and 8** students are better able to understand and use text structures when instruction includes using graphic organizers. Other educators have made similar claims (Biancarosa 2005). Organizers provide a visual tool for students so that they can more easily see the relationships between the main and secondary ideas. They also give students a visual picture for organizing their written work. Dymock (2004, 178) states that "teaching students the many expository [non fiction] text structures that writers use and showing students how to organize material graphically can have a positive effect on comprehension. Demonstrating how to diagram the various expository [nonfiction] text structures enables students to 'see' how texts are constructed … and to understand and remember [them] better." Graphic organizers are also a great benefit to students when they are writing. Teele (2004, 110) has noted that teachers should "use graphic organizers and other visual tools (e.g., concept wheels, sequence-of-events chains, sound wheels, storyboards, word webs) to help students organize their thoughts before starting a writing activity."

I have also come to the conclusion that using different graphic organizers is a very important part of text structure instruction. Thus, in developing my lessons, I like to use many examples, which I have done throughout this book. The purpose is to expose students to a variety of examples of each kind of text structure so they can choose the ones that work best for them. Figure 1 illustrates some examples.

TYPICAL ORGANIZERS FOR SOME TEXT STRUCTURES

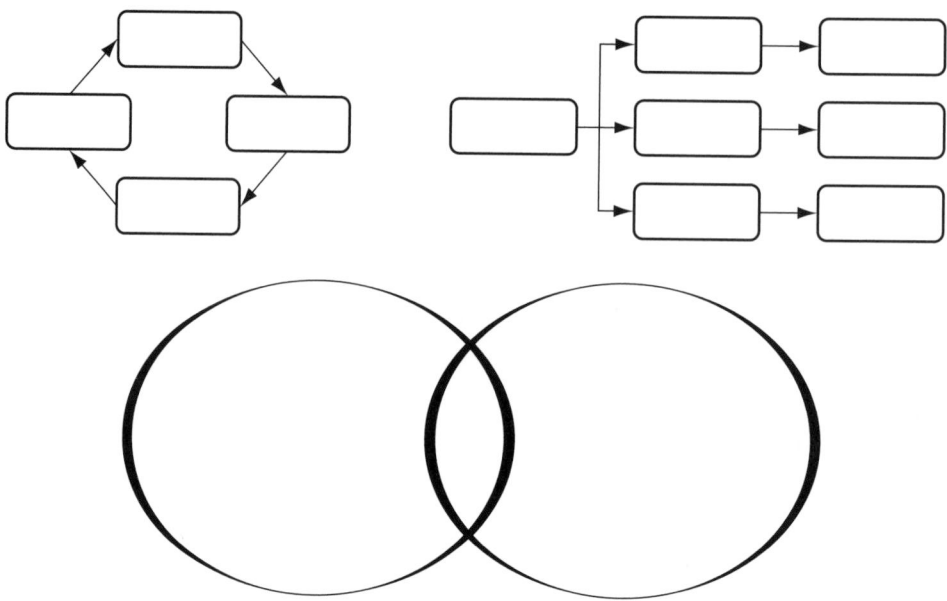

FIGURE 1

Paragraph Features

Topic Sentence

A topic sentence is usually the first sentence in a paragraph. It indicates to the reader what topic or subject will be discussed in the paragraph. It can be something very general such as "The First Nations people taught the pioneers many things." In this enumerative paragraph, the reader would expect to find out some of the things the pioneers learned from the First Nations. For the topic sentence "Let's take a close look at one of the world's most dangerous insects—the mosquito," the reader might expect a descriptive paragraph about some of the characteristics of the mosquito and what makes it so dangerous.

Clincher Sentence

Clincher Sentences—The clincher sentence is the last sentence in the paragraph. Its purpose is to sum up the contents of the paragraph. For example, a basic clincher sentence of a paragraph that has discussed the dangers of hurricanes might be "Hurricanes cause great amounts of damage." It sums up the paragraph without giving specifics. A more com-

Text Structures: Teaching Patterns in Reading and Writing

plex example for a paragraph about the attempts to decrease the problems hurricanes cause might be "It is hoped that all attempts to decrease the devastating damage and loss of life caused by hurricanes will be successful." The sentence indicates that the paragraph discussed a number of issues: the effects of hurricanes and the attempts to minimize their damage. Not all nonfiction paragraphs end in clincher sentences (e.g., magazine and newspaper articles). However, students who use clincher sentences in their writing develop a better understanding of text structures and paragraph organization.

Signal Words

Certain words in expository writing identify to the reader that a particular text structure is being used. As Maxim (1998) and Miller and George (1992) have concluded, "a knowledge of the key words that reveal a specific text structure heightens students' awareness of the structure and according to research, does transfer to students' writing of informational texts such as essays, news and magazine articles, and paragraphs" (Robb, 295). Teaching these signal words to students will help them recognize more easily the structure an author is using. For instance, words such as **because, therefore,** and **as a result** will alert students to the fact that a cause and effect relationship is probably being used.

You can teach signal words as a separate lesson or include them in a mini-lesson when teaching the text structure lesson. For example, when I was asked to go into a **grade 3** classroom to teach compare and contrast, I wondered if I should reduce the list of signal words to a few key words but decided to take in the complete list. After a short discussion of the signal words, only **whereas** was giving students difficulty. So I gave them some examples: "I like vanilla ice cream, whereas your teacher likes chocolate ice cream." "I like cake, whereas your teacher likes pie." Nearly every student used "whereas" in their paragraphs, and most students used it correctly!

The Information Report and Mini-Essay

Once students have a strong understanding of each of the text structures and can identify the various structures in longer texts, it is time to expand their writing ability by teaching them to write reports ("mini-essays") of at least three paragraphs. I have had success with these lessons in essay writing. *Chapter 7, Teaching Description Structures,* is an example of how to guide students from writing a single descriptive paragraph to creating a three-paragraph report, and finally to writing a five-paragraph mini-essay similar to the five-paragraph nonfiction essay that is taught in the later grades.

> The use of the graphic organizer in teaching the essay is critical for student success.

WHAT ARE TEXT STRUCTURES?

Because of its subject-oriented nature, informational text has a variety of text structures, unlike narrative, which basically has one (see Figure 2). Each of these structures has its own purpose and signal words; each is developed differently. I have chosen those structures that **grades 4 to 8** students are most likely to encounter and use. They are listed and outlined below, and are developed more fully in the chapters that follow.

Nonfiction Text Structures
- sequential
- enumerative
- compare and contrast
- cause and effect
- problem and solution
- question and answer
- description

THE NARRATIVE STRUCTURE

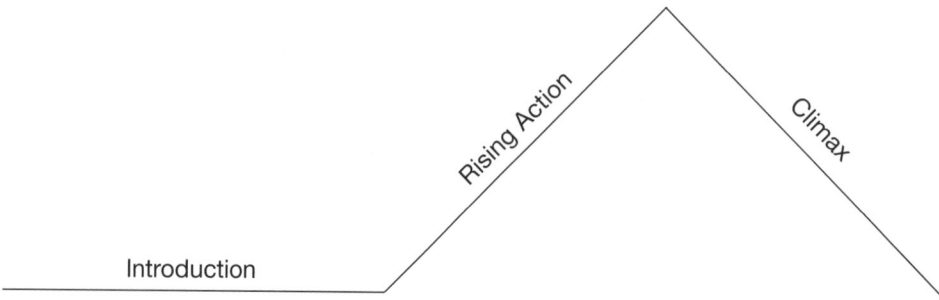

FIGURE 2

TEXT STRUCTURES

Structure	Definition	Signal Words
Sequential	A series of events is presented in temporal order (e.g., chronologically).	first, second, third, next, meanwhile, on [date], not long after, today, tomorrow, once, soon, final(ly), at last, now, before, after, while, then, later
Enumerative	The main idea is listed and supported by examples, but not necessarily in any defined order (e.g., point one is described, then point two).	first, second, third, then, also, for instance, for example, to begin with, furthermore, in addition, most important, more, next, finally, in fact, at last, another, some other
Compare and Contrast	The similarities and differences between two or more subjects are compared and contrasted.	compare, contrast, also (too), between, difference, on one hand, on the other hand, unlike, even though, more ... [than, like, etc.], similar, while, whereas, distinguish, resembles, compared to, instead of, however, but, nevertheless, unless, on the contrary, in common, both, rather, as ... [opposed to, well as, etc.], likewise, although

continued ⎯⎯⎯➔

Text Structures: Teaching Patterns in Reading and Writing

Structure	Definition	Signal Words
Cause and Effect	A cause is stated along with its possible effects, or an effect is given with its possible causes.	as a result, because, due to, this led to, nevertheless, if … then, in order that, unless, since, so that, thus, therefore, accordingly, so, consequently, another reason, some consequences are, for this reason, on account of
Problem and Solution	A problem is presented and one or more solutions are discussed.	a problem is, a solution is, the problem is solved by, propose, conclude, in conclusion, research shows, the evidence is, a/the reason for, one reason is, issues are, propose, conclude, resolved by, an outcome is, issues are, steps can be taken
Question and Answer	A question is asked about a topic, event, or concept. An answer (or answers) to the question is then given.	how, why, when, who, what, how many, where, as a result of, question, answer
Description	A topic is discussed, giving characteristics or attributes of the object, person, animal, or event.	No specific signal words are used with the description structure, but other structures are often part of the description structure; often uses sensory language

FIGURE 3

TEACHING TEXT STRUCTURES

So how do we go about teaching these structures to our students? The difficulty that many children have with informational texts is that they are not always developed with just one structure. Often informational texts combine several structures. In addition, topic sentences may be more complex than those students normally encounter. This is true for many textbooks, especially for **grades 7 to 12**. Also, paragraphs do not always conclude with clincher sentences, and signal words may be phrases rather than single words, or they may not be directly stated. Thus, I agree with Moss (2004, 173) that "each text structure should be taught individually; students need time to master one structure *before* learning another." (Italics added.) Students need to learn each text structure separately before they are able to identify when multiple structures are working together.

I have also discovered that, for many students, these structures need to be taught explicitly. Pressley (2002) and Sweet and Snow (2003) found that "skilled readers use a variety of strategies to comprehend written text" (Dymock 2005, 177). In fact, "many students will not develop these skills without the explicit teaching of comprehension strategies" (ibid.). While all students will benefit from direct teaching of expository text structures, average ability and special education students appear to benefit the most. For example, in my research, a group of special education students that received systematic instruction in expository text structures scored higher in several areas compared to a control group that did not receive text structure instruction (Dillabough 1996). Students showed the most improvement in their ability to

- pick out the main and secondary ideas when reading
- identify and leave out extraneous ideas when reading
- get information for a research assignment
- organize their writing when presenting the material they had researched

Another area that improved for the special education group was their positive attitude toward the tasks compared to the control group. They were much more focused, took less time to do their research, and showed no signs of frustration with the task.

Boys and Nonfiction

Along with average ability and special education students, many boys benefit from direct instruction of language arts skills (Booth 2002; West 2004). "Boys benefit from structured lessons that are based on clear goals and explicit expectations .... Lessons should strike a balance between being teacher-directed and student-directed" (Spence 2006, 47–48). Educators have also concluded that "boys respond best when work is assigned in bite-sized, digestible pieces and when it has a purpose they can understand" (Wilson 2003, 12). By understanding text structures, boys can learn to construct visual representations of main and supporting ideas in a text (Ministry of Education 2004).

When boys learn to focus on what they read, they are able to determine or "uncover" a text's structure and construct visual representations of a text's main and supporting ideas. The steps for teaching text structures that are discussed below, and developed in subsequent chapters, give boys who are struggling readers a "bite-sized" structured approach that they can manage.

RELINQUISHING TEACHER DIRECTION

The "scaffolding" of instruction is extremely important, and it is the basis of the lessons throughout this book. However, as Michael and Bonnie Graves (Kristo and Bamford 2004, 25) have noted, "... effective instruction often follows a progression in which teachers gradually do less of the work and students gradually do more. It is through this process of gradually assuming more responsibility for their learning that students become competent, independent learners."

Figure 4 outlines in general how I teach text structures. Specific steps are listed on page xvi. This outline follows a model of teacher to student direct instruction (scaffolding) that I have found effective.

SCAFFOLDING OF INSTRUCTION

1. Introduce and discuss the pattern, using a sample paragraph and a graphic organizer.

2. Use shared writing to create collaborative paragraphs. *Do this after the features of the pattern have been thoroughly discussed.*

3. Allow students to work in pairs to create a paragraph of the same structure.

4. Share these paragraphs with the class. This is a further check of their understanding.

5. Have students identify which signal words are used, how the topic and clincher sentences explain the paragraph, and what they have learned from the paragraph.

6. Give students the opportunity to write a paragraph independently.

7. Distribute self-assessment sheets, have students assess their own writing, and also have a peer assess it. It is critical that students be given ample opportunity to experience the structure and work with it before any assessment is done.

FIGURE 4

Important Guidelines

Together with this teaching model, there are three guidelines to keep in mind when using graphic organizers to teach text structures:

- **Use writing as an instructional technique.** If students learn to write paragraphs using the structures, they are more able to identify the structure when reading nonfiction texts.
- **Use good models.** Students need to see good models that clearly show the correct form before they read other material that may lack some of the components they have studied. I have tried to include strong examples to help you get started. Your students will provide you with many more great paragraphs after you have taught them the structures.
- **Keep instruction simple.** Use lower-level reading material to teach new concepts. If students are struggling with a paragraph's vocabulary and structure, they will not be able to concentrate on the concept you are trying to teach.

Teaching Steps

These steps will be used throughout the next seven chapters as each structure is examined independently.

1. **Define the structure.** Give students the definition of the structure they will be studying. For example, "Today we will be studying the sequence text structure. Does anyone know what the word 'sequence' means?" Have students give examples, adding a few of your own if necessary.

2. **Examine model paragraphs to identify their most important attributes.** Display several paragraphs on overhead transparencies and ask students to find the common characteristics of each. Use examples from a variety of books to help students see that they will encounter these structures in many informational sources and not just in school materials.

3. **Examine a model paragraph and its graphic organizer to identify the attributes of the organizer and how it links to the paragraph.** Display a paragraph and an organizer on the overhead. Ask students what characteristics they notice in the organizer and how the organizer and paragraph are linked.

4. **Make a graphic organizer to go with a model paragraph.** Have students read a model paragraph and fill in the organizer using point form. (*This is the beginning of students extracting the important information from a paragraph for research.*)

5. **Make a paragraph to go with a graphic organizer.** Give students a completed graphic organizer. Ask them to write a paragraph using the information. (*This is the beginning of students writing a paragraph from their jot notes during research.*)

6. **In pairs, compose an original organizer and paragraph.** After students have been exposed to many examples of the structure, have them work in pairs to compose an original organizer and paragraph.

7. **Ask each student to compose their own organizer and paragraph.** (*This can be a cumulative activity once students have had several experiences writing individual paragraphs, going through the self-and peer-assessment processes, and receiving teacher descriptive feedback.*)

8. **Read expository texts to identify the patterns.** Challenge students to search for examples in trade books, textbooks, and magazines that demonstrate the structure the class has been discussing, afterwards sharing their examples with the class. *This is a critical step.* The activity makes the connection between the writing they have been doing and their reading of expository material.

TEXT STRUCTURES IN THE CONTENT AREAS

The models in this book are "ideal" examples. In other words, they all have a topic sentence, signal words, and clincher sentence, and are in paragraph form. Once students are able to identify these features and write a "pure" form of the paragraph, they should be shown the text pattern in other forms (e.g., the steps in a science experiment might be done in a list with no clincher sentence, but students should still be able to identify the pattern as a sequence one). Most examples in textbooks are missing some of these elements but are still easily recognizable as a particular text structure.

DIFFERENTIATED INSTRUCTION OR ALTERNATIVE ACTIVITIES

Each chapter includes a section with differentiated instruction or alternative activities you can use either to teach the concept or to let students demonstrate their learning. Of course, it is important to offer students alternative approaches and learning strategies to accommodate the diversity of learning styles. For example, auditory learners respond more successfully to lessons and teaching methods that require them to listen. Visual learners "benefit from seeing graphic representations, visual models and demonstrations of skills and concepts" (Mixon 2004, 48–52). Kinesthetic learners benefit from building structures instead of listening or seeing diagrams. I have tried to accommodate all three styles of learning in the lessons and teaching strategies throughout this book. Figure 5 outlines these additional lessons.

Chapter/Text Structure	Lessons	Page Number
1 Sequence Structures	• Cut-up paragraphs • Math sequence line-ups	11
2 Enumerative Structures	• Mystery bag selections • Drama tableaux	39
3 Compare and Contrast Structures	• Photo comparison	66
4 Cause and Effect Structures	• Cause and effect strips/posters • Picture match-ups	93
5 Problem and Solution Structures	• Acting out solutions • Problem/solution game	123
6 Question and Answer Structures	• Twenty questions • What is the question?	153
7 Description Structures	• Class essay	197

FIGURE 5

TEXT STRUCTURES

One note about the order in which I teach these structures: I have found that sequence and enumerative structures are the easiest for students to understand. (I usually start with sequence structures, then do enumerative structures.) However, the order of these structures isn't really important for understanding how text structures work in informational text, and you can match the order of your lessons to the levels and abilities of your students.

Sequence Structures

- A series of events is presented in temporal order. Each event follows in some logical sequence.
- This structure is easy to learn because of children's prior experience in listening to and reading fiction stories, which are most often written in chronological order.

Enumerative Structures

- A main topic is given and supported by a list of examples or details.
- Point one is described, then point two, etc. There is no specific order in how points are listed, although the topic sentence may indicate an order.

Compare and Contrast Structures

- The similarities and/or differences between two or more subjects are compared and/or contrasted.
- Students need to be able to identify the topics or subtopics that are being compared and contrasted. The key is usually the topic sentence, which indicates the subjects to be discussed.

Cause and Effect Structures

- A cause is stated along with its possible effects, or an effect is given with its possible causes.
- These paragraphs show how facts, events, or concepts happen or come into being as a result of other facts or consequences.

Problem and Solution Structures

- Information about a problem is given. Attempts to solve the problem are discussed, and the results of the attempts to solve the problem are stated.
- The problem is usually stated in the topic sentence.

Question and Answer Structures

- A question is posed about a topic, event, concept, or idea. (Other structures might be involved depending on the question asked.)
- If the question is "What caused World War I?" then the answer would be given in a cause and effect format. If the question is "How can you show the phases of the Moon?" then the answer might be developed in a sequence format.
- Signal words often occur only in the question.

Description Structures

- Characteristics or attributes of an object, person, animal, or event are described.
- A main topic is developed by giving several subtopics related to the main topic. In a report or mini-essay form, each subtopic is usually put into a separate paragraph.
- The description structure is one of the most widely used patterns.
- The description structure does not have signal words of its own, although sensory words are frequently used. Since other text structures can be used to develop a description structure, their signal words might also be present.

LINKING ASSESSMENT TO LEARNING

Assessment is a critical component of any unit of study. Students need to be partners in their learning. They need to consistently assess their own achievement over time. They need to be able to "make dependable judgments about their own work" (Stiggins 2000, 11). Self-assessment encourages students to look critically at their own work, allowing them to make changes before the final assessment is done. "Any student who cannot evaluate the quality of his/her own writing and fix it when it isn't working cannot become an independent, lifelong writer" (ibid.). A student's self-assessment gives you an accurate view as to whether the student really understands the criteria that will be marked or assessed, as well as whether the student is able to edit or revise to reflect this understanding.

Peer feedback is also an excellent way for a teacher to see if students are understanding the task and the criteria. (However, this feedback should *not* be used for evaluation.) By critically looking at a partner's work, students become more adept at assessing their own work. The discussion that occurs between the two students as they discuss the criteria is an invaluable part of the assessment process.

I have found that students become much more involved in their learning if they have taken part in developing their own rubrics and assessment checklists. After creating such tools, students can use them to assess their work before handing it in to be marked. A student's self-assessment can help you see if the student understands the criteria well and, if not, where misunderstanding occurs. If there are substantial differences between teacher and student assessments, a conference can be used to see where the problem lies. Given the opportunity, students will become surprisingly accurate at assessing their own work. (See *Chapter 8, Monitoring and Assessing Student Work*, for a more complete discussion of assessment, as well as blackline masters assessment checklists and rubrics.)

TEACHING SEQUENCE STRUCTURES

1

DEFINING THE STRUCTURE

A sequence pattern *presents a series of events in a particular order*. For example:

- *Chronological* is the retelling of the events of a story or relating the events of a special occasion in a time sequence (a recounting).
- *Step-by-Step* are the recipe or how-to books, directions, experiments.
- *Alphabetical/Numerical Order* are the ABC books and counting books for young children.

The sequence structure is usually the one with which students are most familiar. They have likely been exposed to stories written in a time sequence from early childhood. Students who have not been exposed to fiction before attending school are usually aware of the need for some things to be done in a specific order. Getting dressed in the morning, making a sandwich, or operating a device such as a microwave or DVD player are operations that most children probably understand to be sequential.

Paragraph Features

Topic Sentence

The topic sentence in a sequence paragraph tells the reader that some topic is going to be developed sequentially. For example, "This is how you make a peanut butter sandwich" signals that the paragraph will follow some sequence. However, it is a basic **grades 4 to 6** topic sentence, and it lacks creativity and attention-catching vocabulary. A more advanced student might write, "Satisfy your chocolate cravings by following the recipe for this mouth-watering chocolate cake."

Clincher Sentence

The clincher sentence sums up the ideas in the paragraph. It can be as simple as, "These are the steps you need to follow to wash your dog" or it can be more creative and appealing such as, "Following these steps will not only give you a clean dog but will probably result in your becoming very tired and wet."

> Note that, for many examples of written directions and experiments, there are no topic or clincher sentences. Instead, there might be headings (e.g., for a science experiment: purpose, observations, etc) or the information might be numbered to indicate order.

However, it is important for students to realize that clincher sentences are not always found in "real-world" examples of nonfiction writing. For example, textbook writers often use clincher sentences at the end of sections rather than at the end of each paragraph.

Signal Words

Sequence signal words are words that indicate an order or time in which something is to happen. For example, **first, second, third, next, now, after,** and **then** clearly explain which event comes before or after another. A word such as **meanwhile** indicates to the reader that two things are happening at the same time (e.g., "Meanwhile, back at the barn, the animals were getting restless"). Words such as **today, tomorrow,** and **on** [date] indicate that something is happening within a specific time frame.

Grades 4 to 8 Classrooms

When teaching the sequence structure to **grades 4 to 6** students, I like to keep the explanation and the lessons simple. I expect students to be able to write a paragraph with the correct topic sentence, clincher sentence, and signal words. Students at this level often use signal words such as **first, second, next, after,** and **finally.** After they have had more practice with the structure, encourage students to use more descriptive signal words such as **meanwhile, not long after, to begin with** and **following this.**

Grades 4 to 6 students may need very structured lessons when first introduced to sequence structures. They should also be given many opportunities to write in pairs or small groups so they become familiar with the concept of the structure before being asked to write a paragraph independently. As well, students need to be exposed to some of the easier forms of the sequence structures found in their textbooks. They should be able to identify sequence structures such as the life cycle of a frog or the major events of a story.

Grades 7 and 8 students will likely have had a lot of exposure to the sequence structure. If this is evident, then the review of the structure can be fairly brief. Their paragraphs should be more complex, not only in terms of grade-appropriate language but also concept development. The topic and clincher sentences should be stronger and more interesting than those used by **grades 4 to 6** students. Signal words, other than the ones listed above, should also be used (such as **preceding** and **initially**).

It is crucial in **grades 6 through 8** that students be exposed to the many different types of sequence structures commonly found in nonfiction texts. For example, students are likely to encounter sequence structure paragraphs with bulleted or numbered lists as well as paragraph examples with which they might be more familiar. They might also come across introductory paragraphs in nonfiction articles and textbooks that outline steps that are later described under subheadings. **Grades 7 and 8** students need to become familiar with these non-paragraph types of sequence structures.

SIGNAL WORDS FOR SEQUENCE STRUCTURES	
first	once
second	soon
third	final(ly)
next	at last
meanwhile	now
on (date)	before
not long after	after
	while
today	then
tomorrow	later

Additional Instructional Support

From my personal experience, I have found that the English Language Learners (ELL) and special education students benefit a great deal from the structured lessons that are included in this book. The structure gives them a format to follow, while the format models how to approach the task or lesson. For example, when these students begin to write their own paragraphs, I find a fill in the blanks format is helpful. The blanks lead students through the sequence without requiring them to develop the paragraph on their own. Figure 1.1 is one example with the text structure elements highlighted.

Our Class Trip to the Zoo

On our class trip to the zoo, we had many exciting activities. ← topic sentence
The first thing we did was _____. The second activity was _____. After that, signal words
we _____. Finally, we
_____. We had a great time doing all those ← clincher sentence
activities.

FIGURE 1.1

The same can be said for using predefined organizers, which I do in each lesson. As students become more comfortable with the sequence pattern, they can take more responsibility for choosing organizers, eventually creating organizers of their own.

INTRODUCING THE STRUCTURE

Step 1: Start by asking students what the word "sequence" means. Encourage them to give examples. If students are having difficulty explaining the meaning of the word or its concept, try asking them questions to elicit some responses. For example:

- What does *order* have to do with the *sequence* of things?
- In what order do you do things in the morning? Do you go to school before you put on your school clothes and have breakfast?
- Why is the order or sequence of events important?

Step 2: Brainstorm with students some sequence situations or events, such as following a recipe, playing board and card games, or cleaning their rooms. Choose several examples and have students identify these sequences. The following are some examples of sequence situations.

WHAT TO DO WHEN THE FIRE ALARM GOES OFF

To prompt students' thinking about the steps involved, ask questions and write the answers on the board:

- What is the first thing you do if you hear the fire alarm? *(One student closes the windows while everyone else lines up at the door.)*
- Once you are lined up, what would be the next step? *(Walk quietly down the hall and out the door.)*
- Now that you are outside, what do you have to do next? *(Line up quietly in alphabetical order on the grass away from the building.)*
- While we are getting into line, what do the runners do? *(Get the attendance from the secretaries who are waiting by the basketball hoops.)*
- What does the teacher do next? *(Takes attendance to make sure everyone is out safely.)*
- The next thing that is done is … ? *(The runners take the attendance back and say, "Everyone is here.")*
- What is the final step of the fire drill? *(When the bell rings, walk quietly back into the school.)*

HOW TO SIGN OUT A BOOK FROM THE LIBRARY

I like to have students work in small groups to list the steps. You might want to have one group share their results while the other groups check that group's list against their own steps, sharing any steps that the first group may have missed.

Once students understand that the sequence structure involves steps or an order, you can continue by examining model paragraphs as well as looking at topic and clincher sentences.

EXAMINING A MODEL PARAGRAPH

Introduce the Model

Step 1: Project on an overhead transparency or distribute to the class a sequence paragraph. BLM 1.1, "Charlie's Bath," is an example.

Identify Paragraph Elements

Step 2: Ask students to read the paragraph, identify the topic and clincher sentences, and circle the signal words. A marked-up example is shown in Figure 1.2.

Text Structures: Teaching Patterns in Reading and Writing

Charlie's Bath

<u>Washing our dog, Charlie, is a challenge.</u> [First,] he sees the   ←   **topic sentence**
tub and hose and runs away. [Then] we have to catch him and
drag him over to the tub. Our [next] job is to put Charlie into
the tub. That's not an easy task because he braces himself
with all four legs and refuses to move. [Once] he is in the tub,   **signal words**
things don't get any easier. We have to hold him tightly as we
lather him with dog shampoo and give him a good scrub.
[After] we're *all* covered in shampoo, we rinse him off with the
hose. [While] he wriggles and twists, we put conditioner on
him, wait a few minutes, and rinse it off. [At last] we let him out
of the tub, and he shakes himself dry, wetting everyone. Our
[final] challenge is to keep him clean long enough to get him
inside the house. <u>Giving Charlie a bath is a lot of fun but is</u>   ←   **clincher sentence**
<u>also very tiring.</u>

FIGURE 1.2   BLM 1.1

Share and Discuss

Step 3: As a class, discuss students' choices and why this paragraph has a sequential structure.

DEVELOPING A GRAPHIC ORGANIZER

Introduce the Model

Step 1: To help students understand the relationship between a sequence paragraph and its graphic organizer, provide them with a paragraph together with a completed graphic organizer. (Figures 1.3 and 1.4, BLM 1.2, "Catching a Lake Fish" is one example.) When you introduce the graphic organizer for the model paragraph, point out to students that the organizer shows the organization of the paragraph in point form—in this example, the steps or sequence of catching a lake fish. Discuss with students how the organizer matches the sequence of the paragraph.

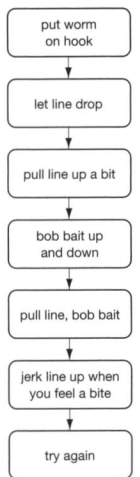

FIGURE 1.3

Catching a Lake Fish

There are a number of things you have to do to catch a lake fish. First, put the worm or other bait securely on the hook. Then, let your line drop to the bottom of the lake. Next, pull the line up a little and wait for a bite. After not getting any bites for a while, bob the bait up and down. If that doesn't work, pull on the line and bob the bait up and down some more. Finally, when you feel a bite, jerk your line up. Hopefully, you've caught a fish! If you haven't, try the whole process again.

FIGURE 1.4   BLM 1.2

Identify Paragraph Elements

Step 2: Have students work in pairs to underline the topic and clincher sentences and circle the signal words. A marked-up example is shown in Figure 1.5.

Catching a Lake Fish

topic sentence ⟶ <u>There are a number of things you have to do to catch a lake fish.</u> First, put the worm or other bait securely on the hook. Then, let your line drop to the bottom of the lake. Next, pull the line up a little and wait for a bite. After not getting any bites for a while, bob the bait up and down. If that doesn't work, pull on the line and bob the bait up and down some more. Finally, when you feel a bite, jerk your line up. Hopefully, you've caught a fish! <u>If you haven't, try the whole process again.</u>

signal words

clincher sentence

FIGURE 1.5

Share and Discuss

Step 3: As a class, compare the model graphic organizer to the written paragraph:

- Is the order the same? Should the order be the same?

Text Structures: Teaching Patterns in Reading and Writing

- Has anything been left out of the paragraph that was included in the organizer?
- Do the signal words help tie the paragraph together? How?

Create the Graphic Organizer

Step 4: Give students another paragraph and have them complete their own graphic organizer. See BLM 1.3, "King Salmon Life Cycle," which includes a blank organizer that students can use. A marked-up example of this paragraph is shown in Figure 1.6.

Step 5: It is important for students to realize that there are not necessarily signal words for each part of the organizer. Remind them, too, that the organizer uses point form—not full sentences—to show the sequence of the paragraph.

King Salmon Life Cycle

There are many stages in the life cycle of the king salmon. ← topic sentence
First, they hatch in cold mountain streams. Then, as young fish, or fingerlings, they begin a long swim downstream to larger streams and rivers. Months later, the young fish reach the Pacific Ocean. After three or four years, the adult salmon begin their trip back to the stream where they were born. They face many hazards on their journey: currents, rapids, grizzly bears, eagles, and humans. When they get to the stream of their birth, the females finally lay their eggs, which are then fertilized by the males. Not long after, the adults die. Their life cycle is over, but another one will soon begin. ← clincher sentence

signal words

FIGURE 1.6 BLM 1.3

Share and Discuss

Step 6: Finally, on an overhead transparency, use descriptive feedback from students to fill in a class organizer. Have them compare their organizers with the class organizer. Figure 1.7 is an example of a completed organizer.

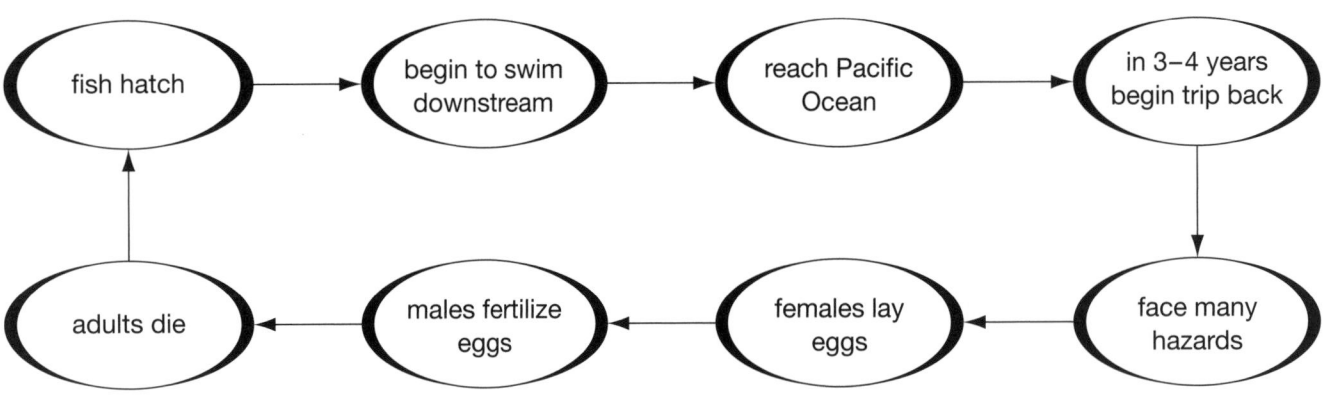

KING SALMON LIFE CYCLE

FIGURE 1.7

WRITING A SEQUENCE PARAGRAPH

Use a Graphic Organizer

Step 1: Students can work in pairs to develop a paragraph based on a given organizer. Figure 1.8, BLM 1.4, is one example. Encourage them first to think about what signal words they will use. Remind them, as well, that their topic sentences need to reflect the type of text structure of their paragraphs. For example, for "How to Make a Sundae," the topic sentence, "Sundaes are my favourite dessert" has little to do with making a sundae. (Note that students may be unfamiliar with this type of organizer. Encourage them to see that there are different types of organizers they can use.)

HOW TO MAKE A SUNDAE

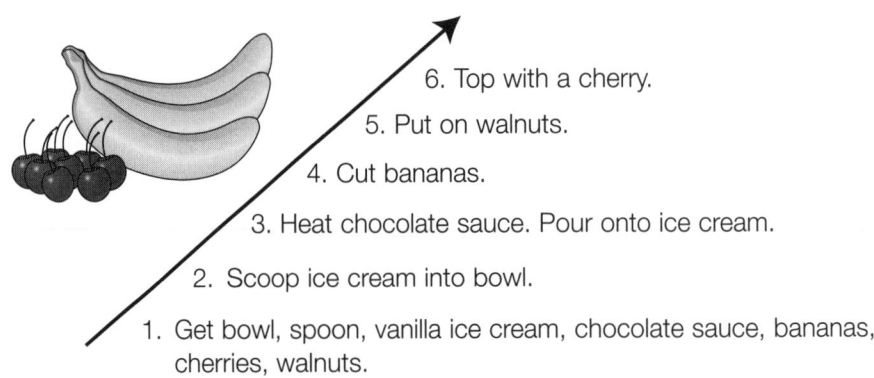

6. Top with a cherry.

5. Put on walnuts.

4. Cut bananas.

3. Heat chocolate sauce. Pour onto ice cream.

2. Scoop ice cream into bowl.

1. Get bowl, spoon, vanilla ice cream, chocolate sauce, bananas, cherries, walnuts.

FIGURE 1.8 BLM 1.4

Step 2: After they have written their paragraphs, ask students to identify their topic sentence, signal words, and clincher sentence. Figure 1.9 is an example of a paragraph based on the "How to Make a Sundae" organizer.

Text Structures: Teaching Patterns in Reading and Writing

How to Make a Sundae

If you want a dessert that's more delicious than you can possibly imagine, follow this simple recipe. First, you will need a bowl, a spoon, vanilla ice cream, chocolate sauce, bananas, cherries, and walnuts. Second, using the spoon, scoop two large scoops of ice cream into the bowl. Next, heat up the chocolate sauce and pour it on top of the ice cream. Then cut the banana into slices and heap them onto the ice cream. Spread walnuts all over the top of the ice cream and top it with a cherry. Finally, pour a bit more chocolate sauce over all of it. Get ready for the most mouth-watering ice cream sundae ever!

topic sentence

signal words

clincher sentence

FIGURE 1.9

Share and Discuss

Step 3: Distribute or display examples of sequence paragraphs to the class (or use a paragraph of your own). After each example, discuss whether

- the paragraph has a suitable topic sentence
- the signal words are appropriate for a sequence paragraph
- the clincher sentence reflects the topic sentence

COMPOSING THEIR OWN PARAGRAPHS

Once students have written jot notes from their paragraphs to make their organizers, and have developed paragraphs from their organizers, have them write their own paragraphs for the sequence structure.

Step 1: Brainstorm topics with the class, writing them on the board or an overhead transparency.

Step 2: Have students work in pairs to select a topic, or invite them to make up a topic of their own. (I have found that, when students write their first original sequence paragraphs, working in pairs is very successful. Students tend to take more risks when working with a partner.)

Step 3: After they have chosen their topics, students can list the steps or sequences that are appropriate and then use their lists to create their organizers and paragraphs. Remind them, when they are writing their paragraphs, to follow the order of their organizers.

Step 4: Finally, have students create their own graphic organizers and sequence paragraphs on a topic of their choosing.

Share and Discuss

Step 5: Have students search for examples of sequence text structures in textbooks, nonfiction books, and magazine articles. Encourage them to compare these examples with the ones they have written and studied. (See *Sequence Structures in the Content Areas*, which follows.)

DIFFERENTIATED INSTRUCTION

In every classroom, there are students who dislike writing or who, for a variety of reasons, have difficulty putting words to paper. Here are some other types of activities that may be successful with these students.

Cut-up Paragraphs

This activity allows teachers to see if students understand the format of a sequence paragraph, but students need not do any writing. I prefer having students work in small groups to allow for rich discussions. However, if you want to know if individual students understand the concept, then they can do the activity independently.

1. Students are given a paragraph written as individual sentences. Each sentence is put onto a separate strip of paper with the signal words missing. The signal words are written on their own pieces of paper. I copy the sentences onto white paper and the signal words onto coloured paper, cutting each up.

2. I ask students to put together the sentences to form a proper paragraph and to include the appropriate signal words. An example on the life cycle of a butterfly is provided by Figures 1.10 and 1.11. BLM 1.5 includes the individual sentences as well as the signal words.

   You might want to review signal words with students. For example, some signal words, such as **next** and **after**, can go in any order in the paragraph, while others, such as **first** and **finally**, have only one correct place in a paragraph.

The following is a cut-up paragraph, including signal words, for "The Life Cycle of a Butterfly."

The Life Cycle of a Butterfly

This stage is called a pupa.

The larva hatches from the egg and is known as a caterpillar.

A butterfly has four stages in its life cycle.

The adult butterfly comes out of the case and waits for its wings to dry so it can fly away, and the cycle begins again.

The adult female butterfly lays her eggs on a plant.

The metamorphosis, or change from a caterpillar to a butterfly, is one of nature's miracles.

The caterpillar makes a case, or chrysalis, around itself for protection as it changes into a butterfly.

Life Cycle Signal Words

first

finally

afterwards

next

FIGURE 1.10

FIGURE 1.10   BLM 1.5

3. As students share their assembled paragraphs with the class, ask groups to compare their paragraphs. If there are differences, have groups tell why they chose the order they did. However, students should realize that there is only *one* correct way for the sentences to be arranged, even though some signal words could go in several different spots.

Figure 1.11 is an example of a paragraph based on "The Life Cycle of a Butterfly."

The Life Cycle of a Butterfly

topic sentence →

A butterfly has four stages in its life cycle. First, the adult female butterfly lays her eggs on a plant. Next, the larva hatches from the egg and is known as a caterpillar. Afterwards, the caterpillar makes a case, or chrysalis, around itself for protection as it changes into a butterfly. This stage is called the pupa. Finally, the adult butterfly comes out of the case and waits for its wings to dry so it can fly away, and the cycle begins again. The metamorphosis, or change from a caterpillar to a butterfly, is one of nature's miracles.

signal words

clincher sentence →

FIGURE 1.11 BLM 1.6

4. Once students understand the correct sentence order for a paragraph, ask them to write one on their own, or with a partner or group. They can cut up the paragraph into individual sentences and paste them onto separate pieces of paper along with suitable signal words. Have students exchange their cut-up paragraphs with another student or group, who will piece it back together. This activity gives descriptive feedback to the students who wrote the paragraph by answering the questions, "Is it a sequence paragraph, and does it makes sense?" It also shows you which students or groups understand the structure well enough to put a paragraph together correctly.

Sequence Lines

1. Have students line up according to their birthdays. This activity shows you which students understand how to put things in an order or sequence.

2. For a math-based line-up activity, you might want to try the following:
   - Give all but five students a decimal or fraction on a card (e.g., 3.1, $2\frac{1}{2}$, 2.6, $2\frac{3}{4}$).
   - The other five students receive a card with a signal word on it (e.g., **first, next, after, then, finally**).
   - Students must arrange themselves in a sequence according to the size of the decimal or fraction.

- The five students with signal words put themselves in appropriate positions along the line. For example, the student with the signal word **first** would place himself or herself at the beginning of the line. A student with the word **next** might go between the fourth and fifth student or any other reasonable place for that signal word. If a student has the signal word **finally,** he or she would be positioned just before the last decimal or fraction.

SUGGESTED CROSS-CURRICULAR TOPICS

Below is a list of topics that involve a sequence and could be used for any of the activities discussed.

Social Studies
- Timeline of medieval times
- The steps in a voting procedure
- How a castle is built
- The order of provinces from east to west or west to east
- The physical regions of Canada

Science
- The life cycle of animals or plants
- The water cycle
- How clouds are made
- How a tornado is formed
- The digestive process
- The rock cycle

Math
- The steps to solve a multiplication or division problem
- The steps involved in problem solving
- Putting numbers in order according to size
- How to find the area of a rectangle

Arts
- The steps involved in doing any arts activity

Physical Education and Health
- How to play a game
- The steps involved in a sports activity (e.g., hitting a badminton shuttlecock or making a layup in basketball)
- The steps involved in buying a bicycle helmet for safe cycling

Language Arts
- Putting the events of a story in order
- Writing instructions on how to do something (e.g., make a cake)

SEQUENCE STRUCTURES IN THE CONTENT AREAS

There are many examples of the sequence structure in textbooks and trade books, but they are not necessarily found in their "pure" form. Often there is a one or two-sentence introduction, and then the sequence is indicated by numbering, bullets, or a combination of both.

Figure 1.12, BLM 1.7, is a good example of paragraph sequence structures found in a **grade 7** science text. The first paragraph introduces the topic, the second and third paragraphs describe the sequence for a fossil to form, and the last sentence of the third paragraph is the clincher sentence. Signal words such as **suddenly, gradually, as** [the layer], **eventually,** and **final** are used.

How Fossils Form

topic sentence ⟶ Fossils are rocklike casts, impressions, or actual remains of organisms that were buried after they died, before they could decompose. Only a tiny fraction of organisms are preserved as fossils. This is because most dead organisms decay or are eaten by scavenging animals. Also, soft tissue, such as muscle and organs, does not fossilize well. Animals that have neither bones nor shells will not leave fossils.

signal words — An organism that is suddenly buried—for example, if it falls into mud or quicksand, or is covered quickly by a landslide of sediment or blowing volcanic ash—may become a fossil. As the layer that contains the organism is covered by other layers of sediment, it gradually becomes sedimentary rock.

As wet sediment becomes rock, minerals that are dissolved in the water gradually replace minerals in the body of any buried organisms. Bone, shell, and parts of plants can all be replaced this way. Eventually, particle by particle, the

clincher sentence ⟶ fossilizing organism is replaced by minerals. The final result is a fossil that looks exactly like the original organism but is in a rocklike form.

B. Ritter, *Nelson Science & Technology 7* (Toronto: Nelson), 2000, 224.

FIGURE 1.12   BLM 1.7

It is important that students be able to identify the sequence structure in its various forms. (See BLMs 1.8 to 1.11 for additional model paragraphs.) As you come across examples in content subject areas, take the time to point them out to students so they begin to make the connection between what they are learning in language arts and what they are learning in other subjects. When you see a student using a text structure paragraph in another subject area without being prompted to do so, celebrate! The student has internalized the use of the structure and can apply it when appropriate. Point out this student's success to the other students so they begin to see the connection as well.

LINKING ASSESSMENT TO LEARNING

The most important traits to focus on for the sequence structure will be *organization* and *ideas*. The organization criteria will include having a topic sentence, clincher sentence, and signal words. The criteria for ideas will include staying on topic and explaining each step clearly.

Students need to set specific criteria to benefit from assessing their work. Ideally, students should help to develop the criteria, because this gives them a more thorough understanding of what they need to know and what is expected of them. (See *Chapter 8, Monitoring and Assessing Student Work*.) At the beginning of the year, **grades 4 to 6** students might suggest criteria such as neat writing, proper capitalization and punctuation (e.g., using periods correctly), and no spelling mistakes. I encourage them to be more specific by asking them questions such as the following:

- How many different signal words do you think we should use? (Three or more is a great start.)
- What is important about the topic sentence? (It tells what the paragraph will be about.)

Once they have had the experience of looking at a number of sequence paragraphs, I have students add a few more important items to their criteria. For example:

- having the steps in the paragraph in a proper sequence
- including the details for each step in a sequence paragraph (**grades 4 to 6** and **grades 7 and 8**) or for each topic that is developed in subsequent paragraphs
- realizing that all the details in the paragraph have to be connected to the topic sentence

Don't panic! It takes **grades 4 to 6** students most of the year to get to this point. **Grades 7 and 8** students should be aware of the important criteria much earlier in the year if they have been exposed to the various structures in the earlier grades. But because participating in choosing the criteria for assessment is often a new experience for students, it does take time.

Traits "are the characteristics or qualities that define good writing" (Trehearne, 2006, 230). These include
- ideas presented
- word choice
- voice (the personality of the writer)
- language conventions (grammar, spelling, etc.)
- sentence fluency (using sentences that make sense and vary in length and structure)

Use read-alouds to point out strong examples that fit the criteria. Also, have students assess various examples of writing before they write and assess their own work. Giving them strong examples will help them see the qualities of good writing.

Student Self-Assessment Checklist for Sequence Structures

Name: _____ Date: _____

Organization		
My graphic organizer fits with my sequence paragraph.	Yes	No
I have a topic sentence.	Yes	No
I have a clincher sentence.	Yes	No

Word Choice		
I used sequence signal words.	Yes	No
I used _____ different sequence signal words. (number)		

Ideas and Content		
My topic sentence: • tells the reader that the topic will be discussed in a specific order. • catches the reader's attention.	Yes Yes	No No
My clincher sentence ties the ideas of my paragraph together.	Yes	No
The supporting sentences in my paragraph describe the steps involved in the sequence.	Yes	No

The strengths in my sequence paragraph include:

The areas that need improvement in my sequence paragraph include:

My goal for future writing is:

Peer Feedback Checklist for Sequence Structures

Author: _____ Peer Editor: _____ Date: _____

Organization		
The graphic organizer fits with the sequence paragraph.	Yes	No
There is a topic sentence.	Yes	No
There is a clincher sentence.	Yes	No

Word Choice		
Sequence signal words were used.	Yes	No
_____ different sequence signal words were used. (number)		

Ideas and Content		
The topic sentence: • tells the reader that the topic will be discussed in a specific order. • catches the reader's attention.	Yes Yes	No No
The clincher sentence ties the ideas of the paragraph together.	Yes	No
The supporting sentences in the paragraph describe the steps involved in the sequence.	Yes	No

The strengths in the sequence paragraph include:

The areas that need improvement in the sequence paragraph include:

My suggested goal for the writer is:

Assessment Rubric for Sequence Structures

Name: _____ Date: _____

	Level 1	Level 2	Level 3	Level 4
Graphic Organizer	Organizer is incomplete and/or does not fit the sequence structure.	Organizer is fairly complete, may have minor errors; indicates a sequence structure is being used.	Organizer is complete; clearly indicate a sequence structure is being used.	Organizer is clearly complete; indicates a sequence structure is being used and is of original design.
Topic Sentence	Weak topic sentence; doesn't indicate that a sequence will be given.	Topic sentence evident, a basic format is used; some indication that a sequence will be given.	Topic sentence indicates that a sequence will be given; captures the reader's attention.	Topic sentence clearly states that a sequence will be given; captures the imagination of the reader.
Signal Words	Sequence signal words are used improperly.	Some sequence signal words used; not always used correctly.	Effective use of sequence signal words.	Effective use of advanced sequence signal words.
Clincher	Weak clincher sentence; no connecting of ideas.	Clincher sentence evident, basic format.	Good clincher sentence, sums up ideas in paragraph.	Strong clincher sentence, ties ideas together well.
Body Sentences	Few points link to the main idea; no supporting details describe the sequence.	Some points link to the main idea; a few supporting details describe the sequence.	All points link to the main idea; supporting details describe the sequence.	All points link to the main idea and have supporting details that clearly describe the sequence.
Understanding of Structure	Shows little understanding of the sequence structure.	Shows some understanding of the sequence structure.	Shows a considerable understanding of the sequence structure.	Shows a thorough understanding of the sequence structure.

To move to the next level, I must ...

Assessment Checklists

As students fill out the sequence peer feedback and self-assessment checklists, it is important that you circulate and ask questions about their assessment. Some students will indicate "yes" without really examining the criteria carefully. For this reason, I not only ask if there is a topic sentence but if the topic sentence catches the reader's attention. This makes the student stop and think about the topic sentence and its effectiveness. I do the same for the signal words. I ask students if the words have been used and also have students indicate how many different words are used. This task helps the students who overuse **then** throughout the paragraphs, encouraging them to go back to their paragraphs and consider using different signal words.

Discussing the self-assessment checklists with students should help you assess their understanding of the structure and indicate where they need to go next. Mini-lessons can then be set up for those students requiring further assistance in particular areas such as

- creating strong topic sentences
- using a variety of sequence signal words
- ensuring that the ideas are clearly stated
- completing the paragraph with a strong clincher sentence

For example, to help students create strong topic sentences, you might

- give students examples of strong topic sentences from sequence paragraphs
- show students a paragraph *without* a topic sentence and have them create a topic sentence for the paragraph
- present as many examples as you find necessary to help students understand what a strong topic sentence looks like and how it points the way for the rest of the paragraph

Assessment Rubrics

The rubric is used for assessment only after students are very familiar with the structure and have had many opportunities to work with the peer and self-assessment checklists. When they write the paragraphs that I will assess, I have them use the rubric for self-assessment so they have the opportunity to revise what they have written before they hand it in. I then mark the paragraph using the same rubric. It quickly shows me who understands the criteria and, more importantly, who can apply the criteria to their own work.

The bottom section of the peer and self-assessment checklists is the most important for students to complete. (See Figure 1.13 for a typical student response. My comments are in italics.) It is only through reviewing this part of the checklist that you will know for sure if students have a thorough understanding of the criteria used, what strengths they have, and what areas still require improvement. Given the opportunity to assess their work, students will take much more interest in their own writing.

To move to the next level, I must...

... try to write a topic sentence that catches the reader's attention. I also need to use different signal words instead of **first**, **next**, **finally**.

*(Try to encourage your students to give more detail, such as, "I will try to use **meanwhile**, **to begin with**, and **not long after**," instead of "I will use different signal words.")*

Students complete the bottom of the rubric after it is returned to them.

FIGURE 1.13

Identifying Text Structures: Reading Like a Writer

When students are comfortable writing the text structure, it is important they make the connection between what they write and what they read. They should now be able to identify the structure when they encounter it in their textbooks and library books. I use BLM 8.23, Checklist for Identifying Text Structure Criteria, to track their progress in identifying structures in content areas.

BLM 8.23

Checklist for Identifying Text Structure Criteria

Name: _____   Date: _____

	Sequence	Enumerative	Compare and Contrast	Cause and Effect	Problem and Solution	Question and Answer	Description
Is able to identify the structure when it is in its basic form in an individual paragraph.							
Is able to identify the characteristics of the structures when reading textbooks and trade books (signal words, topic sentence, clincher sentence, etc.).							

FIGURE 1.14   BLM 8.23

1   Teaching Sequence Structures

Blackline Masters

Name: _____ Date: _____

Read the paragraph, underline the topic and clincher sentences, and circle the signal words.

Charlie's Bath

Washing our dog, Charlie, is a challenge. First, he sees the tub and hose and runs away. Then we have to catch him and drag him over to the tub. Our next job is to put Charlie into the tub. That's not an easy task because he braces himself with all four legs and refuses to move. Once he is in the tub, things don't get any easier. We have to hold him tightly as we lather him with dog shampoo and give him a good scrub. After we're *all* covered in shampoo, we rinse him off with the hose. While he wriggles and twists, we put conditioner on him, wait a few minutes, and rinse it off. At last we let him out of the tub, and he shakes himself dry, wetting everyone. Our final challenge is to keep him clean long enough to get him inside the house. Giving Charlie a bath is a lot of fun but is also very tiring.

Name: _____ Date: _____

Read the paragraph, underline the topic and clincher sentences, and circle the signal words.

Catching a Lake Fish

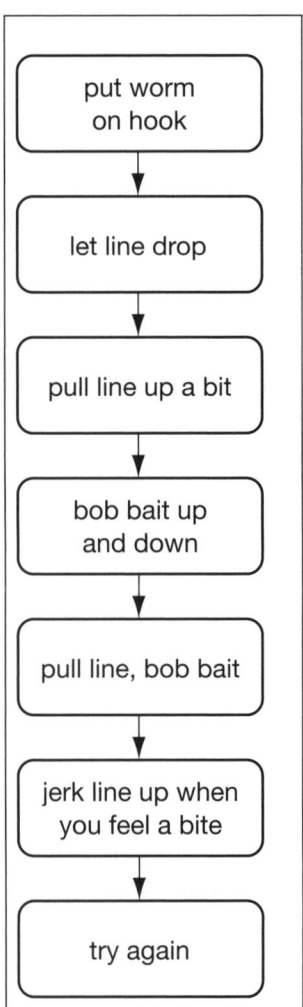

There are a number of things you have to do to catch a lake fish. First, put the worm or other bait securely on the hook. Then, let your line drop to the bottom of the lake. Next, pull the line up a little and wait for a bite. After not getting any bites for a while, bob the bait up and down. If that doesn't work, pull on the line and bob the bait up and down some more. Finally, when you feel a bite, jerk your line up. Hopefully, you've caught a fish! If you haven't, try the whole process again.

Name: _____   Date: _____

Read the paragraph, underline the topic and clincher sentences, and circle the signal words. Then fill out the organizer for the paragraph. Remember to use point form, not full sentences, to fill in the organizer.

King Salmon Life Cycle

There are many stages in the life cycle of the king salmon. First, they hatch in cold mountain streams. Then, as young fish, or fingerlings, they begin a long swim downstream to larger streams and rivers. Months later, the young fish reach the Pacific Ocean. After three or four years, the adult salmon begin their trip back to the stream where they were born. They face many hazards on their journey: currents, rapids, grizzly bears, eagles, and humans. When they get to the stream of their birth, the females finally lay their eggs, which are then fertilized by the males. Not long after, the adults die. Their life cycle is over, but another one will soon begin.

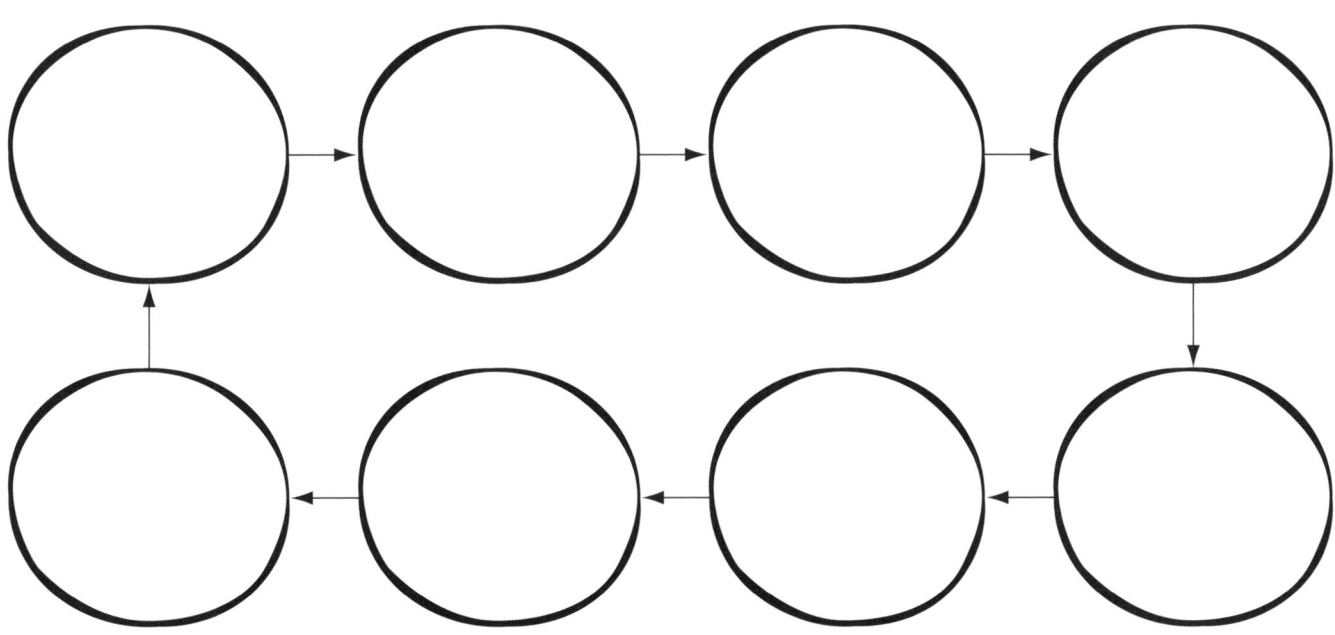

Name: _____ Date: _____

From this graphic organizer, write a paragraph. Then underline the topic and clincher sentences, and circle the signal words.

How to Make a Sundae

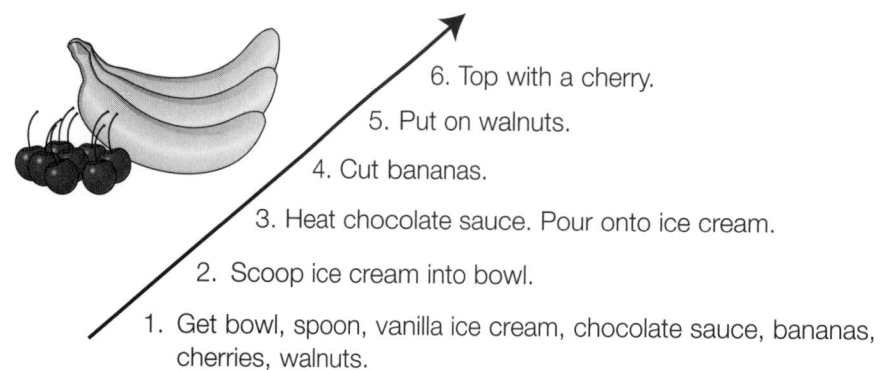

6. Top with a cherry.

5. Put on walnuts.

4. Cut bananas.

3. Heat chocolate sauce. Pour onto ice cream.

2. Scoop ice cream into bowl.

1. Get bowl, spoon, vanilla ice cream, chocolate sauce, bananas, cherries, walnuts.

Name: _____ Date: _____

Cut out each sentence and signal words onto separate strips of paper. Then put together the sentences to form a proper paragraph. Include the signal words.

The Life Cycle of a Butterfly

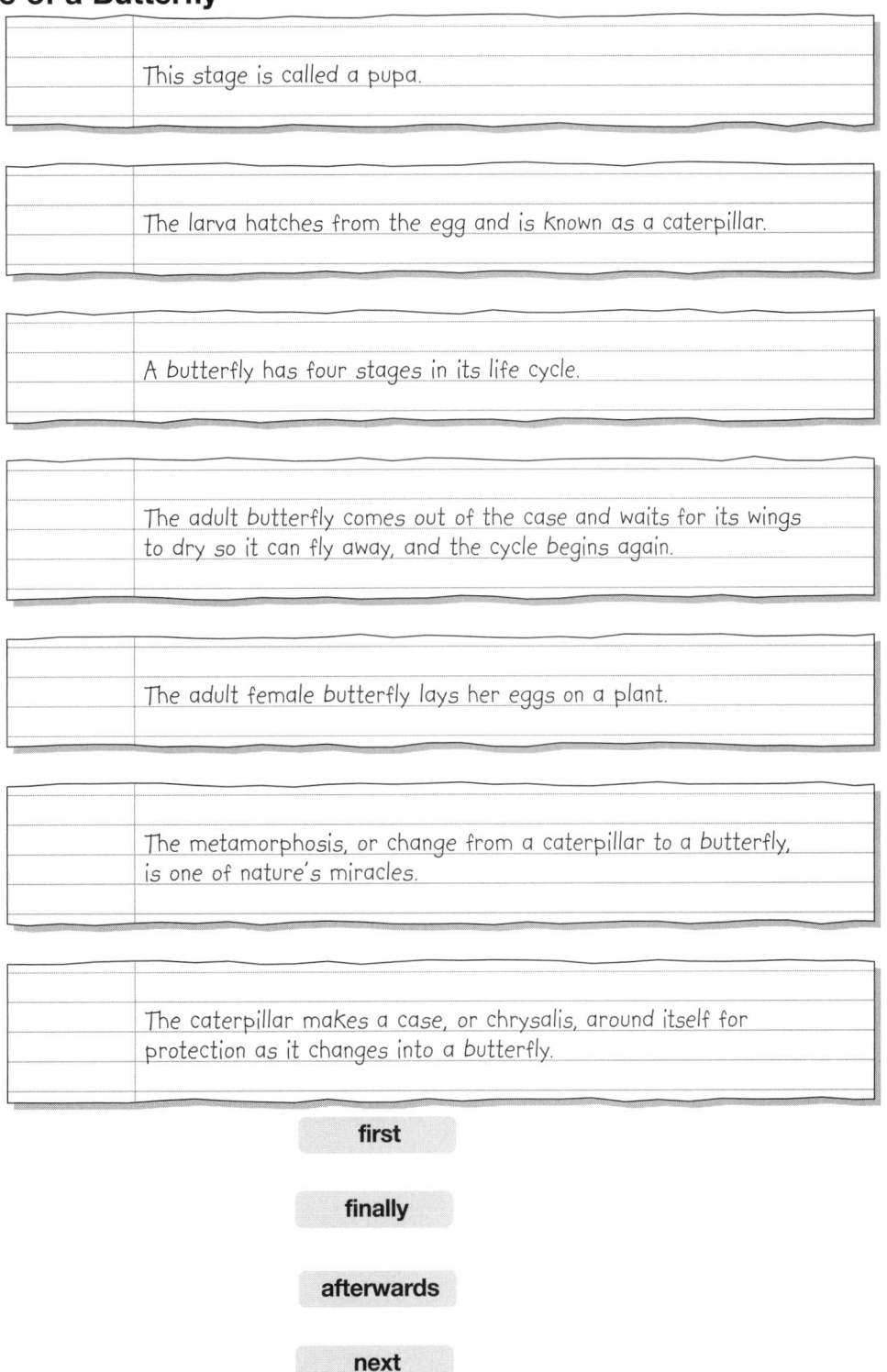

This stage is called a pupa.

The larva hatches from the egg and is known as a caterpillar.

A butterfly has four stages in its life cycle.

The adult butterfly comes out of the case and waits for its wings to dry so it can fly away, and the cycle begins again.

The adult female butterfly lays her eggs on a plant.

The metamorphosis, or change from a caterpillar to a butterfly, is one of nature's miracles.

The caterpillar makes a case, or chrysalis, around itself for protection as it changes into a butterfly.

first

finally

afterwards

next

Name: _____   Date: _____

Read the paragraph, underline the topic and clincher sentences, and circle the signal words.

The Life Cycle of a Butterfly

A butterfly has four stages in its life cycle. First, the adult female butterfly lays her eggs on a plant. Next, the larva hatches from the egg and is known as a caterpillar. Afterwards, the caterpillar makes a case, or chrysalis, around itself for protection as it changes into a butterfly. This stage is called the pupa. Finally, the adult butterfly comes out of the case and waits for its wings to dry so it can fly away, and the cycle begins again. The metamorphosis, or change from a caterpillar to a butterfly, is one of nature's miracles.

Name: _____ Date: _____

Read the paragraph, underline the topic and clincher sentences, and circle the signal words.

How Fossils Form

Fossils are rocklike casts, impressions, or actual remains of organisms that were buried after they died, before they could decompose. Only a tiny fraction of organisms are preserved as fossils. This is because most dead organisms decay or are eaten by scavenging animals. Also, soft tissue, such as muscle and organs, does not fossilize well. Animals that have neither bones nor shells will not leave fossils.

An organism that is suddenly buried—for example, if it falls into mud or quicksand, or is covered quickly by a landslide of sediment or blowing volcanic ash—may become a fossil. As the layer that contains the organism is covered by other layers of sediment, it gradually becomes sedimentary rock.

As wet sediment becomes rock, minerals that are dissolved in the water gradually replace minerals in the body of any buried organisms. Bone, shell, and parts of plants can all be replaced this way. Eventually, particle by particle, the fossilizing organism is replaced by minerals. The final result is a fossil that looks exactly like the original organism but is in a rocklike form.

B. Ritter, *Nelson Science & Technology 7,* (Toronto: Nelson), 2000, 224.

Name: _____ Date: _____

Read the paragraph, underline the topic and clincher sentences, and circle the signal words.

Trip to the Zoo

Our class went to the zoo to see the animals. First, we saw the playful monkeys. Second, we visited the noisy birds. After that, we went to the lion cages. Then we watched the huge elephants. Next, we rode on the ponies. Finally, we saw the tall giraffes. We had a great time at the zoo.

Name: _____ Date: _____

Read the paragraph, underline the topic and clincher sentences, and circle the signal words.

Writing a Science Experiment Report

There are steps you should follow when writing a formal science experiment report. First, you write down your hypothesis—that is, your anticipated result of the experiment. Second, you list the apparatus—the equipment you are using. Third, you write down the method—that is, the step by step process of the actual experiment. Fourth, you include a list of the observations—the things that happened during the experiment. And finally, you make a conclusion based on your original hypothesis. If you complete all these steps, you will have a good scientific report.

Name: _____ Date: _____

Read the paragraph, underline the topic and clincher sentences, and circle the signal words.

Explorers

A thousand years ago, adventurous sailors began to push westward from Europe. The first of these were the Norse explorers, also known as the Vikings. They originally came from Norway, Sweden, and Denmark. In 986, they reached the shores of Newfoundland and Labrador. In the 1400s, other explorers reached North America. The first was Christopher Columbus, who, in 1492, discovered parts of Central and South America for Spain. Soon after, in 1497, John Cabot explored the coast of Newfoundland for England. In the 1500s, more explorers came to North America. Jacques Cartier made his three voyages to North America in 1534, 1535, and 1541, travelling down the St. Lawrence River as far as Montréal. After Cartier, Sir Humphrey Gilbert claimed all of Newfoundland for England in 1583. The last of this group of explorers was Samuel de Champlain. His first trip to New France was in 1603. He helped establish settlements along the St. Lawrence River. All of these explorers played an important role in the exploration and settlement of North America.

Name: _____ Date: _____

Read the paragraph, underline the topic and clincher sentences, and circle the signal words.

How to Solve a Math Problem

So, you walk into your math class and find you have a surprise test. Don't panic, just read on! First of all, you might want to get a piece of scrap paper. After that, read over the problem several times. Then figure out if you need to use addition, subtraction, multiplication, or division. You might be able to find out by searching the problem for key words such as *product, quotient, difference,* or *sum*. Once you have done that, find out what strategy to use. There are several ways: working backwards, estimation, deduction, or trial and error (where you pick answers at random). After that, use the operation and the strategy to figure out the answer. But you don't have to use straight operations. You can draw pictures or make a chart or graph. Now you can begin to solve the problem. Whatever method you use, be patient, and finally, check your answer one to two times after you solve it. Good luck (you're going to need it)!!!!

TEACHING ENUMERATIVE STRUCTURES

2

DEFINING THE STRUCTURE

Enumerative structure paragraphs list things that are examples of a main topic. Point one is described, then point two, and so on. Students will find this listing of examples similar to sequence paragraphs, and they may confuse the two structures. The important difference to emphasize is that, *in a sequence paragraph, there has to be an order to the examples*, whereas *in an enumerative structure, the order is not important*. For example, for the topic of baking a cake, a sequence paragraph might be about how to make the cake, where the order of the steps is very important. An enumerative paragraph on baking a cake might list ingredients needed to make the cake. As long as all the ingredients are purchased, the order in which they are bought is immaterial.

Students will find that enumerative paragraphs are among the most widely used text structures because they are often found in combination with other text structures. For example, a cause and effect paragraph might state one cause along with several effects. An enumerative format would then be used to list these effects (the first effect is ..., another effect is ..., a final effect is). In a problem and solution paragraph, signal words such as **one solution is, another solution is,** and **furthermore** could be used to indicate that there is an enumerative structure within the problem and solution format.

Paragraph Features

Topic Sentence

The topic sentence should tell the reader what types of things will be listed. For example, the topic sentence, "There are several categories of food that you should eat daily" indicates that the paragraph is about the types of food that are important to eat each day.

Clincher Sentence

A clincher sentence for this paragraph might be, "By eating food from each basic food category, you will be making a good start toward meeting your body's nutritional needs."

Signal Words

Because enumerative and sequence structures share some similarities, words such as **first, second, third, then, to begin with, next, finally,** and **at last** can be used in either structure. However, unlike a sequence paragraph, using **first, next,** and **finally** in an enumerative paragraph indicates an arbitrary order the author has chosen rather than an absolute sequence of things. In other words, the first point the author has chosen to discuss could just as easily have been the last point.

Signal words are usually absent when enumerative structures are developed in a list format (e.g., bulleted, numbered, etc).

Grades 4 to 8 Classrooms

Although students will have seen the enumerative text structure often in their reading, they may not be familiar with the actual name of the structure or what it means. Students should be given a variety of examples and many opportunities to write enumerative paragraphs. Have them suggest topics that would suit the structure to ensure their understanding. Because this structure can be confused with the sequence structure, students might find it easier to use those signal words that are different from those used in sequence paragraphs until they become familiar with the structure.

Students in **grades 4 to 6** will need sufficient time studying this text structure to ensure that they understand the differences between sequence and enumerative paragraphs. They should have opportunities to work in pairs or small groups before being asked to write paragraphs independently. They also need to be exposed to some of the simpler forms of the enumerative structure found in their textbooks. Ideally, most **grades 4 to 6** students should be able to identify an enumerative structure when they are working in other content areas such as science and social studies.

In **grades 7 and 8**, students need to be exposed to the many different forms the enumerative structure can take in nonfiction texts. For example, students might see a paragraph that includes a bulleted list, or a paragraph with a list of items that are later described under subheadings.

Grades 4 to 6 students should be able write an enumerative paragraph with a topic sentence, clincher sentence, and suitable signal words. **Grades 7 and 8** students should be expected to write more complex paragraphs using grade-appropriate language. Their topic and clincher sentences will be stronger, and more advanced signal words should be evident.

Additional Instructional Support

Using coloured paper to identify different sentences is a great way to help students who are having difficulty understanding this structure. It helps them see the elements that make up an enumerative paragraph. As you discuss with students the different parts of a model paragraph and create

SIGNAL WORDS FOR ENUMERATIVE STRUCTURES	
first	most
second	important
third	more
then	next
also	finally
for instance	in fact
for example	at last
to begin with	another
	some other
furthermore	in addition

2 Teaching Enumerative Structures

a class paragraph, put each sentence onto different-coloured strips of paper. Here is one example (see Figure 2.1):

- Write the topic sentence on a red strip of paper.
- Write the first item discussed on a blue strip of paper.
- Write the details for that item on a yellow strip of paper.
- Write the next item discussed on another blue strip of paper and its details on yellow paper.
- Write the clincher sentence on a green strip of paper.

On a red strip of paper: Did you know that many of the vegetables you eat are really roots?

On a blue strip of paper: To begin with, there is the carrot.

On a yellow strip of paper: The great taste of this root makes it a very popular snack.

On a blue strip of paper: Another root is the radish.

On a yellow strip of paper: Its vibrant colour brightens up any salad.

On a blue strip of paper: In addition, there is the beet.

On a yellow strip of paper: Beets are often made into pickles.

On a blue strip of paper: Finally, there is the parsnip.

On a yellow strip of paper: It looks similar to a carrot but is light yellow in colour.

On a green strip of paper: Carrots, radishes, beets, and parsnips are roots that are great to eat.

FIGURE 2.1

Text Structures: Teaching Patterns in Reading and Writing

The coloured strips of paper provide visual cues that help students see all the parts needed for the paragraph. After doing this as a guided writing activity, ask students to work in pairs to create their own coloured paragraphs. When circulating around the room, you can see very quickly who understands the structure.

INTRODUCING THE STRUCTURE

Step 1: Start by asking students what the word "enumerative" means. Because this will probably be a new word for them, you might want to ask them to look up the root word, "enumerate," in a dictionary. Discuss its meaning. Point out to students, if their dictionary entry is similar to that in Figure 2.2, that "enumerative" is a form of the word "enumerate." Pose questions such as the following:

- What other text structures list points or items?
- What element is missing in the definition of "enumerate" that was part of the sequence structure definition? (*chronological order*) Or: Why do you think the list in an enumerative structure is different from that in a sequence structure?

e·nu·mer·ate (i nyü′mə rāt′ *or* i nü′mə rāt′)   1 name one by one; give a list of: *She enumerated the days of the week.* 2 count. 3 *Cdn.* make up or enter in a list of voters in an area.   v., **e·nu·mer·at·ed, e·nu·mer·at·ing.**

e·nu·mer·a·tion (i nyü′mə rā′ shən *or* i nü′mə rā′ shən) 1 an enumerating; listing; counting. 2 a list. *n.*

e·nu·mer·a·tive (i nyü′mə rə tiv *or* i nü′mə rə tiv, i nyü′mə rā′ tiv *or* i nü′mə rā′ tiv) that ENUMERATES; having to do with ENUMERATION. *adj.*

e·nu·mer·a·tor (i nyü′mə rā′ tər *or* i nü′mə rā′ tər) 1 *Cdn.* a person appointed to list, prior to an election, the eligible voters in a polling area. 2 any person or thing that lists or counts. *n.*

Gage Intermediate Dictionary. (Toronto: HarperCollins), 2005, 520.

FIGURE 2.2

Step 2: Have students think about the differences and similarities between the two structures as they examine the model paragraphs that follow.

As an alternative, you could simply begin by examining the model paragraph that follows and see if students can figure out its characteristics.

EXAMINING A MODEL PARAGRAPH

Introduce the Model

Step 1: Have students read an enumerative paragraph. BLM 2.1, "Famous Kid Inventions," is an example. Ask them to identify the signal words, topic sentence, and clincher sentence. A marked-up example is shown in Figure 2.3.

Compare Sequence and Enumerative Paragraphs

Step 2: If students have already studied the sequence structure, you might want to have them compare an enumerative paragraph and a previously discussed sequence paragraph. They should identify their similarities and differences, looking at

- signal words (**first, next,** etc.)
- topic sentences
- clincher sentences
- how the paragraphs are developed (e.g., if the order is changed in an enumerative paragraph, it still makes sense)

Famous Kid Inventions

topic sentence →

__Kids have produced some remarkable and useful inventions.__ For example, the popsicle was a kid-created invention. In 1905, an 11-year-old boy accidentally left some homemade soda pop on his back porch. The next morning, he found it frozen with the stirring stick standing straight up.

signal words

Another example was the first snow machine. It was invented by 15-year-old Joseph Bombardier in 1922. A more recent invention took place in a wood-shop class. That's where a Grade 8 student thought of a better way to come down a ski

clincher sentence →

hill—on a snowboard. __Kid inventions like these have changed the way people live and play.__

FIGURE 2.3   BLM 2.1

Share and Discuss

Step 3: As a class, discuss students' choices and why this paragraph has an enumerative structure.

DEVELOPING A GRAPHIC ORGANIZER

Introduce the Model

Step 1: Introduce students to another enumerative paragraph along with its graphic organizer. (See BLM 2.2, "Advertising Techniques," Figures 2.4 and 2.5.) When you introduce the graphic organizer, ask students to explain how it is different from the organizers they have used for sequence structures. For example, there is no order shown for the examples or points given. However, the organizer still uses specific examples, as did the sequence organizer.

Advertising
Techniques

"We're the Best"
Company claims
to be better than
the rest.

**Celebrity
Endorsement**
Famous person
tells about product.

Bandwagon
Everyone is buying
it, you should too.

FIGURE 2.4

> Graphic organizers, such as the one in Figure 2.4, can be used with a variety of text structures depending on the language of the topic sentence. For example, if "Advertising Techniques" is changed to "What are three advertising techniques?", the structure becomes question and answer. However, the paragraph still can be developed using the enumerative structure ("The first technique is...," "The second technique is...," etc).

Advertising Techniques

   There are many advertising techniques companies use to convince people to buy their products. To begin with, there is the bandwagon technique. These ads claim that everyone is buying the product, so you had better do so, too. Otherwise, you will be left out! Another technique is the celebrity endorsement. Famous people get money to endorse a product they say they use themselves. Then there is the "we're the best" technique. This is where the advertiser claims to be better than the rest but doesn't offer any proof. Regardless of which technique advertisers use, their goal is the same—for you to buy their product.

— topic sentence

— signal words

— clincher sentence

FIGURE 2.5   BLM 2.2

Identify Paragraph Elements

Step 2: Have students work in pairs to

- compare the organizer to the paragraph
- circle the signal words
- underline the topic sentence and clincher sentence

Create the Graphic Organizer

Step 3: Give students a different paragraph. Tell them that they will make their own graphic organizer from the paragraph. (See Figures 2.6 and 2.7, and BLM 2.3, "Scuba Diving Equipment.")

Scuba Diving Equipment

topic sentence → <u>Scuba diving requires special equipment.</u> To begin with, you need a wetsuit to keep you warm, because the water can be very cold. You also have to wear fins, which will help you swim quickly. A weight belt goes around your waist to keep you from bobbing to the surface. But the most important item is a scuba tank. It holds air so you can breathe under water. In addition to the tank, you need a hose and a mouthpiece. Your final piece of gear is a diving mask so you can see the fish clearly. <u>Once you have the necessary scuba equipment, you can enjoy scuba diving in many places around the world.</u>

signal words

clincher sentence →

FIGURE 2.6

Step 4: Have students work in pairs to circle the signal words and underline the topic and clincher sentences. A marked-up example is shown in Figure 2.6. Ask students to make an organizer for the paragraph. Emphasize that they should use point form, not full sentences, to fill in the organizer. (You can distribute a blank organizer such as the one in BLM 2.4, or students can develop one of their own.) It is important for students to realize that there are not necessarily signal words for each part of the organizer. Figure 2.7 is an example of a completed organizer:

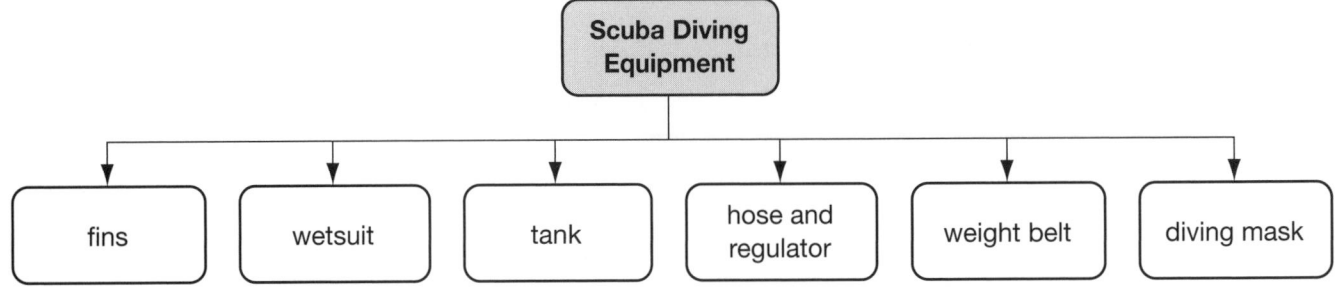

FIGURE 2.7

Text Structures: Teaching Patterns in Reading and Writing

Share and Discuss

Step 5: Complete a class organizer for the paragraph on an overhead transparency using feedback from students. Have students compare their own organizers with the class organizer.

WRITING AN ENUMERATIVE PARAGRAPH

Use a Graphic Organizer

Step 1: Now challenge students to write a paragraph based on a graphic organizer. (For an example, see Figure 2.8, "Eating Well.") Students can work in pairs to write a paragraph using the jot notes on the organizer. Remind them that they must have a topic sentence and clincher sentence as well as appropriate signal words.

EATING WELL

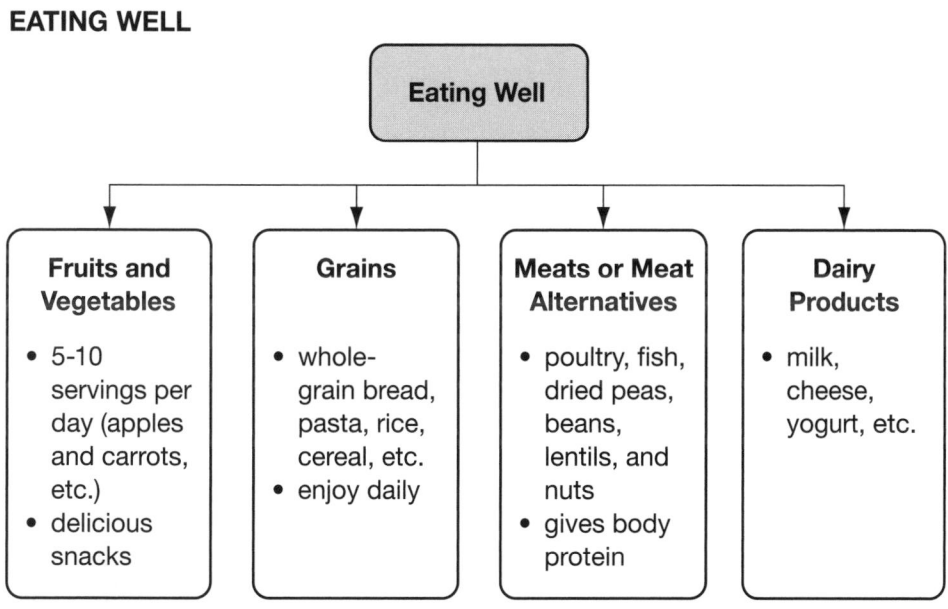

FIGURE 2.8 BLM 2.5

Figure 2.9 is an example that was developed from the above organizer. The paragraph elements have been highlighted.

Eating Well

There are several categories of food that you should eat daily in order to stay healthy. The first is fruits and vegetables. You need five to ten servings of fruit and vegetables each day. For example, you can eat an apple or carrot for a healthy snack. Another category is grains. Food such as whole-grain bread, pasta, rice, and cereals should be enjoyed regularly.

← topic sentence

signal words

continued ——→

However, stay away from cereals that are high in sugar. You also should eat meat or meat alternatives to provide the protein your body has to have. You can enjoy high-protein foods such as poultry and fish, or include dried peas, beans, lentils, and nuts in your diet. The final category is dairy products. Choose low-fat milk, cheese, and yogurt. These products help supply the calcium needed for strong, healthy bones. <u>By eating food in the four basic food categories, you can meet your body's nutritional needs.</u>

clincher sentence

FIGURE 2.9 BLM 2.6

Share and Discuss

Step 2: Share students' examples of enumerative paragraphs and organizers with the class. After each example, discuss whether

- the organizer reflects the paragraph's structure and information
- the paragraph has a suitable topic sentence
- the signal words are appropriate for an enumerative paragraph
- the clincher sentence reflects the topic sentence

COMPOSING THEIR OWN PARAGRAPHS

Once students have written jot notes from their paragraphs to make their organizers, and have developed paragraphs from their organizers, have them write their own paragraphs for the enumerative structure.

Step 1: Brainstorm topics for an enumerative paragraph with the class. Make sure that students are not giving you sequence topics. They may have a tendency to do so until they thoroughly understand the enumerative structure. For example, on the topic of hockey equipment:

Sequence Structure: Putting on hockey equipment—order *is* important.

Enumerative Structure: What equipment you would have to buy to play hockey—order *is not* important.

Step 2: Have students work in pairs to select a topic, or they can make up one of their own.

Step 3: After they have chosen their topics, ask students to list the points or examples that are appropriate, and then use their lists to create their organizers and paragraphs.

Step 4: Finally, have each student create an organizer on a topic of their own choosing and use it to write an enumerative paragraph.

Text Structures: Teaching Patterns in Reading and Writing

Share and Discuss

Step 5: Have students read their enumerative paragraphs to the class. Discuss whether the paragraphs have the necessary parts—topic sentence, signal words, and clincher sentence—and whether they are, in fact, enumerative paragraphs. Have the class compare the paragraphs to their graphic organizers.

Step 6: As a follow-up, and to link their learning to "real-world" examples, have students search in library books and textbooks for paragraphs that contain the enumerative structure. Ask for volunteers to share the examples they found. Discuss with students how the elements in these enumerative paragraphs compare to the examples they have studied and written. (See *Enumerative Structures in the Content Areas* for some examples.)

ALTERNATIVE ACTIVITIES

If you find that some students have difficulty understanding the concept of enumerative structures, you might want to consider the following activities. Each one allows students to explore this structure without requiring them to read or write. They are small-group-based activities, but students could also work in pairs. As an aid to students, you might also display a list of enumerative structure signal words on the board, chart paper, or an overhead transparency.

Mystery Bags

1. Five or six objects are placed in a Mystery Bag. They could be any set of items related to a specific topic of study. (See *Suggested Cross-Curricular Topics* on page 40.) For example, for physical education and health unit, different types of fruit could be in the bag. For science, it might be a selection of types of rocks. For math, geometric objects such as cubes or rectangular prisms might be added.

2. A student takes an item out of the bag. Using a signal word, she or he gives a fact about the object. For example, "**To begin with**, an apple is a red, juicy fruit. It is a popular lunch item."

3. The student (or another student) picks out an additional item and, using a different signal word, tells a fact about the fruit. For example, "**In addition** to the apple, here is a banana. This fruit is often used as a topping for cereal or sundaes."

4. To involve more students at one time, have a Mystery Bag for each group of five or six students. You can walk around the room and observe the groups to ensure that students use the appropriate signal words and give a fact about each object.

5. For follow-up, and as a review of the concept, you could create another Mystery Bag to be used with the whole class. Hold up each object and have students write an enumerative paragraph about the items you show them. Students who experience difficulty writing can give their enumerative example orally.

Drama Tableaux

1. In this activity, students create a tableau illustrating three or more situations based on a topic. A tableau is like a snapshot of an activity. Students go into their positions, which they hold for about three to five seconds before moving into the next position. For example, for the topic "the roles of people in the feudal system," students could create a tableau of the nobility, then the religious leaders, followed by the knights, and finally the serfs. In this example, a tableau could show an activity that each of the groups might do. The nobles could be at a banquet, the knights engaged in a tournament, and so on. Between each tableau, students hold up cards with appropriate signal words (e.g., **to begin with, in addition, furthermore, another, most important**, etc.).

SUGGESTED CROSS-CURRICULAR TOPICS

Here are some topics that would fit with the enumerative pattern:

Social Studies

- What a person needs to have or do to become a Canadian citizen
- Reasons to trade with a certain province or territory
- Celebrations and traditions
- Physical features of Canada
- Roles of people in medieval society
- Various community helpers
- Items in a pioneer home

Science

- Types of motion
- Types of matter (solids, liquids, gases)
- Examples of simple machines
- Causes of erosion
- Tests for rock identification
- Types of weather instruments
- Different habitats of animals

Math

- Types of geometric shapes
- Types of problem-solving strategies (guess and check, draw a diagram, etc.)

- Kinds of graphs
- Different attributes in patterning
- Types of quadrilaterals
- Transformations (translations, rotations, reflections)

Arts

- A discussion of various artists and their styles
- The elements of art (shape, space, line, form, texture, colour)

Physical Education and Health

- A discussion of the sports you do in a gym or outside
- Safety rules for participation in gym activities
- Rules for a particular game or competitive sport
- The four basic food groups
- Things to look for when buying a bicycle helmet

Language Arts

- A discussion of each character in a story
- A discussion of each setting in a novel
- Types of punctuation and their uses
- Kinds of poetry
- Genres of fiction (science fiction, historical fiction, etc.)
- Reading strategies (visualizing, asking questions, etc.)

ENUMERATIVE STRUCTURES IN THE CONTENT AREAS

When you move from teaching the text structures using model paragraphs to showing examples from textbooks, students will likely be confronted with several differences between the two types of examples. In most cases, the length of the textbook examples will be longer. Many examples will be developed over several paragraphs, with topic paragraphs that list topics for subsequent related paragraphs. Instead of signal words, students might see bulleted or numbered lists as well as subheadings for each subtopic. However, the enumerative structure will still be clearly evident: a list of items is given, and each item is discussed.

The examples provided are from a trade book (BLM 2.7), and a **grade 7** textbook (BLM 2.8).

In the trade book example, "The Brain", the three main parts of the brain are discussed. No clincher sentence is given.

In the **grade 7** social studies textbook example, the topic sentence introduces the "Thirteen Colonies" of what would become the United States and how they can be divided into three groups. The three groups are discussed in separate paragraphs. No clincher sentence is given.

LINKING ASSESSMENT TO LEARNING

Encourage students to look at text structure traits such as organization, ideas and content, voice, and word choice.

Similar to the sequence structure, the most important traits to focus on in the enumerative structure will be *organization* and *ideas*. Students should be able to stay on topic while enumerating the list and giving details for each item.

For students to benefit from the assessment of their work, they should set and understand their own specific criteria, similar to those used for the sequence paragraph. The criteria would include having

- a strong topic sentence
- a clincher sentence that sums up the information in the paragraph
- a variety of appropriate signal words

Use read-alouds to point out strong examples that fit the criteria for enumerative paragraphs.

Specific criteria for the enumerative structure would be to include details about each item on their list. Other criteria, such as using proper sentence structure, punctuation, and spelling—as well as effective use of vocabulary—could be added if they have been thoroughly discussed previous to this topic. However, you might find that students are more successful in learning this text structure if the number of criteria are kept to a minimum. Once students have a thorough understanding of this structure, other criteria can be added. Also, have students assess various examples of writing before they are expected to write and assess their own work. Giving them strong examples will assist them to see the qualities contained in good writing.

Assessment Checklists

As students fill out the enumerative peer and self-assessment checklists, it is important that you circulate and ask questions about their assessment. Some students will indicate "yes" without really examining the criteria carefully. For this reason, I not only ask if there is a topic sentence but if the topic sentence catches the reader's attention. This makes the student stop and think about the topic sentence and its effectiveness. I do the same for the signal words. I ask if the words have been used, and I also have students indicate how many different words are used. This task helps students who overuse **then** throughout their paragraphs, encouraging them to go back to their paragraphs and consider using different signal words. (See Figure 2.10, Grade 6 Peer Feedback.)

The strengths in the enumerative paragraph include:

He has good signal words and he included some items in a list. He also included some nice details.

The weaknesses in the enumerative paragraph include:

The topic sentence didn't tell the reader the topic of the paragraph. There is no clincher sentence and no punctuation. There could be more signal words. There needed to be a topic sentence because it just went into what was on the list.

My suggested goal for this writer is:

Make sure your topic sentence clearly tells the reader the topic of your paragraph.

(This peer editor shows an understanding of what is needed in an enumerative paragraph. The editor was able to identify strengths and weaknesses.)

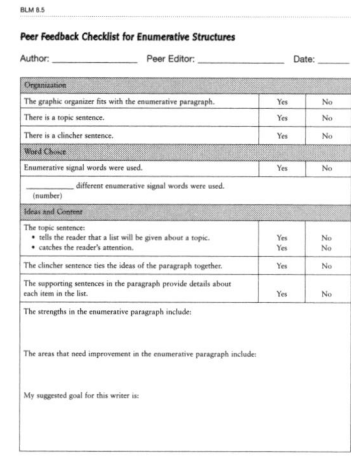

FIGURE 2.10

I feel that the bottom section of the peer feedback and self-assessment checklists is the most important for students to complete (Figure 2.11). It is only through having students fill out this part of the checklist that you will know for sure if students have a thorough understanding of the criteria used, what strengths they have, and what areas still require improvement.

GRADE 6 STUDENTS' SELF-ASSESSMENT

The strengths in my mini-essay include:

I have a good topic sentence and clincher sentence that catches the reader's attention. I used a lot of signal words and a good structure.

(This student has the right idea. I would want to conference with the student to clarify what is meant by "a good structure.")

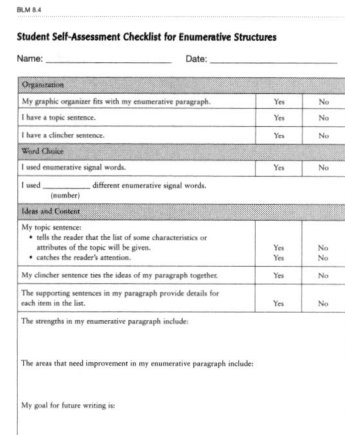

The weaknesses in the enumerative paragraph include:

I don't have enough detail after each item in my list.

My goal for future writing is:

I plan to put another sentence with more detail in my paragraph.

(This student has identified an area where his writing needs more work. If time permits, I would conference with the student to help him or her gain a better understanding of how to put more detail into the paragraphs.)

FIGURE 2.11

Discussing the self-assessment tools with students will help you assess their understanding of the structure and indicate where they need to go next. Mini-lessons can then be set up for those students requiring further assistance in particular areas, such as

- creating strong topic sentences
- using a variety of enumerative signal words when appropriate
- ensuring that the ideas are clearly stated
- finishing off the writing with a strong clincher sentence
- knowing the difference between the enumerative and sequence structures

For example, if you find that some students are still having difficulty understanding the difference between the enumerative and sequence structures, give them a variety of topics and ask them to indicate which of these types of paragraphs (enumerative or sequence) might follow. Start with examples that are easy to compare (such as the first three examples below) and then add topics that are more difficult:

- How to make brownies (*sequence*)
- Ingredients you need to make brownies (*enumerative*)
- How to put on equipment to play football (*sequence*)
- Which equipment to buy before you can play football (*enumerative*)
- The reasons for the War of 1812 (*enumerative* and *cause and effect*)
- The order of events in the War of 1812 (*sequence*)
- Food you eat to stay healthy (*enumerative*)
- What you need to paint your room (*enumerative*)
- Different types of transportation (*enumerative*)
- How to study for a test (*sequence*)
- Steps involved in cleaning your bedroom (*sequence*)

Once students seem to have a good understanding of the differences between these two structures, ask them to suggest topics and explain what type of paragraph (sequence or enumerative) they would write.

Assessment Rubrics

The assessment rubric for Chapter 2 enumerative structures is used for assessment *only* after students are very familiar with the structure and have had many opportunities to work with peer and self-assessment checklists (see BLM 8.6, page 237).

Anecdotal Notes

Keeping anecdotal records from these conferences, samples of students' work, and marks from various assignments will help track students' progress.

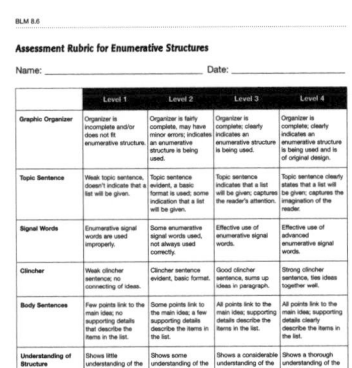

Blackline Masters

Name: _____ Date: _____

Read the paragraph, underline the topic and clincher sentences, and circle the signal words.

Famous Kid Inventions

Kids have produced some remarkable and useful inventions. For example, the popsicle was a kid-created invention. In 1905, an 11-year-old boy accidentally left some homemade soda pop on his back porch. The next morning, he found it frozen with the stirring stick standing straight up. Another example was the first snow machine. It was invented by 15-year-old Joseph Bombardier in 1922. A more recent invention took place in a wood-shop class. That's where a Grade 8 student thought of a better way to come down a ski hill—on a snowboard. Kid inventions like these have changed the way people live and play.

Name: _____ Date: _____

Work in pairs to compare the organizer to the paragraph, then underline the topic and clincher sentences, and circle the signal words.

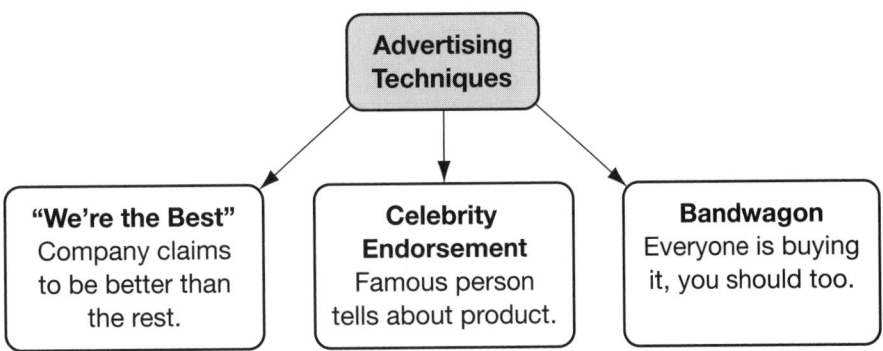

Advertising Techniques

There are many advertising techniques companies use to convince people to buy their products. To begin with, there is the bandwagon technique. These ads claim that everyone is buying the product, so you had better do so, too. Otherwise, you will be left out! Another technique is the celebrity endorsement. Famous people get money to endorse a product they say they use themselves. Then there is the "we're the best" technique. This is where the advertiser claims to be better than the rest but doesn't offer any proof. Regardless of which technique advertisers use, their goal is the same—for you to buy their product.

Name: _____   Date: _____

Work in pairs to circle the signal words and underline the topic and clincher sentences. Then make an organizer for the paragraph. Remember to use point form, not full sentences, to fill in the organizer.

Scuba Diving Equipment

Scuba diving requires special equipment. To begin with, you need a wetsuit to keep you warm, because the water can be very cold. You also have to wear fins, which will help you swim quickly. A weight belt goes around your waist to keep you from bobbing to the surface. But the most important item is a scuba tank. It holds air so you can breathe under water. In addition to the tank, you need a hose and a mouthpiece. Your final piece of gear is a diving mask so you can see the fish clearly. Once you have the necessary scuba equipment, you can enjoy scuba diving in many places around the world.

Name: _____ Date: _____

Create a graphic organizer for BLM 2.3, "Scuba Diving Equipment." Remember to use point form, not full sentences, to fill in the organizer.

Scuba Diving Equipment

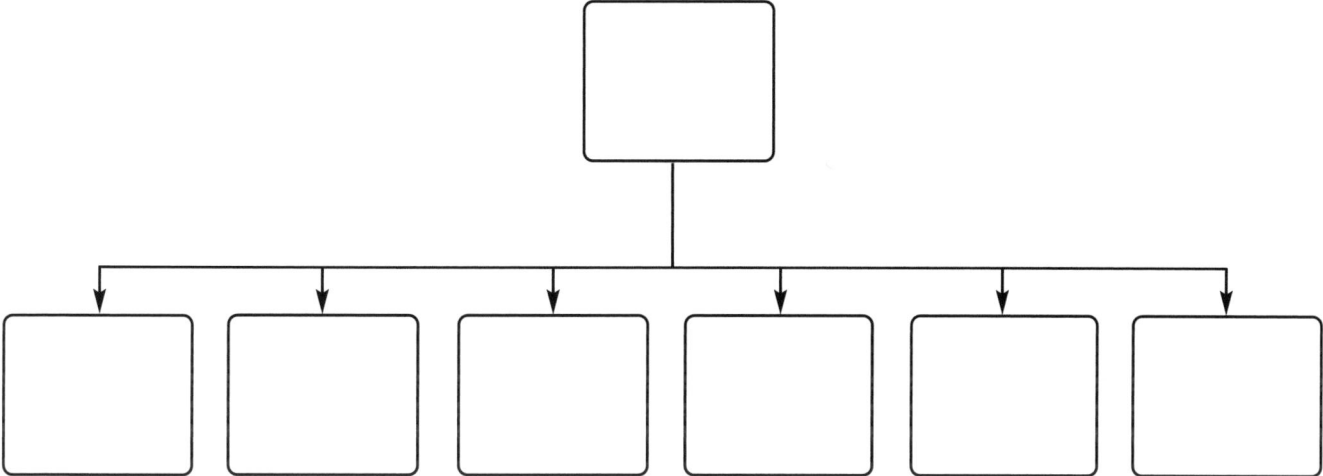

Name: _____ Date: _____

From this graphic organizer, write a paragraph, underline the topic and clincher sentences, and circle the signal words.

Eating Well

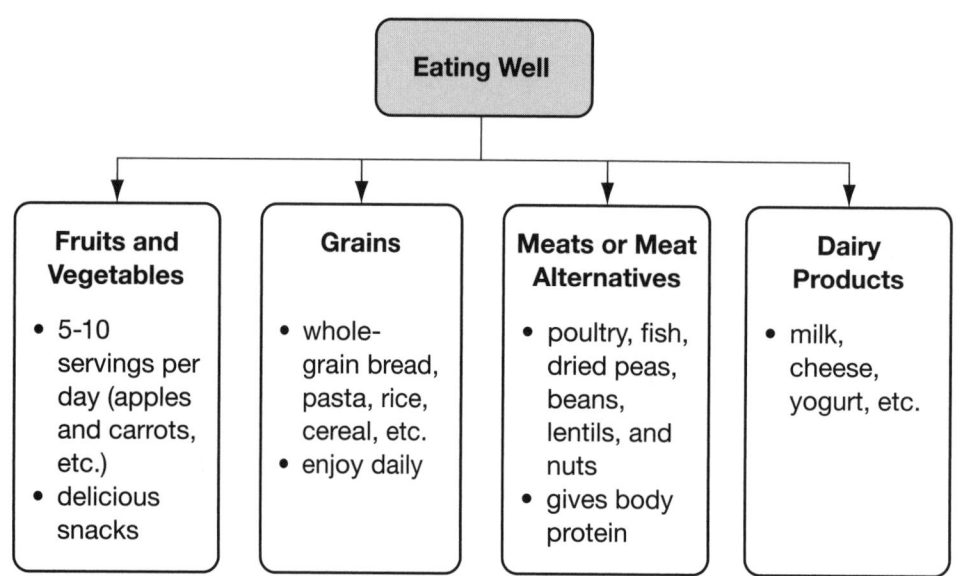

Name: _____ Date: _____

Read the following paragraph, underline the topic and clincher sentences, and circle the signal words. Then compare the paragraph you wrote based on the jot notes from your graphic organizer with this paragraph. How do they compare? Are your topic and clincher sentences similar? Did you use some of the same signal words?

Eating Well

There are several categories of food that you should eat daily in order to stay healthy. The first is fruits and vegetables. You need five to ten servings of fruit and vegetables each day. For example, you can eat an apple or carrot for a healthy snack. Another category is grains. Food such as whole-grain bread, pasta, rice, and cereals should be enjoyed regularly. However, stay away from cereals that are high in sugar. You also should eat meat or meat alternatives to provide the protein your body has to have. You can enjoy high-protein foods such as poultry and fish, or include dried peas, beans, lentils, and nuts in your diet. The final category is dairy products. Choose low-fat milk, cheese, and yogurt. These products help supply the calcium needed for strong, healthy bones. By eating food in the four basic food categories, you can meet your body's nutritional needs.

Name: _____ Date: _____

Share and Discuss

The Brain

The brain is the most complex organ in the human body. It is made of 15 trillion neurons and has three main parts: cerebrum, cerebellum, and brainstem. The cerebrum regulates emotions and conscious action; the cerebellum coordinates involuntary movements; and the brainstem links the brain to the spinal cord.

Name: _____ Date: _____

Share and Discuss

The Thirteen Colonies

Each of the Thirteen Colonies was different, but they can be divided into three groups based on their location.

New England

Most of the New England settlers came from England and Scotland. These colonies were first settled by religious groups whose beliefs were not accepted in England. The economy was based on wheat farming and trade with the islands in the Caribbean Sea to the south. The seaport towns were prospering. Boston had a population of 15 000. Many people in the seaport towns made their living from the sea or as craftspeople and merchants.

The Middle Colonies

The Middle Colonies had many different religions and nationalities compared to the other colonies. They were settled by Dutch, Swedes, English, Germans, Scots, and Irish, as well as others. These colonies were known as the "breadbasket" of the New World because most people were farmers. Ships loaded with crops from the Middle Colonies left from the harbours of New York and Philadelphia. These crops were sold in Britain and the West Indies.

The Southern Colonies

Many of the Southern colonists were from England. Others were Scots, French, and Germans. The main industry was agriculture. Many workers were needed for the huge tobacco, sugar, and rice farms, which were called plantations. These plantations were owned by a small, powerful group of people. Few settlers were willing to work for wages on the plantations when they could have small farms of their own, so the plantation owners used slaves from Africa as workers. At that time, slavery was still legal in much of Europe, North America, and elsewhere. It was not entirely abolished in the states, colonies, and territories of North America until 1865.

P. Clark et. al. *Canada Revisited*, 7th ed. (Edmonton: Arnold Publishing Ltd.), 1999, 125.

TEACHING COMPARE AND CONTRAST STRUCTURES

3

DEFINING THE STRUCTURE

The compare and contrast structure *shows similarities and/or differences between two or more items, such as objects, events, people, or ideas.* There are a number of ways these paragraphs can be developed:

- *Similarities* of two or more things are discussed (e.g., a discussion about the similarities of two ancient civilizations).
- *Differences* between two or more things are discussed (e.g., the differences between rocks and minerals. This is a more common type of paragraph for this structure).
- *Similarities* and *differences* are both discussed in the same paragraph. This can be developed in two ways. All the similarities can be given first, followed by all the differences (see Figure 3.7, "Moths and Butterflies," on page 60). Alternatively, similarities and differences can be presented for one feature at a time (see Figure 3.9, "Downhill Skiing and Water Skiing," on page 62).

Paragraph Features

Topic Sentence

The topic sentence should tell the reader what is being compared or contrasted. For example, for the topic sentence, "There are many similarities between a frog and a toad," what the frog and toad have in common will be discussed, not their differences. Conversely, if the topic sentence is, "There are many differences between a moth and a butterfly," the reader would expect to find out about the differences between moths and butterflies, not their similarities. "Street and ice hockey are not the same, but they have several similarities" would indicate that both similarities and differences will be identified.

These are simple examples where the words "similarity" and "difference" are usually stated in the topic sentence. Older students are likely to encounter compare and contrast topic sentences that are less direct. Here are a few examples:

- Ecosystems and habitats are related, but they are not the same.
- Portable MP3 players offer listeners a number of advantages over full-sized stereo systems.
- Squirrels and chipmunks compete for the same food sources.
- Professional hockey has changed over the last 10 years.

Clincher Sentence

The clincher sentence sums up the paragraph and usually restates the similarities and/or differences.

Signal Words

Signal words used for similarities include **compare**, **similar**, and **resembles**. To indicate differences, students might encounter words such as **contrast**, **between**, and **differences**. They will also come across comparatives and superlatives (greater, fastest, darker, largest, smaller, etc.). Students need to be taught these forms so they can recognize them when they encounter them in their reading (see Figure 3.1).

SIGNAL WORDS FOR COMPARE AND CONTRAST STRUCTURES

also (too)	*similar*
although	*different*
as ... [opposed to, well as, etc.]	*similar* or *different*
between	*similar* or *different*
both	*similar* or *different*
but	*different*
compare	*similar* or *different*
compared to	*similar* or *different*
contrast	*different*
difference	*different*
distinguish	*different*
even though	*different*
however	*different*
in common	*similar*
instead of	*different*
likewise	*similar*
more ... [than, like, etc.]	*different*
nevertheless	*different*
on one hand	*different*
on the contrary	*different*
on the other hand	*different*
rather	*different*
resembles	*similar*
similar	*similar*
unless	*different*
unlike	*different*
whereas	*different*
while	*similar* or *different*

COMPARATIVES AND SUPERLATIVES

great   (comparative)
greater
greatest   (superlative)

fast   (comparative)
faster
fastest   (superlative)

FIGURE 3.1

Grades 4 to 8 Classrooms

Grades 4 to 6 students should be able to identify and write compare and contrast paragraphs. However, I have found that it is important to keep lessons simple, using clear and direct examples. If students are discussing a topic that fits well into the compare and contrast structure, point that out to them and have them work in pairs to write a compare and contrast paragraph. When studying Canada, for example, comparing two provinces would be an appropriate assignment. Students might compare weather, physical regions, or natural resources. When studying fiction, students might be asked to compare themselves to a character in a book they are reading. At **grade 4,** students should not be expected to write more than a single paragraph using this structure, but encourage them to see that compare and contrast topics in textbooks are often developed in more than one paragraph. By the time students reach **grades 7 and 8,** they should start making connections to other subject areas and apply their knowledge of the compare and contrast structure to assignments they are given.

Figure 3.2 is an example of an early **grade 4** compare and contrast paragraph. It is written by a student who is of low average ability in writing. This is the student's first individual attempt. Notice the effort to use new signal words such as **on one hand, on the other hand,** and **whereas.** It is also evident that this student knows that there should be a clincher sentence but will require more instruction in how to write one that ties in with the rest of the paragraph. The topic sentence mentions the bicycle and skateboard but does not indicate that their similarities and differences will be discussed.

> This is a grade 4 student example. Note that spelling and other errors have not been corrected.

Do you have a bicycle or a skateboard? If you do heres some information on them. First on a bike you peddle on the other hand a skateboard you push with your feet. Another difference is on a bike you sit on it whereas on a skateboard you stand on it. The other diffreance is a bike is big whereas a skateboard is small. The similar thing about these items is they both have wheels. I wish you learned something.

FIGURE 3.2

A **grade 7** student paragraph is shown in Figure 3.3. It has much more advanced vocabulary than the **grade 4** paragraph. The writing style is also much stronger, and the student's "voice" is evident. The use of signal words is more developed. The student uses a topic sentence and clincher sentence, although both could be improved with further instruction.

"Voice refers to [the] feelings [of the writer]. It is the heart of the piece. It is what moves the reader." (Trehearne, 2006, 278).

Comparing Sharks

Is it a whale shark or a basking shark? Well you be the judge. Similarities include the fact that they both eat plankton by straining it out of the water through their teeth. (Yuck!) They're both found in all temperate oceans, and of course they're both sharks. On one hand they both reach lengths between 13m and 15m but on the other hand the whale shark is definitely longer, and bigger weighing up to 18 metric tonnes! Whale sharks much prefer to stay beneath the surface while eating, whereas the basking sharks would rather swim on the surface while eating. (They both eat all day to eat enough to survive.) Even though whale sharks have never been hunted the basking shark was once heavily hunted for the large quantities of oil found in its liver. Another distinguishing feature is that basking sharks do not pump water so they have to rely on their swimming to pass water over the gills. The whale shark, however, is able to pump water over its gills so does not need to swim forward when eating. I bet you'll never look at any shark the same way again.

This is a grade 7 student example. Note that spelling and other errors have not been corrected.

FIGURE 3.3 BLM 3.9

The example in Figure 3.4 is from a **grade 3** student. This paragraph was completed after a one-hour lesson on compare and contrast structures. (The class had received instruction in the sequence and enumerative structures prior to this lesson.) The student has a good understanding of comparing and contrasting and has made an excellent effort at using signal words.

Do you have a brother and a dog. Well then I am going to compare and contrast them. My dog and brother are the same in most ways. Here's an exmple: they both are pigs, they both are scared of taking a bath even tho my dog is 8 months and my brother is 5 years old. My dog barks a lot and my brother talks a lot. Here's an exmpel of what there different for: My dog has fur but my brother dosen't, my brother weres clothes most of the time but my dog dosen't and my dog eats with his mouth but my brother eats with his hands. On the other hand I like my dog better. I just compared and contrast my dog and brother.

FIGURE 3.4

When students first attempt to use new signal words, they often include them incorrectly, but with further instruction and practice, they can use the signal words effectively.

Additional Instructional Support

Breaking down the structure further for English Language Learners (ELL) and special education students is highly recommended. You might begin by writing on the board or chart paper simple sentences that use basic signal words (**similar, different, same, unlike**, etc.). It is helpful to read the sentences to students as they read along. For example, give them a sentence such as, "The whale is huge, but a perch is small," and have them create other sentences using this pattern. Some student examples are shown in Figure 3.5.

The/A ____ is [large/expensive/etc.], but the/a _____ is [tiny/cheap/etc.].

That child wears glasses, but that girl wears contact lenses.

The boy turns into the Hulk, but the girl turns into Wonder Woman.

The rabbit is fast, but the turtle is slow.

The dolphin is fast, but a shark is faster.

I have a television in my room, but my friend doesn't.

Chocolate brownies are yummy, but pencils are not.

FIGURE 3.5

Write the sentences on the board as students contribute their ideas orally. Once they have an understanding of the concept of comparing one thing to another, introduce some unfamiliar signal words (e.g., **whereas, on one hand**, and **on the other hand**). Give them examples using these new signal words, and then ask students to work in pairs to create comparisons using the words. (See Figure 3.6 for examples of comparisons students have created. Signal words are in bold.)

The wind is cold, **however** a winter blizzard is colder.

The elephant is big **compared to** the giraffe.

This flag has a maple leaf **as opposed to** the other flag, which has a circle.

On one hand, chalk is messy, **on the other hand** pencils are not.

I like French fries **whereas** my friend likes hamburgers.

FIGURE 3.6

Here are some examples of comparisons students have created. Signal words are in bold.

When students are comfortable comparing one thing to another using one example, introduce more examples for comparison. For instance, ask students to choose two contrasting items, such as a spoon and a fork, and have them compare the two items in as many ways as they can. You can jot their comparisons on the board. For example:

- The fork has three tongs, whereas the spoon has none.
- The fork is used to eat solid food such as potatoes, but, on the other hand, the spoon is used for eating soup.

Other comparisons could be made between a pen and marker, a t-shirt and a hat, and so on. After students have given a few comparisons, you could ask them to add a topic sentence and clincher sentence to the paragraph.

INTRODUCING THE STRUCTURE

Step 1: Start by asking students about times when they have compared or contrasted something. For example:
- comparing prices of an item they want to buy (e.g., $10 in one store, $8 in another store)
- deciding which t-shirt to wear (e.g., "The green and white striped one is warmer than the blue one, so I should wear it today.")
- choosing books to read or movies to see (e.g., "This movie is supposed to have more action than that one, so I think I will like it better.")

Step 2: Write students' suggestions on the board. Ask them to explain what is being compared (price, warmth, amount of action, etc.). Have them orally make up a sentence that shows that comparison (e.g., "The price of this basketball is less than the price of that one"). Once students understand the concept of comparing one thing to another, move on to comparisons developed in a single paragraph.

EXAMINING A MODEL PARAGRAPH

Introduce the Model

Step 1: Provide a compare and contrast paragraph. BLM 3.1, "Moths and Butterflies," is one example.

Identify Paragraph Features

Step 2: Ask students to read the model paragraph and identify
- what is being compared and contrasted
- the similarities and differences, compared to other structures they have studied

Ask students to
- circle the compare and contrast signal words
- underline the topic sentence and clincher sentence

Note that, while the topic and clincher sentences should be easily identifiable, the signal words may be a bit more of a challenge for this text structure. However, most students should be able to identify them quickly if they are familiar with the other text structures. Figure 3.7 shows the highlighted paragraph elements.

Moths and Butterflies

topic sentence → Even though moths and butterflies have a lot of things in common, they also have important differences. One similarity is that they belong to the insect family. Another characteristic they share is that both emerge from cocoons after being caterpillars. In addition, moths and butterflies each have four wings. As for differences, moths have short, thick bodies, whereas butterflies have long slender ones. Moths are usually busy at night, but butterflies are active by
clincher sentence → day. It is these differences that help you tell them apart.

FIGURE 3.7 BLM 3.1

signal words

Share and Discuss

Step 3: As they become more familiar with the concepts of topic sentences, clincher sentences, and signal words, you should start to see some students using these compare and contrast paragraph features when working in other subject areas. When you notice this happening, bring it to the attention of all the students and celebrate this accomplishment. When you do so, other students will also start making the connection between writing in language arts lessons and writing in other subjects.

DEVELOPING A GRAPHIC ORGANIZER

Introduce the Model

Step 1: Give students a compare and contrast paragraph, together with its graphic organizer. (See "Downhill Skiing and Water Skiing," Figures 3.8 and 3.9, and BLM 3.2.) When you introduce the graphic organizer to students, point out that it shows the comparison and/or contrast of the paragraph. Like earlier organizers, it also uses point form.

DOWNHILL SKIING AND WATER SKIING

	Downhill Skiing	Water Skiing
Similarities	• Can go fast/slow • Do turns and tricks • Use skis	• Can go fast/slow • Do turns and tricks • Use skis
Differences	• Skis are narrower • More control of speed • Winter, snow-covered hills • Ski anywhere on hill	• Skis are wider • Less control of speed • Summer, water • Ski where the tow boat goes

FIGURE 3.8 BLM 3.2

Identify Paragraph Elements

Step 2: Have students identify the topic sentence, clincher sentence, and signal words in the accompanying paragraph. (See Figure 3.9, BLM 3.2, for a marked-up example.) Challenge them to identify the similarities between the organizer and the finished paragraph.

Downhill Skiing and Water Skiing

topic sentence ⟶ <u>Downhill skiing and water skiing are two sports that have less in common than you think.</u> While both use skis, their widths and shapes are not similar. Downhill skis are narrower and more contoured. Water skis are more like snowboards, shorter and wider than downhill skis. For both sports, you can go fast or slow and do tricks, but there are important differences. Downhill skiers have more control than water skiers. That's because they are not being pulled by anything. They can choose any run on the hill. On the other hand, water skiers can only go where the tow boat takes them. However, the biggest difference is when and where each sport takes place. We downhill ski in winter on snow-covered hills. We

signal words

clincher sentence ⟶ water ski in summer on warm lakes. <u>Still, winter or summer, these sports are great ways to spend our free time.</u>

FIGURE 3.9 BLM 3.2

Create the Graphic Organizer

Step 3: Ask students to make their own graphic organizer based on a paragraph you will give them. (See "Earth and Us," Figure 3.10, BLM 3.3, for a marked-up example.) You can distribute a blank organizer such as BLM 3.4, or students can develop one of their own. Emphasize to students that, rather than full sentences, point form is used to fill in the organizer and that there will not necessarily be signal words for each part of the organizer.

Step 4: Have students work in pairs to circle the signal words and underline the topic and clincher sentences.

Earth and Us

topic sentence ⟶ <u>Comparing the human body to Earth is not as strange as it sounds.</u> Did you know that both can suffer from sunburn? We use suntan lotion to protect us from the Sun. Earth has similar protection, but instead of suntan lotion, it has the ozone layer. If we don't protect our skin, it burns. If the ozone layer develops holes, plants and animals may get burned by the

signal words

continued ⟶

Text Structures: Teaching Patterns in Reading and Writing

Sun's harmful radiation. Acid indigestion is [another] thing both have in common. When we eat something that has too much acid, our stomachs experience pain and heartburn. Car exhaust and industrial pollution act like too much acid, [as well.] In fact, they produce acid rain. It kills living things in lakes, destroys plants, and even eats away at buildings. [Another] way the human body resembles Earth is that both can get a fever. When we are sick, our temperature goes up. Earth's temperature can [also] rise when air pollution acts like a greenhouse and traps the Sun's heat. <u>We must take care of ourselves and Earth to prevent sunburn, indigestion, and fever</u>.

——————————— **clincher sentence**

FIGURE 3.10   BLM 3.3

Share and Discuss

Step 5: Use descriptive feedback from students to create a class organizer for the paragraph. Have students check their own organizers against the class's. An example of a completed organizer is shown in Figure 3.11.

EARTH AND US

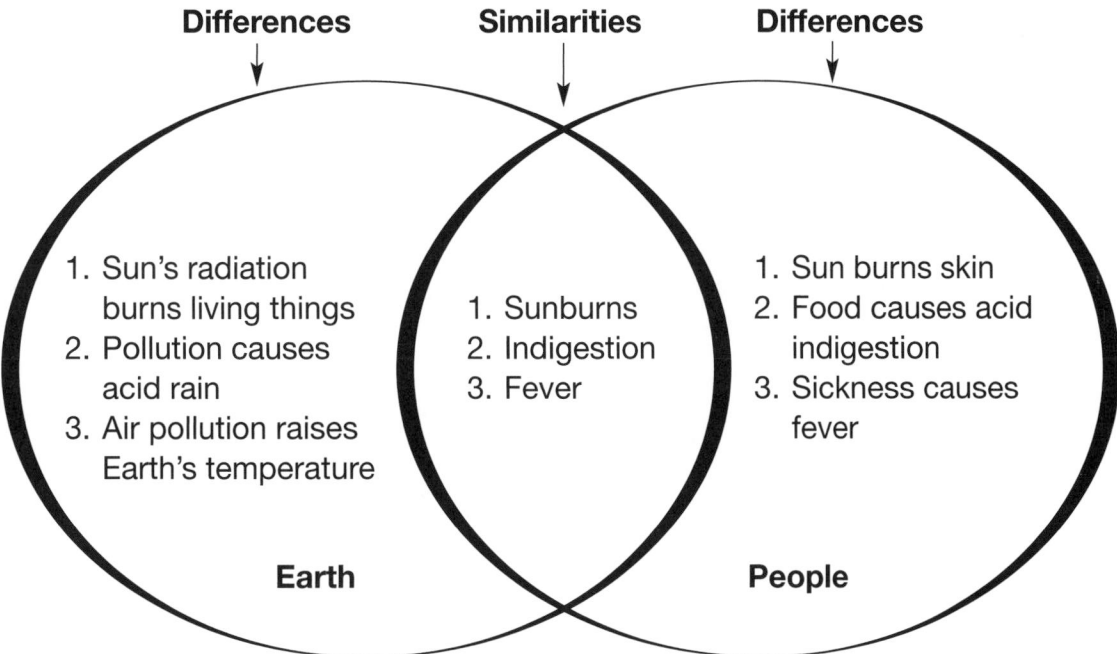

FIGURE 3.11   BLM 3.4

WRITING A COMPARE AND CONTRAST PARAGRAPH

Use a Graphic Organizer

Step 1: Have students work in pairs to write a paragraph using the jot notes on an organizer. (See the "Frogs and Toads" organizer, Figure 3.12, BLM 3.5.) Remind them that they must have a topic sentence, clincher sentence, and signal words for their paragraphs.

FROGS AND TOADS

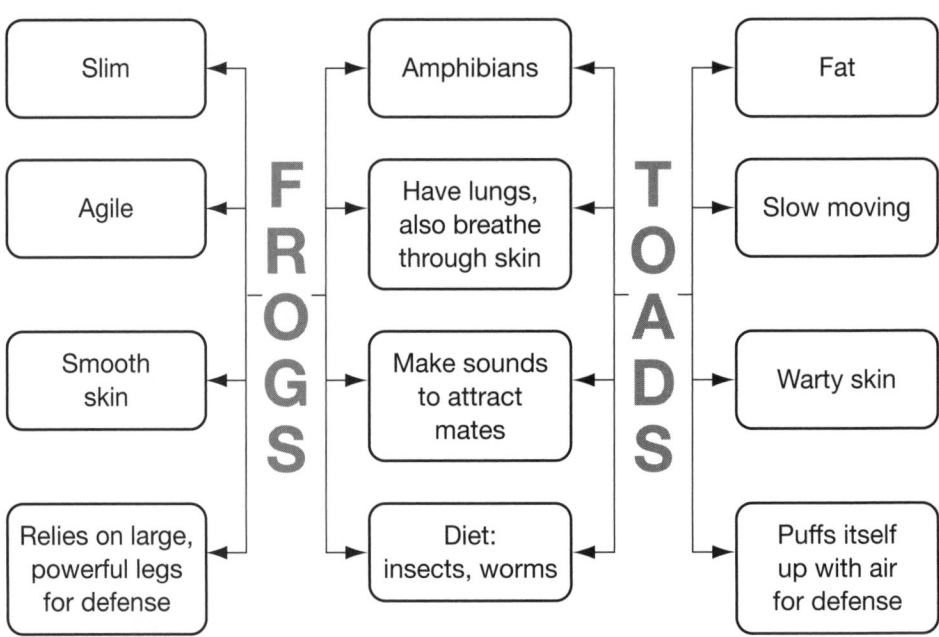

FIGURE 3.12   BLM 3.5

Share and Discuss

Step 2: Distribute compare and contrast paragraphs to the class (or use an overhead transparency or LCD projector). After each example, discuss whether the rules for compare and contrast paragraphs were followed:

- Is there a comparison being made? a contrast? What criteria are used?
- Does the paragraph match the graphic organizer?
- Does the paragraph have a topic sentence, clincher sentence, and signal words?
- If some paragraph elements are missing, how could the paragraph be revised to include them?

Step 3: Ask students to compare their own paragraphs with a model paragraph developed from the graphic organizer and discuss their similarities and differences. Figure 3.13, BLM 3.6, is a paragraph developed from the graphic organizer.

Frogs and Toads

Frogs and toads—how can you tell them apart? Even though they are similar in appearance, frogs and toads do have some notable differences. On one hand, the frog is slim, agile, and has smooth skin. On the other hand, the toad is fat, slow moving, and has warty skin. Another difference is how each defends itself. When threatened, the frog relies on its large, powerful back legs to leap to safety, whereas the toad puffs itself up with so much air it is impossible for a small snake to swallow it. However, the frog and toad do have a lot in common. They are both amphibians, which means that they live in the water and on land. Each has lungs and can breathe by absorbing oxygen through its skin. The sounds they make are also similar. Male frogs and toads croak to attract females in the breeding season. Both of these amphibians eat almost anything, with their usual diet being insects. Knowing these characteristics should help you the next time you are trying to decide if the amphibian you are looking at is a frog or a toad.

topic sentence

signal words

clincher sentence

FIGURE 3.13 BLM 3.6

COMPOSING THEIR OWN PARAGRAPHS

Once students have written jot notes from their paragraphs to make their organizers, and have developed paragraphs from their organizers, have them work in pairs to create their own paragraphs for the compare and contrast structure.

Step 1: Brainstorm topics for a compare and contrast paragraph with the class. Have the partners select a topic, or they can make up one of their own.

Step 2: After they have chosen their topics, have students create their organizers and write their paragraphs.

Step 3: Have each student create another organizer on a topic of his or her choosing and use it to write a compare and contrast paragraph.

Share and Discuss

Step 4: Ask for volunteers to read their paragraphs to the class, or, alternately, distribute compare and contrast paragraphs to the class. Discuss with the class whether the paragraph has the necessary parts—topic sentence, signal words, and clincher sentence—and whether it is a compare and contrast paragraph. Have the class compare the paragraph to its graphic organizer.

Step 5: Link students' learning to "real-world" examples by having them search in library books and textbooks for paragraphs that contain the compare and contrast structure. Ask for volunteers to share the examples they found. Discuss with students how the elements in these paragraphs compare to the examples they have studied and written. (For some additional model paragraphs, see pages 81–84.)

DIFFERENTIATED INSTRUCTION
Photo Comparisons

1. Show students pictures of two different people and have them compare and contrast them. For example:

   - Both people are wearing jeans and a t-shirt.
   - One person is taller than another person.
   - This person has red hair and that person has brown hair.
   - This person is holding an apple and that person is holding a pear.

2. Once they can pick out similarities and differences, show them another picture. Ask students to compare the pictures, but this time add signal words. For example:

   - This picture is about winter, whereas that picture is a spring scene.
   - Both pictures have three people in them.

3. As students get better at making comparisons, have them compare the art techniques used in two different paintings (e.g., "This painting is an impressionist-style painting that Claude Monet might have done, whereas this one is in the cubist style of Pablo Picasso").

SUGGESTED CROSS-CURRICULAR TOPICS

Many topics allow for comparing and contrasting in the **grades 4 to 6** and **grades 7 and 8** curricula. They include the following:

Social Studies

- Compare students' lives to those of children in medieval times
- Compare today's social and environmental concerns to those of medieval times
- Compare and contrast how two or more early civilizations were governed
- Compare modern life to life in an ancient civilization
- Compare social and cultural characteristics of two First Nations
- Explain the differences between First Nations people and early explorers
- Compare two or more regions of Canada
- Compare past attitudes to the fur industry to present-day attitudes
- Compare Canada in 1867 to today
- Compare the North West Mounted Police of the past to the Royal Canadian Mounted Police of today
- Compare the challenges faced by farmers at the beginning of the twentieth century to the challenges faced by farmers today
- Compare and contrast the characteristics of communities with high population density to communities with low density

Science

- Compare the life cycles of different kinds of plants or animals
- Explain the differences between sand, clay, humus, and other soil components
- Compare soil samples from two locations
- Compare natural and artificial light sources
- Compare a single pulley system to a multiple pulley system
- Explain the differences between rocks and minerals
- Compare cold-blooded and warm-blooded animals
- Compare vertebrates and invertebrates
- Give the similarities and differences between fossils and animals of the present
- Explain the differences in design between various types of flying devices
- Explain the differences between pure substances and mixtures using the particle theory
- Compare renewable and non-renewable resources
- Compare the automatic functions of the human eye to functions in an automatic camera

Math

- Compare a fraction and a decimal
- Compare two methods of adding, subtracting, multiplying, or dividing
- Compare two three-dimensional figures
- Compare and contrast similar and congruent figures
- Compare various quadrilaterals (e.g., equal sides, length of sides, angles, parallel sides)
- Compare and contrast two patterns
- Compare and contrast the areas and perimeters of two shapes

Arts

- Compare two works of art according to the elements of design
- Compare the techniques of two artists
- Compare cool colours and warm colours

Physical Education and Health

- Compare a bounce pass to a chest pass in basketball
- Compare good sportsmanship to poor sportsmanship
- Compare a healthy diet to an unhealthy diet

Language Arts

- Compare two characters in a book
- Compare the themes of two books
- Compare two books or two authors
- Compare two authors for ideas, organization, voice, conventions, effective use of language
- Compare two videos on the same topic
- Compare two newspaper articles on the same topic

COMPARE AND CONTRAST STRUCTURES IN THE CONTENT AREAS

As with the other structures, textbook and nonfiction examples will not necessarily fit the "ideal" models we have dealt with in this book. However, students learn to recognize the structure if given enough practice. Here are some examples that you could use with students.

What's the difference?

Viruses and bacteria are **both** microscopic germs, but they're **different** in many ways. Bacteria are like tiny animals—they can move around, and they can reproduce.

continued ——→

In this example, the title gives the first indication that something is being compared. The first sentence in the paragraph tells us what will be compared. Signal words (highlighted in bold) are used throughout the paragraph. There is no clincher sentence.

Viruses **aren't** anything **like** animals. Some scientists don't think viruses are even alive. A virus can't reproduce or move without help. It has to hang out waiting to be swept along by a sneeze or a wave of body fluid. Which are **more** dangerous? Viruses and bacteria can **both** be deadly, but in a battle between the two, certain viruses win. They're so small they can get inside bacteria and make them sick.

T. Romanek, *Achoo, The most interesting book you'll ever read about germs* (Toronto: Kids Can Press) 2003, 10.

FIGURE 3.14   BLM 3.7

Cheetahs and Leopards

If you have trouble telling a cheetah from a leopard, you're not alone. Spotting the **differences between** these big spotted cats can be tricky.

Cheetahs are the **fastest** mammals in the world. A cheetah has long legs for chasing gazelles, zebras, and other quick-moving animals that it eats. Over short distances, a cheetah can race as fast as a car zooming down the highway. A leopard has **shorter** legs and can't run **as quickly**. It catches its prey by sneaking up behind another animal, then pouncing on it.

Cheetahs and leopards have **different** faces, too. A cheetah has dark stripes that run down both sides of its face, from its eyes to its upper lip. A leopard doesn't have these markings. Its face is **broader and heavier**.

Another way to tell a cheetah from a leopard is to see which big cat climbs trees. You'll never see a full-grown cheetah up a tree. Its claws, which cannot completely draw back (or retract), are not suited for tree-climbing. All leopards, **on the other hand**, have claws that retract. Most leopards spend lots of time in trees, eating, sleeping, or waiting to pounce on animals that walk on the ground below.

Some leopards, called panthers, have dark-coloured skin with spots that can be seen only in bright sunlight. You'll never spot a cheetah that looks like that!

Diehl, Judy & Plumb, David, *What's the difference? 10 animal look-alikes* (Toronto: Annick Press Ltd.) 2000, 5.

FIGURE 3.15   BLM 3.8

The topic sentence clearly states what the paragraph is about. The use of signal words, such as **different, on the other hand, fastest,** and **shorter,** identify this as a compare and contrast paragraph.

LINKING ASSESSMENT TO LEARNING

As with the other text structures, the most important traits to focus on will be *organization* and *ideas*.

- Successful organization would include having good topic and clincher sentences, as well as suitable signal words.
- The ideas developed in a paragraph should mirror the topic sentence, and the similarities and/or differences should be clearly stated.
- The comparison should be evident in the paragraph; there should be no doubt about what is being compared and/or contrasted.

For students to benefit from the assessment of their work, specific criteria must be set. Ideally, students should help to develop their own criteria because this gives them a more thorough understanding of what they need to know and what is expected of them. If they have previously studied the sequence and enumerative structures and are familiar with the criteria used for them, many students will likely suggest similar organizational criteria, such as

- having a topic sentence that clearly tells what will be discussed in the paragraph
- having a clincher sentence that ties up the ideas in the paragraph
- using a variety of signal words

If this is the first structure students are learning, they might suggest criteria such as neat writing, proper capitalization and punctuation (e.g., using periods correctly), and no spelling mistakes. However, encourage them to think about what is needed for the text structure instead of simply language conventions. If they suggest very general text structure criteria, encourage them to be more specific by asking them questions such as the following:

- How many different signal words do you think we should use? *(For compare and/or contrast, it will depend on the number of characteristics being compared.)*
- What is important about the topic sentence? *(It tells what the paragraph will be about.)*

It is important to be aware that students will not learn to identify criteria overnight. It takes **grades 4 to 6** students most of the year to be able to do so. **Grades 7 and 8** students should understand the important criteria much earlier in the year if they have been exposed to the various structures in the earlier grades. But it does take time, since participating in choosing the criteria for assessment is often a new experience for students.

Assessment Checklists

As students fill out the self-assessment checklists, compare and contrast peer feedback checklists, and compare and constrast assessment rubric, it

Nelson

Comprehensive Literacy Resource

for Grades 3–6 Teachers

Senior Author
Miriam P. Trehearne

Traits "are the characteristics or qualities that define good writing" (Trehearne, 2006, 230). These include
- ideas presented
- word choice
- voice (the personality of the writer)
- language conventions (grammar, spelling, etc.)
- sentence fluency (using sentences that make sense and vary in length and structure)

is important that you circulate and ask questions about their assessments. (See BLM 8.7 to BLM 8.9 for the checklists.) Some students will indicate "yes" without really examining the criteria carefully. For this reason, I not only ask if there is a topic sentence but if the topic sentence catches the reader's attention. This makes the student stop and think about the topic sentence and its effectiveness. I do the same for the signal words. I ask if the words have been used and I also have students indicate how many different words are used.

Discussing the self-assessment checklists with students should help you assess their understanding of the structure and indicate where they need to go next. Mini-lessons can then be set up for those students requiring further assistance in particular areas such as

- creating strong topic sentences
- using a variety of compare and contrast signal words
- ensuring that the ideas are clearly stated and there is a comparison taking place
- completing the paragraph with a strong clincher sentence

For example, below is a mini-lesson that might help students understand the use of clincher sentences.

Mini-Lesson: Clincher Sentences

1. To help students create strong clincher sentences, show them a compare and contrast paragraph without a clincher sentence.

2. Offer them three clincher sentences they could use to finish the paragraph.

3. Discuss the strengths of each ending and have students choose the one that best sums up the ideas in the paragraph. Ask them to explain their reasons.

4. Show students a paragraph without a clincher sentence and have them write their own clincher sentence.

5. Present as many examples as necessary to help students understand what a strong clincher sentence looks like.

Figure 3.17 on page 72 is an example of a checklist I give to students to use for self-assessment. I use the same checklist for assessing their work. It quickly shows me who understands the criteria and, more importantly, who can apply the criteria to their own work.

BLM 8.7

Student Self-Assessment Checklist for Compare and Contrast Structures

Name: _____ Date: _____

Organization		
My graphic organizer fits with my compare and contrast paragraph.	Yes	No
I have a topic sentence.	Yes	No
I have a clincher sentence.	Yes	No
Word Choice		
I used compare and contrast signal words.	Yes	No
I used _____ different compare and contrast signal words. (number)		
Ideas and Content		
My topic sentence: • tells the reader what will be compared and contrasted. • catches the reader's attention.	Yes Yes	No No
I compared and contrasted using the same criteria.	Yes	No
My clincher sentence ties the ideas of my paragraph together.	Yes	No
The supporting sentences in my paragraph give details about what is being compared and contrasted.	Yes	No

The strengths in my compare and contrast paragraph include:

The areas that need improvement in my compare and contrast paragraph include:

My goal for future writing is:

BLM 8.8

Peer Feedback Checklist for Compare and Contrast Structures

Author: _____ Peer Editor: _____ Date: _____

Organization		
The graphic organizer fits with the compare and contrast paragraph.	Yes	No
There is a topic sentence.	Yes	No
There is a clincher sentence.	Yes	No
Word Choice		
Compare and contrast signal words were used.	Yes	No
_____ different compare and contrast signal words were used. (number)		
Ideas and Content		
The topic sentence: • tells the reader what will be compared and contrasted. • catches the reader's attention.	Yes Yes	No No
The same criteria was used to compare and contrast.	Yes	No
The clincher sentence ties the ideas of the paragraph together.	Yes	No
The supporting sentences in the paragraph give details about what is being compared and contrasted.	Yes	No

The strengths in the compare and contrast paragraph include:

The areas that need improvement in the compare and contrast paragraph include:

My suggested goal for this writer is:

Student Self-Assessment Checklist for Compare and Contrast Structures

Name: _____ Date: _____

Organization		
My graphic organizer fits with my compare and contrast paragraph.	(Yes)	No
I have a topic sentence.	(Yes)	No
I have a clincher sentence.	(Yes)	No

Word Choice		
I used compare and contrast signal words.	(Yes)	No
I used ___2___ different compare and contrast signal words. (number)		

Ideas and Content		
My topic sentence: • tells the reader what will be compared and contrasted. • catches the reader's attention.	(Yes) (Yes)	No No
I compared and contrasted using the same criteria.	(Yes)	No
My clincher sentence ties the ideas of my paragraph together.	(Yes)	No
The supporting sentences in my paragraph give details about what is being compared and contrasted.	(Yes)	No
The strengths of my compare and contrast paragraph include:		

I used signal words I haven't used before such as whereas. My topic sentence tells that I am talking about hockey and street hockey. People who read my paragraph will learn lots about street and ice hockey.

FIGURE 3.17   BLM 8.7

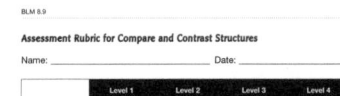

Assessment Rubrics

When students write the paragraphs that I will assess, I use the rubric for self assessment so that they have the opportunity to revise what they have written before they hand it in. I mark the paragraphs using the same rubric.

After I hand back the paragraph, students fill in the bottom of the rubric, which asks them to look at the criteria and explain how they will move up to the next level. (See Figure 3.18 for an example.) My comments are in italics.

GRADE 5 STUDENT SELF-ASSESSMENT

> **Students complete the bottom of the rubric after it is returned to them.**

To move to the next level, I must …

add more detail when I compare two things. I compared my mom and me but didn't give any examples about the facts I gave.

(This student is on the right track. She realizes she has to add more detail to her paragraph to make it more effective. This provides an excellent opportunity for student/teacher conferencing.)

FIGURE 3.18

Identifying Text Structures: Reading Like a Writer

After students have had practice with compare and contrast paragraphs, they need to make the connection between their writing and the text structures they find in their reading. See Figure 3.19, BLM 8.23, for a tool that allows you to track their progress in this area of reading.

BLM 8.23

Checklist for Identifying Text Structure Criteria

Name: _____   Date: _____

	Sequence	Enumerative	Compare and Contrast	Cause and Effect	Problem and Solution	Question and Answer	Description
Is able to identify the structure when it is in its basic form in an individual paragraph.							
Is able to identify the characteristics of the structures when reading textbooks and trade books (signal words, topic sentence, clincher sentence, etc.).							
Is able to identify the structure when reading textbooks or trade books even though it is not in its basic form (bullets used instead of signal words, no clincher sentence, etc.).							

Comments

FIGURE 3.19   BLM 8.23

Anecodotal Records

Keeping anecdotal records from teacher–student conferences, as well as samples of students' work and marks from various assignments, helps track students' progress over the year. When students turn in compare and contrast structure assignments, most marks will be for organization and ideas. However, marks could also be given for language conventions and effective use of vocabulary if those traits have been discussed earlier in the year.

Blackline Masters

Name: _____ Date: _____

Read the paragraph. Underline the topic and clincher sentences, and circle the signal words.

Moths and Butterflies

Even though moths and butterflies have a lot of things in common, they also have important differences. One similarity is that they belong to the insect family. Another characteristic they share is that both emerge from cocoons after being caterpillars. In addition, moths and butterflies each have four wings. As for differences, moths have short, thick bodies, whereas butterflies have long slender ones. Moths are usually busy at night, but butterflies are active by day. It is these differences that help you tell them apart.

Name: _____ Date: _____

With a partner, read the paragraph. Underline the topic and clincher sentences, and circle the signal words. Then discuss the similarities between the organizer and the finished paragraph.

Downhill Skiing and Water Skiing

	Downhill Skiing	**Water Skiing**
Similarities	• Can go fast/slow • Do turns and tricks • Use skis	• Can go fast/slow • Do turns and tricks • Use skis
Differences	• Skis are narrower • More control of speed • Winter, snow-covered hills • Ski anywhere on hill	• Skis are wider • Less control of speed • Summer, water • Ski where the tow boat goes

Downhill skiing and water skiing are two sports that have less in common than you think. While both use skis, their widths and shapes are not similar. Downhill skis are narrower and more contoured. Water skis are more like snowboards, shorter and wider than downhill skis. For both sports, you can go fast or slow and do tricks, but there are important differences. Downhill skiers have more control than water skiers. That's because they are not being pulled by anything. They can choose any run on the hill. On the other hand, water skiers can only go where the tow boat takes them. However, the biggest difference is when and where each sport takes place. We downhill ski in winter on snow-covered hills. We water ski in summer on warm lakes. Still, winter or summer, these sports are great ways to spend our free time.

Name: _____ Date: _____

Create a graphic organizer based on this paragraph.

Earth and Us

Comparing the human body to Earth is not as strange as it sounds. Did you know that both can suffer from sunburn? We use suntan lotion to protect us from the Sun. Earth has similar protection, but instead of suntan lotion, it has the ozone layer. If we don't protect our skin, it burns. If the ozone layer develops holes, plants and animals may get burned by the Sun's harmful radiation. Acid indigestion is another thing both have in common. When we eat something that has too much acid, our stomachs experience pain and heartburn. Car exhaust and industrial pollution act like too much acid, as well. In fact, they produce acid rain. It kills living things in lakes, destroys plants, and even eats away at buildings. Another way the human body resembles Earth is that both can get a fever. When we are sick, our temperature goes up. Earth's temperature can also rise when air pollution acts like a greenhouse and traps the Sun's heat. We must take care of ourselves and Earth to prevent sunburn, indigestion, and fever.

Name: _____ Date: _____

In pairs, make your own organizer for the "Earth and Us" paragraph. Remember to use point form, not full sentences, to fill in the organizer.

Earth and Us

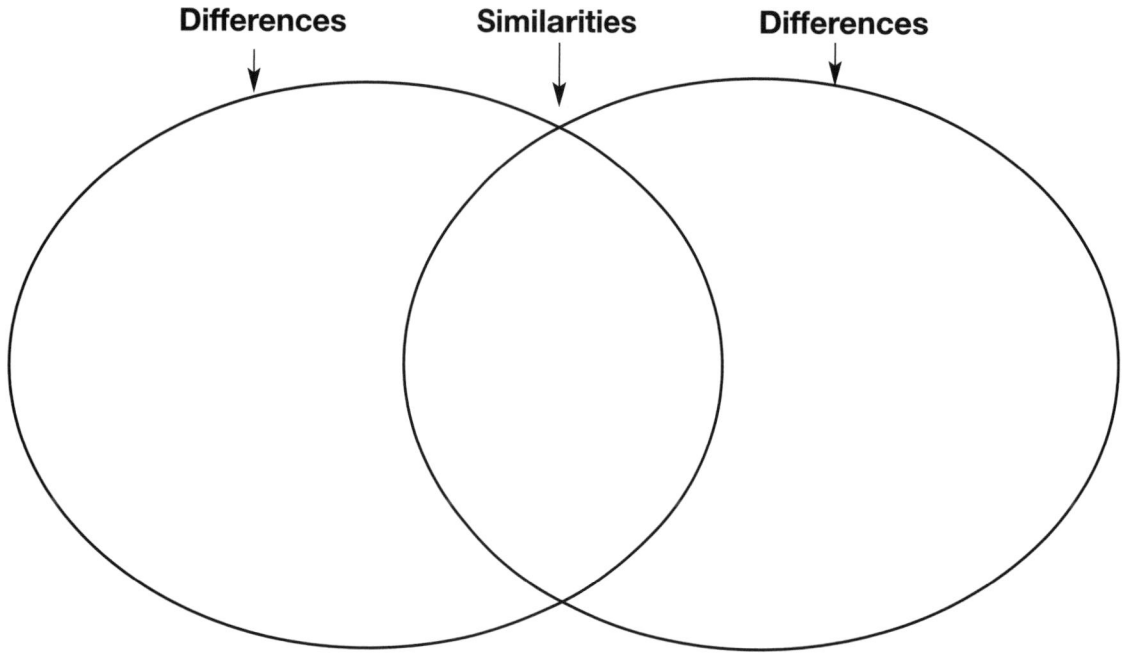

Name: _____ Date: _____

In pairs, using this graphic organizer, write a paragraph. Underline the topic and clincher sentences, and circle the signal words.

Frogs and Toads

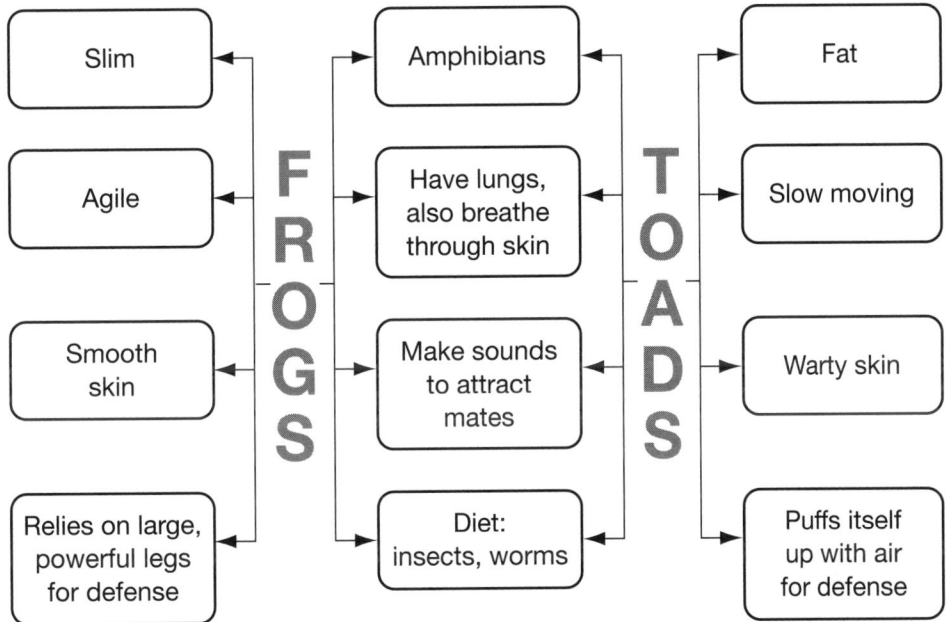

Name: _____ Date: _____

In pairs, compare your paragraphs with this model paragraph developed from the graphic organizer. Discuss their similarities and differences.

Frogs and Toads

Frogs and toads—how can you tell them apart? Even though they are similar in appearance, frogs and toads do have some notable differences. On one hand, the frog is slim, agile, and has smooth skin. On the other hand, the toad is fat, slow moving, and has warty skin. Another difference is how each defends itself. When threatened, the frog relies on its large, powerful back legs to leap to safety, whereas the toad puffs itself up with so much air it is impossible for a small snake to swallow it. However, the frog and toad do have a lot in common. They are both amphibians, which means that they live in the water and on land. Each has lungs and can breathe by absorbing oxygen through its skin. The sounds they make are also similar. Male frogs and toads croak to attract females in the breeding season. Both of these amphibians eat almost anything, with their usual diet being insects. Knowing these characteristics should help you the next time you are trying to decide if the amphibian you are looking at is a frog or a toad.

Name: _____ Date: _____

Underline what is being compared in this paragraph. Then circle the signal words.

What's the difference?

Viruses and bacteria are both microscopic germs, but they're different in many ways. Bacteria are like tiny animals—they can move around, and they can reproduce. Viruses aren't anything like animals. Some scientists don't think viruses are even alive. A virus can't reproduce or move without help. It has to hang out waiting to be swept along by a sneeze or a wave of body fluid. Which are more dangerous? Viruses and bacteria can both be deadly, but in a battle between the two, certain viruses win. They're so small they can get inside bacteria and make them sick.

T. Romanek, *Achoo, The most interesting book you'll ever read about germs* (Toronto: Kids Can Press) 2003, 10.

Name: _____ Date: _____

Is there a topic sentence in this paragraph? If so, underline it. Then circle the signal words.

Cheetahs and Leopards

If you have trouble telling a cheetah from a leopard, you're not alone. Spotting the differences between these big spotted cats can be tricky.

Cheetahs are the fastest mammals in the world. A cheetah has long legs for chasing gazelles, zebras, and other quick-moving animals that it eats. Over short distances, a cheetah can race as fast as a car zooming down the highway. A leopard has shorter legs and can't run as quickly. It catches its prey by sneaking up behind another animal, then pouncing on it.

Cheetahs and leopards have different faces, too. A cheetah has dark stripes that run down both sides of its face, from its eyes to its upper lip. A leopard doesn't have these markings. Its face is broader and heavier.

Another way to tell a cheetah from a leopard is to see which big cat climbs trees. You'll never see a full-grown cheetah up a tree. Its claws, which cannot completely draw back (or retract), are not suited for tree-climbing. All leopards, on the other hand, have claws that retract. Most leopards spend lots of time in trees, eating, sleeping, or waiting to pounce on animals that walk on the ground below.

Some leopards, called panthers, have dark-coloured skin with spots that can be seen only in bright sunlight. You'll never spot a cheetah that looks like that!

Diehl, Judy & Plumb, David, *What's the difference? 10 animal look-alikes* (Toronto: Annick Press Ltd.) 2000.

Name: _____ Date: _____

Read the paragraph. Underline the topic and clincher sentences, and circle the signal words.

Comparing Sharks

Is it a whale shark or a basking shark? Well you be the judge. Similarities include the fact that they both eat plankton by straining it out of the water through their teeth. (Yuck!) They're both found in all temperate oceans, and of course they're both sharks. On one hand they both reach lengths between 13m and 15m but on the other hand the whale shark is definitely longer, and bigger weighing up to 18 metric tonnes! Whale sharks much prefer to stay beneath the surface while eating, whereas the basking sharks would rather swim on the surface while eating. (They both eat all day to eat enough to survive.) Even though whale sharks have never been hunted the basking shark was once heavily hunted for the large quantities of oil found in its liver. Another distinguishing feature is that basking sharks do not pump water so they have to rely on their swimming to pass water over the gills. The whale shark, however, is able to pump water over its gills so does not need to swim forward when eating. I bet you'll never look at any shark the same way again.

Name: _____ Date: _____

Read the paragraph. Underline the topic and clincher sentences, and circle the signal words.

Rugged vs. Light

One important difference between a mountain bike and a road bike is the design of their frames. Because a mountain bike is designed for rough riding on uneven dirt paths that may have obstacles such as rocks or logs, it is essential that the frame is durable and rugged. Durability means having a thick, heavy frame. Mountain bikes usually weigh several kilograms more than road bikes do. Because a road bike is designed for pavement, it is lighter and can go much faster. However, hitting even a small rock on a road bike can result in a dented wheel. So, when purchasing a bike, make sure you consider where you are going to ride it.

TEACHING CAUSE AND EFFECT STRUCTURES

4

DEFINING THE STRUCTURE

In the cause and effect structure, *facts, events, or concepts are described as happening or coming into being as a result of other factors.* Frequently found in nonfiction books, including textbooks for middle school students, it uses several different forms:

- *One cause* and *one effect* are given: "Not brushing your teeth may result in cavities." The *cause* is not brushing teeth; the *effect* is cavities.
- *One effect* and a list of *many causes* are given: If the *effect* is erosion, *causes* might include erosion by water, wind, ice, and living things.
- *One cause* leading to *several effects* is given: If the *cause* is over-logging, the *effects* might be changes to habitats, smaller populations of some animals, migration of animals, and soil being washed away so new plants cannot grow.

Paragraph Features

Topic Sentence

In a cause and effect paragraph, the topic sentence states that a particular cause will result in certain effects (e.g., "Riding without a helmet can have serious consequences"). It might also indicate that the reader should be watching for several causes for an effect (e.g., "The Winnipeg General Strike was caused by several factors").

Clincher Sentence

As in other text structure formats, the clincher sentence sums up the paragraph and connects back to the topic sentence. However, for cause and effect, it often tells the reader what to do to avoid the results discussed (e.g., "Always do your homework to avoid these unpleasant consequences").

Signal Words

As we move into the structures that are not as familiar to students, it is important to take time to introduce the signal words and how to use them. Students may tend to use only familiar signal words. Encourage them to be risk takers and to try signal words they have never used before. (See list of signal words below.) You can begin by having students include the signal words in simple sentences before asking them to use the words in paragraphs.

SIGNAL WORDS FOR CAUSE AND EFFECT STRUCTURES	
as a result	thus
because	therefore
due to	accordingly
this led to	so
nevertheless	consequently
if ... then	another reason
in order that	some consequences are
unless	for this reason
since	on account of
so that	

Grades 4 to 8 Classrooms

For many **grades 4 to 6** students, this will be their first encounter with the cause and effect structure. They will need to do oral exercises about cause and effect *before* they are expected to write their own paragraphs or independently identify the structures in textbooks. As they become more familiar with the structure, they can begin to identify it in nonfiction texts. They can also begin to write basic paragraphs, perhaps using a template such as the following:

- The cause is ...
- The effect is ...
- Another effect is ...

While **grades 7 and 8** students may be more familiar with this structure, they will still require time and instruction to recognize it in its various forms and be able to write suitable paragraphs. Take the time to ensure that students understand the cause/effect relationship, and invite them to give examples orally before having them write paragraphs.

Additional Instructional Support

As this is one of the more difficult structures for students to understand, it is important to build strong scaffolding into the lessons for English Language Learners (ELL) and special education students. Orally introduce the structure and have students relate the cause and effect structure to their own lives first, before you teach its written form. For example:

1. Begin by putting a cause on the board. For example, "I fell on the ice."

2. Have students tell you the effects of the action, and write the effects down using an arrow to indicate that the cause is related to the effect. For example:

"I fell on the ice." → "I broke my arm."

3. Next, have students suggest more than one effect for a cause (see Figure 4.1.).

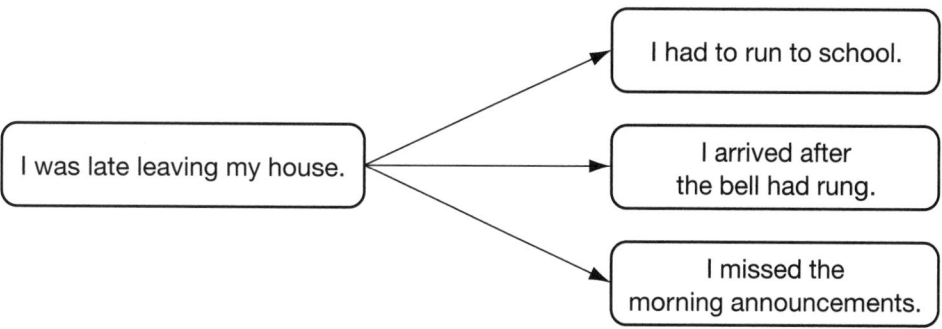

FIGURE 4.1

4. Show students a list of signal words, and have them create a sentence by replacing one of the arrows with a signal word. For example:

- I was late leaving my house **so** I had to run to school.

After students have the idea of the structure, you can have them work in pairs to create their own cause and effect sentences. You can also introduce some of the other signal words once students are confident using this form of the structure.

INTRODUCING THE STRUCTURE

Step 1: If students are not familiar with cause and effect, begin with a simple activity to ensure that they understand the concept.

Step 2: Ask students for the cause(s) and effect(s) for a number of cause and effect topic sentences. Have them also identify the signal words in each of the sentences. For example:

Due to the heavy rain we were unable to play baseball.

Cause: heavy rain

Effect: we were unable to play baseball

Signal words: Due to

Figure 4.2, BLM 4.1, is an example of this type of activity. The causes are circled, the effects are underlined and the signal words are in bold.

Circle the cause and underline the effect in each of the following sentences. Identify the signal words.

1. (Because I arrived late,) I missed the play.

2. (Since you were not at home today,) we decided to visit you another time.

3. (Due to the fact that it was raining,) our baseball game was cancelled.

4. We came home early (because it was too hot to play football.)

5. (The choir practiced for hours) so the members would sing well at the concert.

6. The flowers died (as a result of not getting enough water.)

7. Some homes in Manitoba were destroyed (because of the vast flooding.)

8. The people in Québec were without power for weeks (due to the ice storm.)

FIGURE 4.2 BLM 4.1

Step 3: Once students have a basic understanding of the structure, ask them to think of cause and effect statements from their own experiences (e.g., "I was late for school because I slept in").

EXAMINING A MODEL PARAGRAPH

Introduce the Model

Step 1: Distribute to the class a cause and effect paragraph. BLM 4.2, "Brushing Your Teeth," is one example.

Identify Paragraph Elements

Step 2: Ask students to read the paragraph and underline the topic sentence, the clincher sentence, and circle the signal words. A marked-up example of "Brushing Your Teeth" is shown in Figure 4.3.

Brushing Your Teeth

topic sentence ⟶ If you don't brush your teeth, you may end up in a great deal of pain. Within 20 minutes of eating, the sugars in the food combine with invisible bacteria in your mouth to form acids. As a result, your teeth will begin to decay. When the signal words — sugars and bacteria are not removed, plaque forms on the

continued ⟶

Text Structures: Teaching Patterns in Reading and Writing

teeth. ⌐If⌐ it builds up, ⌐then⌐ the acids produced by the plaque eat a hole in the enamel. This is known as a cavity. ⌐Unless⌐ a dentist treats the cavity, it spreads into the soft, bony material under the enamel and enters the centre of the tooth called the pulp. ⌐Consequently,⌐ the tooth becomes infected, and you end up with a toothache. <u>Brushing your teeth daily is a great way to prevent the discomfort of tooth decay.</u> ←——— **clincher sentence**

FIGURE 4.3 BLM 4.2

Share and Discuss

Step 3: You might have students who are familiar with the compare and contrast text structure compare two cause and effect paragraphs. For example, they could use a graphic organizer to compare similarities in signal words, and topic and clincher sentences.

DEVELOPING A GRAPHIC ORGANIZER

Introduce the Model

Step 1: Distribute a cause and effect paragraph along with a graphic organizer. See Figure 4.4, BLM 4.3, "Bike Helmets," for one example.

Step 2: When introducing the graphic organizer, point out to students that it shows a cause and effect relationship and uses point form.

BIKE HELMETS

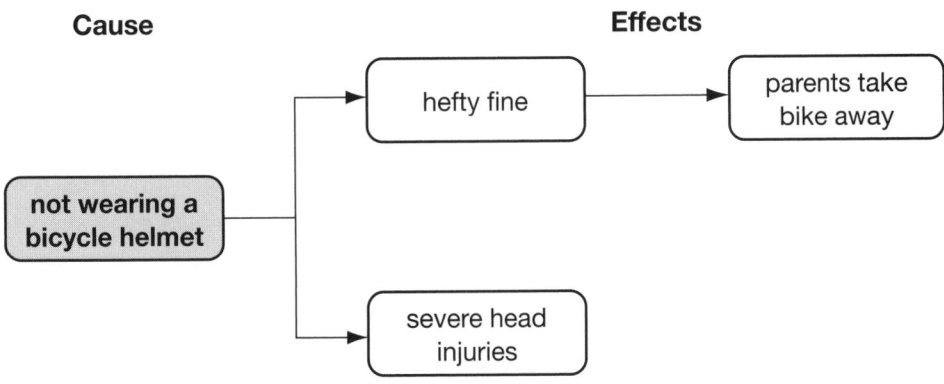

FIGURE 4.4 BLM 4.3

Identify Paragraph Elements

Step 3: Have students identify the topic and clincher sentences, and all the signal words. Note similarities between the points in the organizer and the development of the paragraph (see Figure 4.5).

Bike Helmets

topic sentence ⟶ <u>Riding without a bicycle helmet can have serious effects.</u> You may have to pay a hefty fine, [because] it is against the law to ride your bike without a helmet. This might [lead to] your parents removing your bike privileges for a period of time. The most critical [result,] of course, is that if you are in an accident, you could receive severe head injuries. <u>Wearing a bicycle helmet cannot only save you a lot of grief, it might even save your life!</u>

signal words

clincher sentence

FIGURE 4.5 BLM 4.3

Create the Graphic Organizer

Step 4: Have students make a graphic organizer (see Figure 4.6) to go with a model paragraph. Figure 4.7, BLM 4.4, "Pesticides," is one example. Students can use the organizer provided or make one of their own. It is important for students to realize there will not necessarily be signal words for each part of the organizer.

PESTICIDES

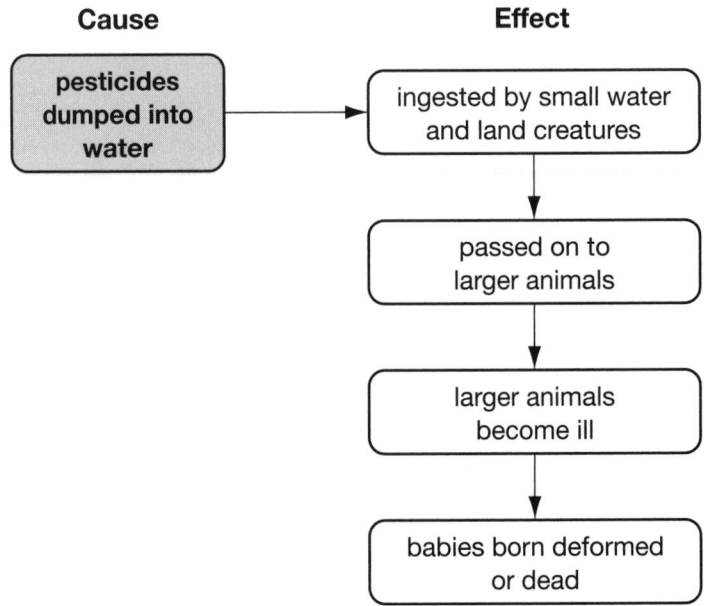

FIGURE 4.6

Text Structures: Teaching Patterns in Reading and Writing

Step 5: Have students work in pairs to circle the signal words and underline the topic and clincher sentences of the paragraph. (Pairs of students will need only one copy of the paragraph between them.)

Pesticides

<u>Pesticides that are dumped into lakes, rivers, and oceans can be very dangerous to marine and animal life.</u> These substances pollute the water. This leads to shellfish and other small water creatures taking in the substances. Consequently, the toxins enter the food chain. When the larger sea creatures eat the smaller creatures, the pesticides are passed on to the larger animals. As a result, the larger animals become very ill. Another effect of this pesticide pollution is that the babies of these larger marine creatures and animals often are born deformed or dead. <u>It is important to stop the dumping of pesticides into the oceans so that marine and animal life can be preserved.</u>

topic sentence

signal words

clincher sentence

FIGURE 4.7 BLM 4.4

Share and Discuss

Step 6: Fill in a class organizer on an overhead transparency using feedback from students. Have them check their own organizers against the class example.

WRITING A CAUSE AND EFFECT PARAGRAPH

Use a Graphic Organizer

Step 1: Have pairs of students write a paragraph using the jot notes from a completed organizer. ("Ice Storm!" in Figure 4.8, BLM 4.6, is one example.) Remind students that their paragraphs must have a topic sentence, clincher sentence, and suitable signal words.

ICE STORM!

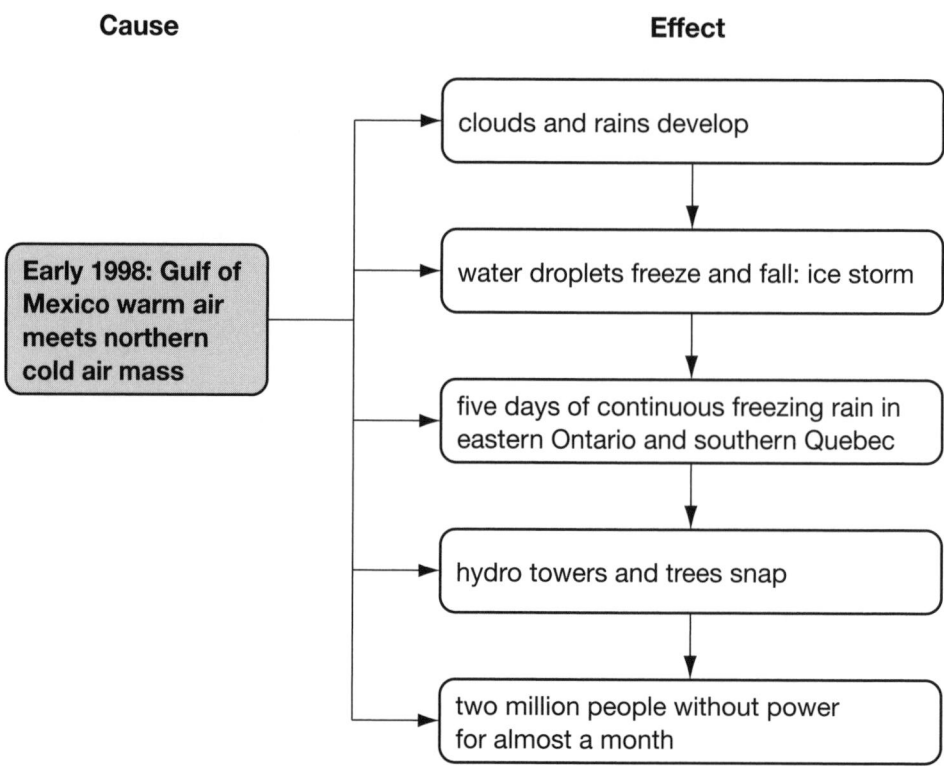

FIGURE 4.8   BLM 4.6

Share and Discuss

Step 2: Distribute to the class a paragraph you have written based on the organizer. Alternately, have volunteers share their paragraphs with the class. For the paragraph, discuss whether the rules for cause and effect paragraphs were followed. Is there a topic sentence, clincher sentence, and signal words? If not, how can the paragraph be revised to include the missing features?

Step 3: Ask students to compare their work to this paragraph. Have them discuss their comparisons as a class or in pairs. Figure 4.9, BLM 4.7, shows an example of a paragraph based on the "Ice Storm!" organizer. The paragraph elements are highlighted.

Ice Storm!

topic sentence ⟶ In early 1998, parts of eastern Ontario and southern Quebec experienced five continuous days of freezing rain that paralyzed the entire region. The cause of this rain was a large, warm air mass from the Gulf of Mexico. It was swept northward by a jet stream, where it met a cold air mass.

signal words

Consequently, clouds and rain developed, and the water droplets froze wherever they landed. The consequences were

continued ⟶

that the layers of ice snapped and bent hydro towers and trees. As a result, two million people were left without power in wintertime for almost a month. This severe weather and environmental destruction has been called Canada's "Storm of the Century."

← clincher sentence

Adapted from Paul Aves et al. *Connections 7: Exploring Physical Geography* (Toronto: Pearson Education), 2000.

FIGURE 4.9 BLM 4.7

COMPOSING THEIR OWN PARAGRAPHS

After students have practised developing cause and effect jot notes and paragraphs from assigned material, have them write their own paragraphs for the cause and effect structure.

Step 1: Brainstorm topics with the class for a cause and effect paragraph. Have students work in pairs to select a suitable topic.

Step 2: After they have chosen their topics, students can develop a list of causes and effects in the form of a graphic organizer. Remind them when they are writing their paragraphs to follow the order of their organizers.

Share and Discuss

Step 3: Read some of your sample paragraphs to the class. Distribute the paragraphs' organizer. Engage the class in a discussion of whether the paragraph has the necessary parts: topic sentence, signal words, and clincher sentence. Ask students to compare each paragraph to its graphic organizer (e.g., Does the organizer reflect the cause and effect structure in the paragraph?). (See *Chapter 8, Monitoring and Assessing Student Work*, for self-assessment checklists and rubrics.) Ask for volunteers to share their paragraphs and graphic organizers with the class.

Step 4: Have students search for "real-world" examples of cause and effect text structures in textbooks, nonfiction books, and magazine articles. Encourage them to compare these examples with the ones they have written and studied. (See *Cause and Effect Structures in the Content Areas* on page 96.)

DIFFERENTIATED INSTRUCTION

The following activities are designed to help raise awareness of causal relationships. They can be given as follow-up activities or used to introduce cause and effect situations and examples.

Cause and Effect Strips

1. Distribute strips of paper that have causes and effects written on them (Figure 4.10).

2. Ask students to match a cause and an effect and then create a sentence using the two strips. Students can work independently or in small groups. Remind them that they should add a suitable signal word between the parts of each sentence. Once they have successfully written a few sentences, challenge students to make some cause and effect strips of their own. They can then exchange the strips with other students to match up and complete.

EXAMPLES:

> The grade five class decided they wanted to help out endangered animals

so

> they raised money and donated it to the World Wildlife Federation.

> The Hornets won the opening game of the tournament

because

> every member of the team played their hardest.

FIGURE 4.10

Picture Match-ups

1. A variation on cause and effect strips is to write causes on strips of paper and use pictures to illustrate the effects (see Figure 4.11, BLM 4.8). Students match a cause with one or more effects. Here is one example:

> "The hurricane hit the land with incredible force."

FIGURE 4.11 BLM 4.8

2. Have students complete the cause and effect sentence using the appropriate effect (or effects). For example:

The hurricane hit the land with incredible force resulting in trees being uprooted, roofs being damaged, and serious flooding.

Cause and Effect Posters

1. In this activity, students create a poster showing a cause and effect relationship. On one side of the poster is the cause, on the other side, the effect. Students include an appropriate signal word to connect the two sides of the poster. See Figure 4.12 for an example.

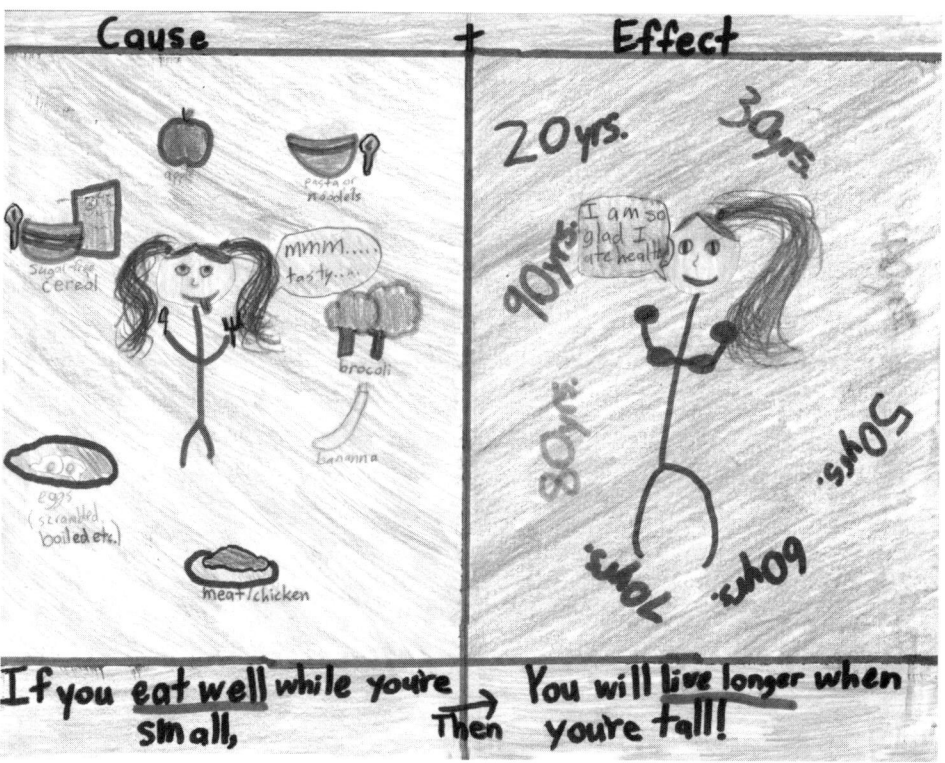

FIGURE 4.12

2. Display the posters in the classroom and challenge students to write cause and effect sentences based on them.

SUGGESTED CROSS-CURRICULAR TOPICS

Here are some topics that might fit the cause and effect pattern:

Social Studies

- Effects on medieval society of expanding contact with other parts of the world
- Muslim influence on the arts, architecture, and science
- Effects of contact with European explorers on First Nations

- Effects of contact with First Nations on European explorers
- Effects of cooperation between First Nations and European explorers
- Reasons for the early travels of explorers and the effects of their travels
- How the St. Lawrence River and Great Lakes influence human activity
- Causes of key events of a period (e.g., causes and effects of the War of 1812)
- Reasons for early settlement of English Canada
- Impact of the War of 1812 on the development of Canada
- Causes and effects of the Rebellions of 1837–1838
- Causes and effects of the Red River Rebellion of 1869–1870
- Factors that led to Laurier's electoral defeat in 1911

Science

- Climate patterns and their causes
- Why animals live in a specific habitat
- Ways humans can affect the natural world
- Effects of wind, water, and ice on the landscape
- The cause of eclipses
- Causes and effects of natural events (e.g., tornadoes, earthquakes)
- How structures are affected by the geometric shapes within them
- Effects of physical features on land use
- Cause and effect relationships between the environment and economy of a province or territory

Physical Education and Health

- Disorders affected by diet (e.g., diabetes)
- Effects of physical activity

Language Arts

- A discussion about which event in a fiction story caused another event or situation
- A discussion about what action of a character caused another action to occur

CAUSE AND EFFECT STRUCTURES IN THE CONTENT AREAS

As with the other structures, textbook examples are not "ideal" examples like the ones included in this book. However, students do learn to recognize the structure involved if they are introduced to enough examples. Most cause and effect structures in textbooks are longer than one para-

Text Structures: Teaching Patterns in Reading and Writing

graph. Often there is a topic paragraph, a clincher paragraph, and signal words. Signal words are sometimes replaced with bullets that show the causes and/or effects.

The first selection following the blackline master section at the end of this chapter (BLM 4.9, page 110) is a single-paragraph example. Each has topic and clincher sentences and signal words. BLM 4.9, "Desertification," is a **grade 8** example. Note that the word **resulted** indicates a cause and effect relationship.

BLM 4.10, "The Impact of Logging," is characteristic of a longer cause and effect structure that students might encounter in textbooks. This one is from a **grade 5** science book. Here there is an introductory paragraph and a clincher paragraph rather than topic and clincher sentences. The two middle paragraphs explain the causes and the effects and use appropriate signal words.

Textbooks often use bulleted lists instead of paragraphs to explain and give information. BLM 4.11, "Winnipeg General Strike, 1919," is one example. Although few signal words are used, bullets show the causes and some of the effects of the strike.

LINKING ASSESSMENT TO LEARNING

As with the other text structures, the most important traits on which to focus will be *organization* and *ideas*.

Successful organization includes having good topic and clincher sentences, as well as suitable signal words.

- The ideas developed in a paragraph should mirror the topic sentence and the cause(s), and the effect(s) should be clearly stated.
- For students to benefit from the assessment of their work, specific criteria must be set. Ideally, students should help to develop the criteria because this gives them a more thorough understanding of what they need to know and what is expected of them. (See *Chapter 8, Monitoring and Assessing Student Work*, for more details.)

Organization Criteria

The criteria that students should focus on for the organization of the cause and effect structure include the following:

- having a strong topic sentence that tells the cause or effect, depending on how the paragraph is organized; sometimes the topic sentence states a *cause,* and then effects are discussed throughout the paragraph, while other times, the topic sentence states the *effect*, and the *causes* are discussed throughout the paragraph
- having a variety of signal words that indicate there is a cause and effect
- having a clincher sentence that sums up the main idea of the paragraph

> Traits "are the characteristics or qualities that define good writing" (Trehearne, 2006, 230). These include
> - ideas presented
> - word choice
> - voice (the personality of the writer)
> - language conventions (grammar, spelling, etc.)
> - sentence fluency (using sentences that make sense and vary in length and structure)

Ideas Criteria

The criteria for the ideas trait should include

- the details that are connected to the main idea
- a discussion of the cause(s) and effect(s)

Assessment Checklists

Peer feedback and self-assessment checklists give students a chance to reflect on their own work and make changes to improve their paragraphs (see BLM 8.10 and BLM 8.11, pages 241–242).

As students fill out these tools, it is important that you circulate and ask questions about their assessments. Some students will indicate "yes" without really checking the criteria carefully. For this reason, I not only ask if there is a topic sentence but if the topic sentence clearly indicates what will be discussed in the paragraph, and if it catches the reader's attention. This makes the student stop and think about the topic sentence and its effectiveness. I do the same for the signal words. I ask if the words have been used and I also have students indicate how many different words are used.

I feel that the bottom section of the peer feedback and self-assessment checklists is the most important. (See Figure 4.13. My comments are in italics.) It is only through having students fill out this part of the form that you will know for sure if students have a thorough understanding of the criteria used, what strengths they have, and what areas still require improvement.

GRADE 7 STUDENT PEER FEEDBACK

(Below are some of the strengths Grade 7 students gave their partners.)

The strengths in the cause and effect paragraph include:

He gave lots of good ideas, super details and used a lot of interesting words.

(This is a bit brief compared to what I would hope for from a Grade 7 student, but he has the right idea. At this level, I would expect him to give me proof for his statements.)

It is so good, it has the periods and everything.

(This response indicates to me that the student does not understand the criteria and is focusing strictly on conventions, and even that is very weak. Further lessons would be required to help this student understand the structure.)

The supporting sentences are interesting and they give the effects of global warming on the Polar Bear. She had all the parts the paragraph should have such as a topic and clincher sentence. The topic sentence introduced the topic that was discussed in the paragraph, (What is causing Polar Bears to become endangered.) Her organizer was very neat and she used jot notes, not full sentences. She could have used a few more signal words.

(This student has a good understanding of the criteria. She gave strengths and an area for improvement. She had done quite a few assessments on other structures before this one. Do not expect this kind of response the first few times you ask students to do peer assessments.)

FIGURE 4.13

Text Structures: Teaching Patterns in Reading and Writing

Discussing the self-assessment checklists with students will help you assess their understanding of the structure and indicate where they need to go next. Mini-lessons can then be set up for those students requiring further assistance in particular areas such as

- creating strong topic sentences
- using a variety of cause and effect signal words
- ensuring that the ideas are clearly stated and there is a cause and effect relationship in the paragraph
- completing the paragraph with a strong clincher sentence

Assessment Rubrics

The assessment rubric for Chapter 4 cause and effect structures is used for assessment *only* after students are very familiar with the structure and have had many opportunities to work with the peer and self-assessment checklists (see BLM 8.12, page 243). They should have had various opportunities to discuss the criteria and read good examples for this structure. When students write the paragraphs that I will assess, I have them use the rubric for self-assessment so they have the opportunity to revise what they have written before they hand it in. I mark the paragraph using the same rubric. It quickly shows me who understands the criteria and, more importantly, who can apply the criteria to their own work.

After I hand back the paragraph, I have students fill in the bottom of the rubric. It asks them to look at the criteria they used and explain how they will move up to the next level. For me, this is the most important part of any assessment. It ensures that students are thinking about their learning and making decisions about what the next steps will be in the learning process. Figure 4.14 shows a typical **grade 7** response. My comments are in italics.

GRADE 7 STUDENT SELF-ASSESSMENT

To move to the next level, I must …

improve my topic sentence. My partner said he didn't know what my topic was when he read the sentence. The effects I put in were not all connected to the main topic. I was talking about the results of smoking but I put in not exercising enough. I was trying to say that you get out of breath easy but my partner didn't understand that part.

(This student knows what he has to improve on and seems to have realized that his writing is somewhat confusing for the reader. The peer editor seems to have given helpful and honest advice in his assessment of the paragraph.)

Students complete the bottom of the rubric after it is returned to them.

FIGURE 4.14

Identifying Text Structures: Reading Like a Writer

When students are familiar with the text structure, having read and written many examples, it is important that they make the connection between what they learned and what they read. They should now be able to identify the structure when they encounter it in their textbooks and library books. A tracking form (Figure 4.15) can be used to monitor their progress in this area.

BLM 8.23

Checklist for Identifying Text Structure Criteria

Name: _____ Date: _____

	Sequence	Enumerative	Compare and Contrast	Cause and Effect	Problem and Solution	Question and Answer	Description
Is able to identify the structure when it is in its basic form in an individual paragraph.							
Is able to identify the characteristics of the structures when reading textbooks and trade books (signal words, topic sentence, clincher sentence, etc.).							
Is able to identify the structure when reading textbooks or trade books even though it is not in its basic form (bullets used instead of signal words, no clincher sentence, etc.).							

Comments

FIGURE 4.15

Anecdotal Records

Keeping anecdotal records from teacher and student conferences, as well as samples of students' work and marks from various assignments, helps track students' progress over the year. When students turn in cause and effect structure assignments, most marks will be for organization and ideas. However, marks could also be given for language conventions, effective use of vocabulary, and voice if those traits have been discussed earlier in the year.

Blackline Masters

Name: _____ Date: _____

Circle the cause and underline the effect in each of the following sentences. Identify the signal words by underlining them in a different colour.

Student-Suggested Cause and Effect Topic Sentences

1. Because I arrived late, I missed the play.

2. Since you were not at home today, we decided to visit you another time.

3. Due to the fact that it was raining, our baseball game was cancelled.

4. We came home early because it was too hot to play football.

5. The choir practised for hours so the members would sing well at the concert.

6. The flowers died as a result of not getting enough water.

7. Some homes in Manitoba were destroyed because of the vast flooding.

8. The people in Québec were without power for weeks due to the ice storm.

Name: _____ Date: _____

Read the paragraph. Underline the topic sentence and clincher sentence, and circle the signal words.

Brushing Your Teeth

If you don't brush your teeth, you may end up in a great deal of pain. Within 20 minutes of eating, the sugars in the food combine with invisible bacteria in your mouth to form acids. As a result, your teeth will begin to decay. When the sugars and bacteria are not removed, plaque forms on the teeth. If it builds up, then the acids produced by the plaque eat a hole in the enamel. This is known as a cavity. Unless a dentist treats the cavity, it spreads into the soft, bony material under the enamel and enters the centre of the tooth called the pulp. Consequently, the tooth becomes infected, and you end up with a toothache. Brushing your teeth daily is a great way to prevent the discomfort of tooth decay.

Name: _____ Date: _____

This graphic organizer is for the paragraph on Bike Helmets. Notice that it is created in point form.

BIKE HELMETS

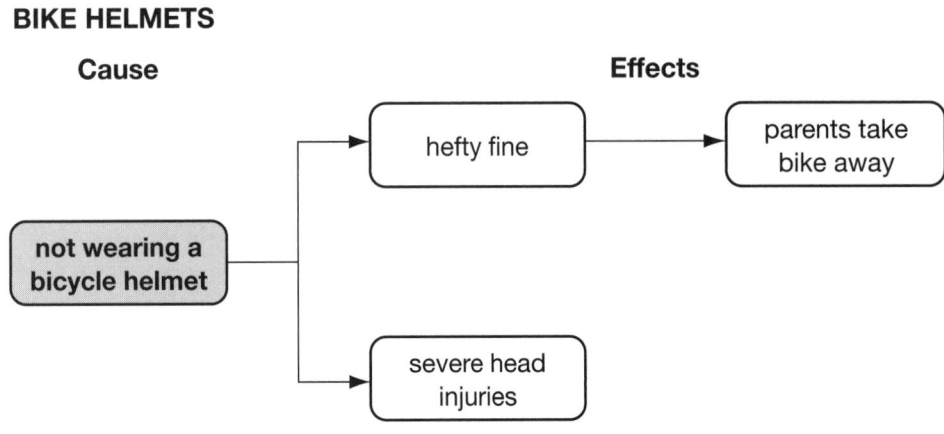

Read the paragraph. Underline the topic and clincher sentences, and circle the signal words.

Bike Helmets

Riding without a bicycle helmet can have serious effects. You may have to pay a hefty fine, because it is against the law to ride your bike without a helmet. This might lead to your parents removing your bike privileges for a period of time. The most critical result, of course, is that if you are in an accident, you could receive severe head injuries. Wearing a bicycle helmet cannot only save you a lot of grief, it might even save your life!

Name: _____ Date: _____

In pairs, create a graphic organizer to go with the model paragraph. Remember that there will not necessarily be signal words for each part of the organizer.

Then, still working in pairs, circle the signal words.

Pesticides

Pesticides that are dumped into lakes, rivers, and oceans can be very dangerous to marine and animal life. These substances pollute the water. This leads to shellfish and other small water creatures taking in the substances. Consequently, the toxins enter the food chain. When the larger sea creatures eat the smaller creatures, the pesticides are passed on to the larger animals. As a result, the larger animals become very ill. Another effect of this pesticide pollution is that the babies of these larger marine creatures and animals often are born deformed or dead. It is important to stop the dumping of pesticides into the oceans so that marine and animal life can be preserved.

Name: _____ Date: _____

In pairs, make your own organizer for the "Pesticides" paragraph. Remember to use point form, not full sentences, to fill in the organizer.

Pesticides

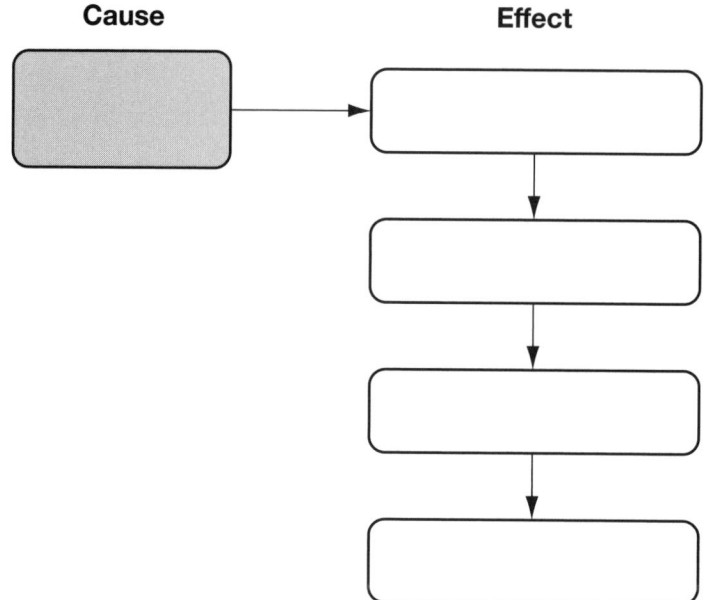

Name: _____ Date: _____

Write a paragraph using the jot notes from a completed organizer. Your paragraph must have a topic sentence, a clincher sentence, and suitable signal words.

Ice Storm!

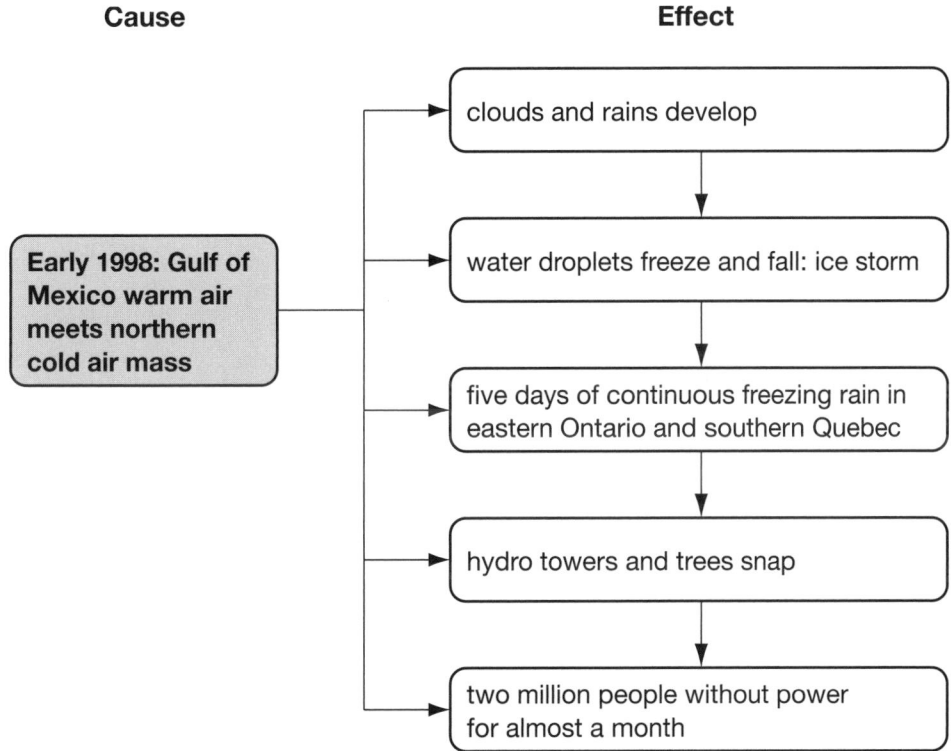

4   Teaching Cause and Effect Structures

Name: _____ Date: _____

In pairs, compare each other's work with the paragraph below. How do they compare? Did you follow the rules for cause and effect paragraphs? Did you include topic and clincher sentences, as well as signal words?

Ice Storm!

In early 1998, parts of eastern Ontario and southern Quebec experienced five continuous days of freezing rain that paralyzed the entire region. The cause of this rain was a large, warm air mass from the Gulf of Mexico. It was swept northward by a jet stream, where it met a cold air mass. Consequently, clouds and rain developed, and the water droplets froze wherever they landed. The consequences were that the layers of ice snapped and bent hydro towers and trees. As a result, two million people were left without power in wintertime for almost a month. This severe weather and environmental destruction has been called Canada's "Storm of the Century."

Adapted from P. Aves et al. *Connections 7: Exploring Physical Geography* (Toronto: Pearson Education), 2000.

Name: _____ Date: _____

Match a cause with one or more effects. Complete the cause and effect sentence using the appropriate effect (or effects).

Picture Match-up

"The hurricane hit the land with incredible force."

Name: _____ Date: _____

Share and Discuss

Desertification

   Overgrazing and the greater use of water from wells
have resulted in desertification. With plants eaten by
herds, winds can easily blow away the thin soil. The lack
of roots means that soil is washed away when it does
rain. In the end, there is less vegetation and more bare,
infertile land that cannot grow crops or graze herds.

Name: _____ Date: _____

Share and Discuss

The Impact of Logging

When only a few trees are harvested at a time, the impact on the local environment is small. The local environment includes all the living and non-living things in a particular area.

As more trees are harvested, more of the local environment is affected. Bark, twigs, and mud can collect in the streams and rivers near logging sites. This can cause changes to the habitats of animals and plants that live in and along the rivers. Many places where salmon go to lay their eggs are destroyed.

When logging is not done carefully, soil may wash away. As a result, new plants cannot grow and animal habitats are changed. This can cause the populations of some animals to get smaller. Other animals may move to new habitats.

As logging increased, the government of British Columbia realized that laws were needed to make sure that forest ecosystems were protected. For example, there are now certain areas that cannot be logged and other areas that are logged less. Areas that are logged are replanted to speed up the growth of new trees. Many Aboriginal peoples are taking a greater role in managing the forests in their traditional areas.

Name: _____ Date: _____

Share and Discuss

Winnipeg General Strike, 1919

Working conditions for many Manitobans after the First World War (1914–1918) were not good:

- Soldiers were returning from the war, and there were not enough jobs for everyone.

- The cost of food was rising, but workers were not making enough money to keep up with the rising prices.

- Relationships between the bosses and the workers were strained. Companies were getting rich, but workers were not well paid. They had to work long hours, often in unsafe conditions.

Workers began to protest. In May 1919, the building and metal workers in Winnipeg went on strike. They wanted better wages, safer working conditions, and shorter work days. They urged other workers to strike too. More than 30 000 people followed their lead:

- Workers stopped delivering newspapers, mail, and milk.

- Taxi drivers, streetcar drivers, and firefighters joined the strike.

- Most stores and restaurants closed.

The Canadian government got involved. It ordered the striking workers to return to work immediately or lose their jobs. Immigrants were told they would be sent out of Canada if they did not do as they were told. The strike organizers were arrested and put in prison.

On June 21, a riot broke out between police and the strikers, who were protesting the arrest of their leaders. Two demonstrators were killed, 34 were injured, and 80 were arrested. The strikers went back to work and the strike leaders were put in jail. This day became known as "Bloody Saturday."

Name: _____ Date: _____

Share and Discuss

Weather Disturbances

There are many weather disturbances that cause serious problems. To begin with, there is flooding, which can lead to the destruction of peoples' homes and farms along with animal habitats. Floods are caused by rivers that overflow their banks after an excessive rainfall. Next, there are hurricanes. They begin as ordinary storms over the warm ocean waters. They grow bigger and bigger as they absorb heat and water from the ocean below. This results in spiralling winds, huge waves, and torrential rainfall, which cause coastal homes and habitats to be destroyed. Third, there can be hail and ice storms that cause property damage. Last, there are tornadoes. They are funnel-like swirling winds that often form during thunderstorms. As the tornado storms across fields and towns, it sucks up everything in its path—homes, animals, cars, trees, people, and buildings—just like a giant vacuum cleaner gone mad. Weather disturbances can result in millions of dollars of property damage and environmental destruction each year.

TEACHING PROBLEM AND SOLUTION STRUCTURES

5

DEFINING THE STRUCTURE

Problem and solution structures *give information about a problem and offer suggestions for its solution.* A problem is stated in the topic sentence followed by the supporting details that describe the problem, its causes, and its solutions. This structure is often found in **grades 7 and 8** textbooks.

Students might encounter this structure in a number of different configurations as outlined in Figure 5.1.

Configuration	Example
One <u>problem</u> with one *solution*	For the <u>problem of garbage</u>: one possible solution is offered: *cut down on packaging.*
One <u>problem</u> with several *solutions*	For the <u>problem of forest fires:</u> several solutions are offered: *put out campfires* and *don't throw cigarette butts out of car windows.*
Several <u>problems</u> and several *solutions*	For the question of why the panda is becoming extinct, several problems are given: <u>bamboo being cut down</u>, <u>hunters killing pandas</u>, and <u>the low reproductive rate of pandas</u>. Several solutions are suggested to increase the panda population: *nature reserves, tough sentences for those convicted of poaching*, and *breeding pandas in captivity.*

FIGURE 5.1

Paragraph Features

Topic Sentence

Topic sentences differ in complexity for **grades 4 to 6** and **grades 7 and 8** students writing this structure. **Grades 4 to 6** students are probably more focused on themselves and the world in which they live. A typical topic sentence at this level might be, "One of the problems I have is not getting

Text Structures: Teaching Patterns in Reading and Writing

my homework done." **Grades 7 and 8** students should demonstrate more advanced vocabulary and discuss more mature concepts. For example, "A major concern to the environment is that the number of whales in the oceans has declined."

Clincher Sentence

The clincher sentence in a problem and solution paragraph sums up the solutions that have been discussed in the paragraph. For example, for the above topic sentence on whales, a possible clincher sentence might be, "Nations and people can work together to save the whales from becoming an endangered species."

Signal Words

The signal words that are most commonly used for the problem and solution structure are fairly simple to identify because they often have the words "problem" and/or "solution" in them: **a problem is, a solution is, the problem is solved by,** and so on. (See list at right.)

Grades 4 to 8 Classrooms

For many **grades 4 to 6** students, this will be the first time they have encountered the problem and solution structure. They no doubt will be familiar with having a problem and what they can do about it, but they probably will not have done much writing using this format. It is important that students be introduced to the structure using simple problems *before* they are expected to write their own paragraphs or independently identify the structures in textbooks. As they become more familiar with the structure, they can begin to identify it in nonfiction texts. They can also begin to write basic paragraphs, perhaps using a template such as the following:

- The problem is …
- One solution is …
- Another way this can be solved is …

While **grades 7 and 8** students may be more familiar with this structure, they will still require time and instruction to recognize it in its various forms, as well as be able to write suitable paragraphs.

Additional Instructional Support

As this is one of the more difficult structures for students to understand, it is important to build strong scaffolding into the lessons for English Language Learners (ELL) and special education students. Orally introducing the structure before teaching its written form can be a successful teaching strategy for these students. For example:

SIGNAL WORDS FOR PROBLEM AND SOLUTION STRUCTURES

a problem is	a/the reason
a solution is	for
the problem	one reason
is solved	is
by	propose
in conclu-	conclude
sion	resolved by
research	an outcome
shows	is
the evidence	steps can be
is	taken
issues are	

1. Begin by asking students to think about problems they have had. Write their problems on the left side of the board.

2. Have students suggest possible solutions for each problem, recording them on the right side of the board.

3. Next, demonstrate writing sentences by taking a statement from the right side, matching it to one on the left side, and adding a signal word.

4. After giving several examples, ask students to write their own sentences. A template like the one below will help them get started:

The problem is _____. The solution to this problem is _____.

The problem is _____. This problem can be solved by _____.

FIGURE 5.2

5. Arranging the problem and solution examples in a chart (Figure 5.3) can also help students see these relationships.

Problem	Solution	Example
I didn't realize that the film started so early so I arrived an hour late.	I need to check movie times in the paper or on the Internet.	The problem is I didn't realize that the film started so early so I arrived an hour late. The solution to this problem is to check movie times in the paper or on the Internet.
Rain threatens to cancel the school's outdoor playday.	Plan indoor events in the gym and other school rooms.	The problem is rain threatens to cancel the school's outdoor playday. This problem can be solved by planning indoor events in the school.

FIGURE 5.3

After students understand the nature of the structure, you can have them work in pairs to create their own problem and solution sentences. You can also introduce more signal words once they are confident using this form of the structure.

INTRODUCING THE STRUCTURE

Ask students what they think a problem and solution structure will be about. After working with the other structures, particularly the cause and effect structure, students should be able to make a fairly accurate prediction. Encourage them to give some examples from their own lives. For example:

Text Structures: Teaching Patterns in Reading and Writing

Problem: I want to go to the movies, but I don't have enough money.

Solution: I will mow people's lawns to earn some money.

EXAMINING A MODEL PARAGRAPH

Introduce the Model

Step 1: Distribute to the class one or more examples of problem and solution paragraphs. Figure 5.4, BLM 5.1, "Garbage," is one example. Notice that this paragraph also uses an enumerative structure to develop the solutions.

> The enumerative signal words for Figure 5.4 are **one**, **another**, and **third**.

Identify Paragraph Elements

Step 2: Ask students to read the paragraph and identify the topic sentence, the clincher sentence, and circle the signal words. A marked-up example of "Garbage" is shown in Figure 5.4.

Garbage

Garbage is becoming a major problem in many communities. Several things can be done to help solve the problem. One solution is to reuse materials instead of throwing them away. For example, instead of throwing out your grocery bags, reuse them. Another solution is to recycle. It is much cheaper and also easier on the environment to recycle products such as newspapers, pop cans, and bottles than make new ones. A third solution is to reduce the amount of garbage we throw out. Take out materials that will decompose, like vegetables and fruit, and put them into the composter instead of the trash bin. If we all reuse, recycle, and reduce, we can cut down the amount of garbage going to our dumps.

— topic sentence

signal words

— clincher sentence

FIGURE 5.4 BLM 5.1

Share and Discuss

Step 3: As a class, discuss students' choices and what features of the model paragraph make it a problem and solution structure.

DEVELOPING A GRAPHIC ORGANIZER

Introduce the Model

Step 1: Provide students with a graphic organizer along with its paragraph. (See Figures 5.5 and 5.6, BLMs 5.2 and 5.3, "Pandas," for example.) When you introduce the graphic organizer for the model paragraph, point out to students that it shows the organization of the paragraph in point form. Also discuss with students the format of the organizer: its two columns or rows that represent the problem(s) and solution(s), and the notes that belong to each category. You might also want to point out to students that an organizer's format can be either horizontal or vertical. Figure 5.5 shows these two formats.

PANDAS

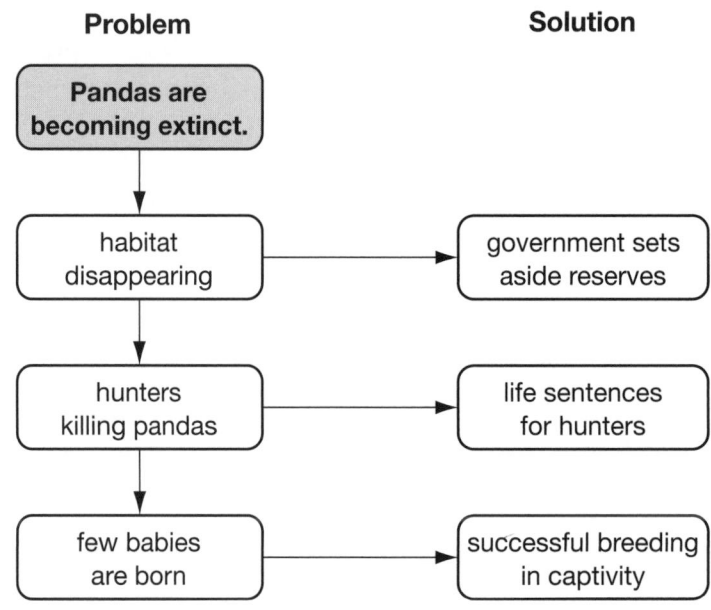

FIGURE 5.5 BLM 5.2

Step 2: Ask students to read the paragraph (BLM 5.3) and have them underline the topic and the clincher sentences, and circle the signal words. See Figure 5.6 for a marked-up example of "Pandas."

◤Pandas

topic sentence ⟶   In China, pandas are very popular animals but they are in danger of becoming extinct. There are several reasons for this

signal words   problem. Their main food source, bamboo, is being cut down because people want the land for farms. Hunters are killing pandas for their valuable skins. Pandas produce fewer babies than most other bears, so their reproductive rate is low.

continued ⟶

Text Structures: Teaching Patterns in Reading and Writing

Several actions have been taken to try to solve these problems. The Chinese government, with the help of the World Wildlife Fund, has set aside 12 nature reserves where bamboo is plentiful. More reserves are planned. Another action is that the government has imposed life sentences for people convicted of poaching. One promising solution is that pandas are successfully being bred in captivity. This should help increase their numbers in the world. Hopefully, pandas will not become extinct if governments and people continue to work together. ← clincher sentence

FIGURE 5.6   BLM 5.3

Share and Discuss

Step 3: As a class, compare the model graphic organizer to the written paragraph. Ask questions such as the following:

- Has anything been left out of the paragraph that was included in the organizer?
- How do the signal words help tie the paragraph together? Are there other signal words that can be used? Are signal words needed for each note on the organizer?
- Does the topic sentence point out that the paragraph is about a problem?

Create the Graphic Organizer

Step 3: Have pairs of students create a graphic organizer from a different model paragraph, for example Figure 5.7, BLM 5.4, "Forest Fires."

Step 4: Have students work in pairs to circle the signal words and underline the topic and clincher sentences.

Step 5: Then have them fill in a graphic organizer. (They can use the blank organizer on BLM 5.5 or they can develop one of their own.) It is important for students to realize that there will not necessarily be signal words for each part of the organizer. More advanced paragraphs (ones that **grades 7 and 8** students might write) and examples in nonfiction texts often use few signal words. It is the information provided in the sentences that indicate a problem or solution.

Forest Fires

topic sentence → <u>Many of the fires that rage through our forests every summer, causing widespread damage and sometimes death, could be prevented.</u> The [problem is] often one of carelessness. Some campers let their campfires burn when they leave their campsites. It only takes one gust of wind to carry hot sparks to the grass and trees, and a fire begins. The [solution is] for campers to douse their fires completely. They should pour many buckets of water on the embers, cover them with dirt to prevent them from starting up again, and check to make sure the coals are cold before leaving the site. Careless smokers are another [problem.] When they throw hot cigarette butts out car windows, the burning tobacco can land on roadside grass, and a fire could start. The [solution to this problem is] simple: smokers should always "butt out" cigarettes in their ashtrays. <u>Forest fires can be prevented if people are careful about fire.</u>

signal words (label for boxed words)

clincher sentence → (points to final underlined sentence)

FIGURE 5.7 BLM 5.4

Share and Discuss

Step 6: Use feedback from students to fill in a class organizer. Ask students to check their own organizers against the class example. Figure 5.8, BLM 5.6, is one example of a completed organizer based on BLM 5.4, "Forest Fires."

FOREST FIRES

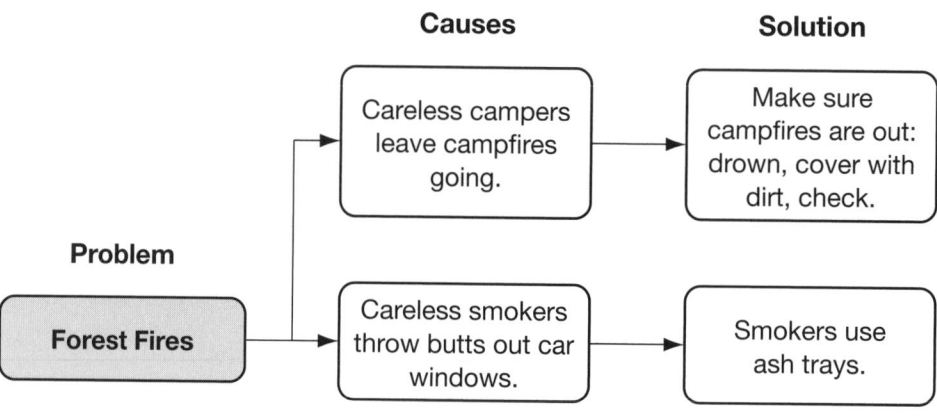

FIGURE 5.8 BLM 5.6

Text Structures: Teaching Patterns in Reading and Writing

WRITING A PROBLEM AND SOLUTION PARAGRAPH

Use a Graphic Organizer

Step 1: Have students work in pairs to write their own paragraphs using the jot notes on another organizer. "Bullying" in Figure 5.9, BLM 5.7, is one example.

Step 2: Remind students that they must have a topic sentence that indicates a problem, as well as a suitable clincher sentence and signal words for their paragraphs.

BULLYING

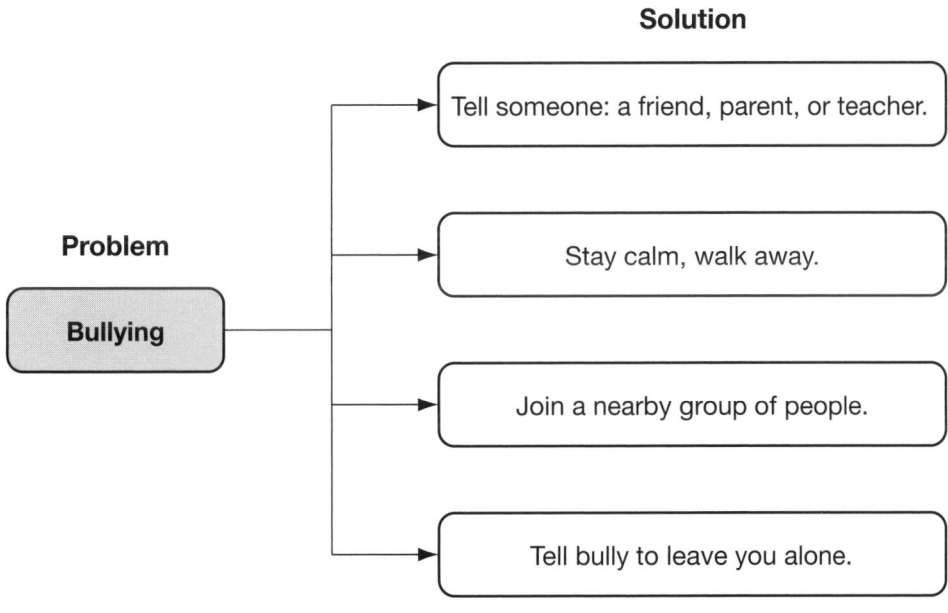

Solution

Tell someone: a friend, parent, or teacher.

Stay calm, walk away.

Problem

Bullying

Join a nearby group of people.

Tell bully to leave you alone.

FIGURE 5.9   BLM 5.7

Share and Discuss

Step 3: Distribute to the class some paragraphs you have written based on the organizer in Figure 5.9, or BLM 5.7. Alternatively, ask for volunteers to share their paragraphs with the class. After each example, discuss whether the rules for text structures have been followed.

- Do paragraphs have the correct elements—topic sentence, clincher sentence, and signal words?
- Is a problem raised in the topic sentence?
- Are solutions given for the problem(s)?

Step 4: Have students compare these paragraphs to the ones they have written. Figure 5.10 is an example of a paragraph based on the "Bullying" organizer. The paragraph elements have been highlighted.

Bullying

topic sentence →

The problem of schoolyard bullying can be a concern for students. However, if you are being bullied, there are several actions you can take. Tell someone: a friend you can trust, your parents, or, if you are at school, a teacher. Also, try to stay calm and walk away from the bully if that is possible. Another solution might be to join a group of people that are nearby. Bullies like to pick on people who are by themselves. Another way this problem can be solved is to stand up straight, look the bully in the eye, and say in a firm voice, "Leave me alone." Bullies do not expect this reaction, and that might be enough to make them stop. Everyone needs to work together to prevent bullying.

signal words

clincher sentence →

FIGURE 5.10   BLM 5.8

COMPOSING THEIR OWN PARAGRAPHS

Once students have created jot notes from a paragraph and a paragraph from jot notes, have them work in pairs to write their first original paragraphs.

Step 1: Start by asking the class to brainstorm topics for problem and solution paragraphs. Record their ideas on the board or an overhead transparency.

Step 2: Ask pairs of students to select a topic, or have them make up one of their own.

Step 3: After they have chosen their topics, each pair will jot down items (problems, solutions, examples, etc.) that they can use to create their organizers. Then they can use these notes first to create their organizers and then to write their paragraphs.

Step 4: When students feel confident writing their paragraphs with a partner, have them work individually to choose a topic, create an organizer, and write their own problem and solution paragraph.

Share and Discuss

Step 5: Distribute student-written paragraphs to the class. Discuss with the class whether these paragraphs have the necessary parts: topic sentence, signal words, and clincher sentence. (You could display paragraphs and organizers on overhead transparencies so the class can more easily review what has been written.) Ask students to compare each paragraph to its graphic organizer (e.g., Does the paragraph reflect the problem and solution organization of the organizer?).

DIFFERENTIATED INSTRUCTION

I have found the following activities to be successful in helping students understand and develop ideas for problem and solution paragraphs. Because these are small-group activities, individual students are able to rely on the collective abilities of their group members rather than feel solely responsible for completing the tasks.

Acting Out Solutions

1. Divide students into small groups of three or four. Give each group a problem.

2. Have them come up with *three* solutions to their problem and act out the solutions for the rest of the class. They must then tell students which solution they feel is the best one and explain their choice.

3. An alternative to this activity is to have students in the class write problem and solution sentences for each part of the solution skit using appropriate signal words. Figure 5.11 illustrates one example.

Problem/Solution Game

1. This activity can be done in small groups or individually. (I would suggest you do it in small groups the first time.) Read a problem to the class for students to solve. It could be something that actually needs to be discussed in class or something you have created.

2. Give students a one- to two-minute time limit to record as many solutions as they can.

3. Have them share their responses with the class. Students get one point for each solution they present that no one else has offered. When they are presenting their solutions, encourage students to use signal words in the sentences (e.g., **one solution is** ..., **another solution is** ..., **this can be solved by** ..., etc.).

> Consider using the problem and solution template discussed on page 116.

Problem:	Bullies on the school ground.
Solutions:	Walk away, tell a teacher, stand up to bully.
Example:	The problem is that bullies bother us at recess. One solution would be to walk away from the bully and join a nearby group of students.

FIGURE 5.11

SUGGESTED CROSS-CURRICULAR TOPICS

Below is a list of topics that involve a problem and solution, which could be used for any of the activities discussed.

Social Studies

- Problems of limited natural resources and possible solutions
- Problems of over-logging and possible solutions
- Problems of overfishing on the Grand Banks
- Problems faced by medieval peasants and how they tried to solve them
- Problems of sanitation and health in medieval towns and cities
- Problems faced by First Nations as a result of contact with European explorers
- Problems with trade between provinces/countries and possible solutions
- Problems faced by early settlers and how they solved them
- Problems faced by people during the Klondike gold rush and how they solved them
- Problem of child labour and how to solve it
- Problems of urban sprawl and possible solutions
- Problems faced by immigrants today and possible solutions

Science

- Problems caused by space exploration (e.g., space junk) and possible solutions
- Problems caused by pollution of water sources and possible solutions
- Problems caused by erosion and possible solutions
- Problems of using too much electricity and possible solutions
- Problems caused by the lack of care for the environment and possible solutions
- Problems caused by oil spills and possible solutions

Math

- Math puzzles, such as logic puzzles that present a problem where students use clues to figure out a solution
- Steps involved in solving a mathematical problem

Physical Education and Health

- Problems of poor sportsmanship and possible solutions
- Problems and solutions of Internet safety
- Problems related to friends, peers, and family, and possible solutions
- Problems caused by smoking and possible solutions

Language Arts

- Problems characters face and how they solve them

PROBLEM AND SOLUTION STRUCTURES IN THE CONTENT AREAS

Like many text structures, examples of problem and solution structures found in nonfiction books and textbooks are often in an essay form. Thus, each developing paragraph illustrates or explains a point in the problem or its solution. See BLM 5.9, "The Human Threat," for an example. Note that the clincher sentence comes at the end of the selection rather than at the end of each paragraph. A **grades 4 to 6** paragraph is shown below (Figure 5.12).

The paragraph is developed using the enumerative structure. The topic is actually stated in the first two sentences. Three different problems are discussed, and enumerative signal words are used to indicate that there is a list of problems (e.g., **as well, also**). There is no clincher sentence.

Underground Mining

Underground mining does not destroy large areas of land on the surface. It causes other problems, however. The groundwater that flows through the rocks can be polluted by the mining, and this can pollute water far away from a mine. As well, underground mining is very expensive. It costs a lot of money to build underground tunnels and to move equipment to them. Underground mining is also dangerous. Harmful gases can build up in the tunnels and cause explosions. Workers in many underground mines must wear breathing equipment to protect themselves from breathing in harmful dust and gases.

← topic sentence

signal words

S. Doyle et al., *B.C. Science Probe 5* (Toronto: Nelson), 2006, 209.

FIGURE 5.12 BLM 5.10

LINKING ASSESSMENT TO LEARNING

For students to benefit from the assessment of their work, specific criteria must be set. Ideally, students should help to develop the criteria because this gives them a more thorough understanding of what they need to know and what is expected of them. (See *Chapter 8, Monitoring and Assessing Student Work* for more details.) The organizational criteria that students should focus on for the problem and solution structure include:

• having a strong topic sentence that sets out the problem
• having a variety of signal words that indicate that a problem is stated and solutions are offered
• having a clincher sentence that sums up the solutions given in the paragraph

The criteria for the **ideas presented** trait should include

• details that are connected to the topic
• details that explain the solutions to the problem

Assessment Checklists

The peer and self-assessment checklists give students a chance to reflect on their own work and make changes to improve their paragraphs (see BLMs 8.13 and 8.14 on pages 244 and 245).

As students fill out the problem and solution checklists, it is important that you circulate and ask questions about their assessments. Some students will indicate "yes" without really checking the criteria carefully. For this reason, I not only ask if there is a topic sentence but if the topic sentence clearly indicates what will be discussed in the paragraph and if it catches the reader's attention. This makes the student stop and think about the topic sentence and its effectiveness. I do the same for the signal words. I ask if the words have been used and I also have students indicate how many different words are used.

Figure 5.13 shows two **grade** 8 students' responses to the checklist. My comments are in italics.

BLM 8.14

Peer Feedback Checklist for Problem and Solution Structures

Author: _____ Peer Editor: _____ Date: _____

Organization		
The graphic organizer fits with the problem and solution paragraph.	Yes	No
There is a topic sentence.	Yes	No
There is a clincher sentence.	Yes	No
Word Choice		
Problem and solution signal words were used.	Yes	No
_____ different problem and solution signal words were used. (number)		
Ideas and Content		
The topic sentence:		
• tells the reader what problem and solution will be discussed.	Yes	No
• catches the reader's attention.	Yes	No
The clincher sentence ties the ideas of the paragraph together.	Yes	No
The supporting sentences in the paragraph give details about the problem and the possible solutions.	Yes	No

The strengths in the problem and solution paragraph include:

The areas that need improvement in the problem and solution paragraph include:

My suggested goal for this writer is:

BLM 8.13

Student Self-Assessment Checklist for Problem and Solution Structures

Name: _____ Date: _____

Organization		
My graphic organizer fits with my problem and solution paragraph.	Yes	No
I have a topic sentence.	Yes	No
I have a clincher sentence.	Yes	No
Word Choice		
I used problem and solution signal words.	Yes	No
I used _____ different problem and solution signal words. (number)		
Ideas and Content		
My topic sentence:		
• tells the reader what problem and solution will be discussed.	Yes	No
• catches the reader's attention.	Yes	No
My clincher sentence ties the ideas of my paragraph together.	Yes	No
The supporting sentences in my paragraph give details about the problem and the possible solutions.	Yes	No

The strengths in my problem and solution paragraph include:

The areas that need improvement in my problem and solution paragraph include:

My goal for future writing is:

The strengths in my problem and solution paragraph include:

I clearly stated the problem and then I discussed the solutions to the problem. I actually had an enumerative structure with my problem and solution structure because I had a list of three solutions. I used both enumerative and problem solution signal words such as another solution and also. I kept to the topic and gave great detail about each solution.

(This is an excellent assessment by the student. He wrote a very strong paragraph and was able to clearly state his strengths and how he can improve. He has also understood the use of several structures at one time.)

The strengths in my problem and solution paragraph include:

I did everything it said on the paper.

The weaknesses in my problem and solution paragraph include:

My clincher sentence wasn't really strong because it didn't tell what could happen if my solutions were followed.

(This student needs to give a lot more detail, but she was a very reluctant writer so I was pleased she completed the form. I would sit down with her and discuss her ideas orally so I can see what she really understands about the structure.)

FIGURE 5.13

Discussing the self-assessment checklists with students will help you assess their understanding of the structure and indicate where they need to go next. Mini-lessons can then be set up for those students requiring further assistance in particular areas such as

- creating strong topic sentences
- using a variety of problem/solution signal words
- ensuring that the ideas are clearly stated and there is a problem with one or more solutions offered
- completing the paragraph with a strong clincher sentence

Assessment Rubrics

As with other text structures, the assessment rubric for the Chapter 5 problem and solution structure is used for assessment only after students are very familiar with the structure and have had many opportunities to work with the peer and self-assessment checklists and the rubric (see BLM 8.15). When students write the paragraphs that I will assess, I have them use the rubric for self-assessment so that they have the opportunity to revise what they have written before they hand it in. I mark the paragraph using the same rubric. It quickly shows me who understands the criteria and, more importantly, who can apply the criteria to their own work.

Figure 5.14 is a **grade 8** student's response to the rubric (the bottom of the sheet). My comments are in italics. This part of the rubric is an important section of the tool. It ensures that students are thinking about their learning and making decisions about what the next steps will be in the learning process.

BLM 8.15

Assessment Rubric for Problem and Solution Structures

Name: _____ Date: _____

GRADE 8 STUDENT SELF-ASSESSMENT

To move to the next level, I must ...

try to have more than one solution to the problem or give a lot more detail on the one solution I gave. I only used one signal word so I will have to try to use other ones next time.

(This was done by a special education student. He got the first idea from his peer editor; the second one was his own idea.)

> Students must complete the bottom of the rubric after it is returned to them.

FIGURE 5.14

Identifying Text Structures: Reading Like a Writer

When students are familiar with writing the text structure, it is important that they make the connection between what they have learned and what they read. Having written paragraphs using the problem and solution structure, they should now be able to identify the structure when they encounter it in their textbooks and library books. The tool below (Figure 5.15) can be used to track their progress in this area.

Checklist for Identifying Text Structure Criteria

Name: _____ Date: _____

	Sequence	Enumerative	Compare and Contrast	Cause and Effect	Problem and Solution	Question and Answer	Description
Is able to identify the structure when it is in its basic form in an individual paragraph.							
Is able to identify the characteristics of the structures when reading textbooks and trade books (signal words, topic sentence, clincher sentence, etc.).							
Is able to identify the structure when reading textbooks or trade books even though it is not in its basic form (bullets used instead of signal words, no clincher sentence, etc.).							

Comments

FIGURE 5.15   BLM 8.23

Anecdotal Records

Keeping anecdotal records helps track students' progress over the year. When students turn in problem and solution structure assignments, most marks will be for organization and ideas. However, marks could also be given for language conventions and effective use of vocabulary and voice, if those traits have been discussed earlier in the year.

Blackline Masters

Name: _____ Date: _____

Read the paragraph. Underline the topic and clincher sentences and circle the signal words.

Garbage

Garbage is becoming a major problem in many communities. Several things can be done to help solve the problem. One solution is to reuse materials instead of throwing them away. For example, instead of throwing out your grocery bags, reuse them. Another solution is to recycle. It is much cheaper and also easier on the environment to recycle products such as newspapers, pop cans, and bottles than make new ones. A third solution is to reduce the amount of garbage we throw out. Take out materials that will decompose, like vegetables and fruit, and put them into the composter instead of the trash bin. If we all reuse, recycle, and reduce, we can cut down the amount of garbage going to our dumps.

Name: _____ Date: _____

Read the paragraph. Underline the topic and clincher sentences and circle the signal words.

Pandas

In China, pandas are very popular animals, but they are in danger of becoming extinct. There are several reasons for this problem. Their main food source, bamboo, is being cut down because people want the land for farms. Hunters are killing pandas for their valuable skins. Pandas produce fewer babies than most other bears, so their reproductive rate is low. Several actions have been taken to try to solve these problems. The Chinese government, with the help of the World Wildlife Fund, has set aside 12 nature reserves where bamboo is plentiful. More reserves are planned. Another action is that the government has imposed life sentences for people convicted of poaching. One promising solution is that pandas are successfully being bred in captivity. This should help increase their numbers in the world. Hopefully, pandas will not become extinct if governments and people continue to work together.

Name: _____ Date: _____

Read and Discuss

Pandas

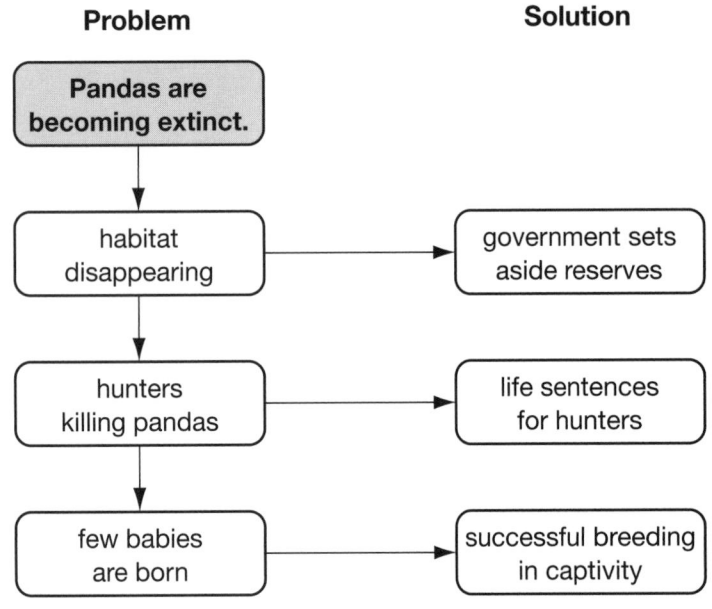

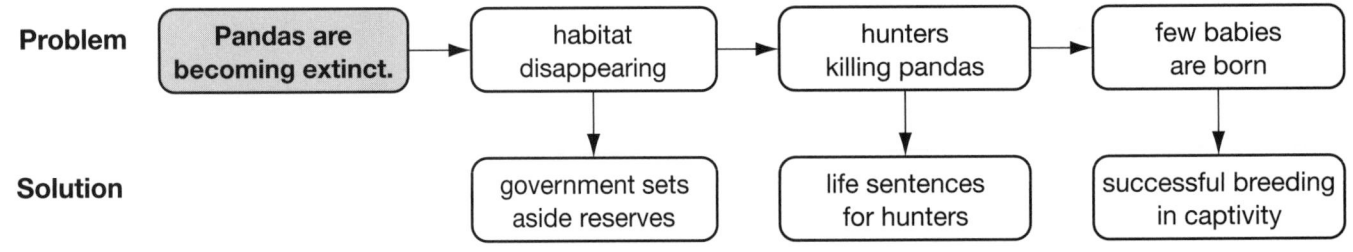

Name: _____ Date: _____

Work in pairs to underline the topic and clincher sentences and circle the signal words.

Forest Fires

Many of the fires that rage through our forests every summer, causing widespread damage and sometimes death, could be prevented. The problem is often one of carelessness. Some campers let their campfires burn when they leave their campsites. It only takes one gust of wind to carry hot sparks to the grass and trees, and a fire begins. The solution is for campers to douse their fires completely. They should pour many buckets of water on the embers, cover them with dirt to prevent them from starting up again, and check to make sure the coals are cold before leaving the site. Careless smokers are another problem. When they throw hot cigarette butts out car windows, the burning tobacco can land on roadside grass, and a fire could start. The solution to this problem is simple: smokers should always "butt out" cigarettes in their ashtrays. Forest fires can be prevented if people are careful about fire.

Name: _____ Date: _____

In pairs, make your own organizer for the "Forest Fires" paragraph. Remember to use point form, not full sentences, to fill in the organizer.

Note that there will not always be signal words in each part of the organizer.

Forest Fires

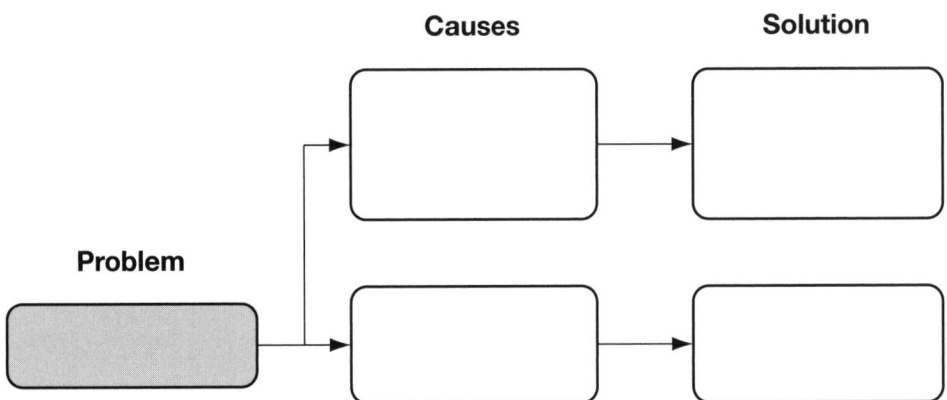

Name: _____ Date: _____

Compare your graphic organizer against this example.

Forest Fires

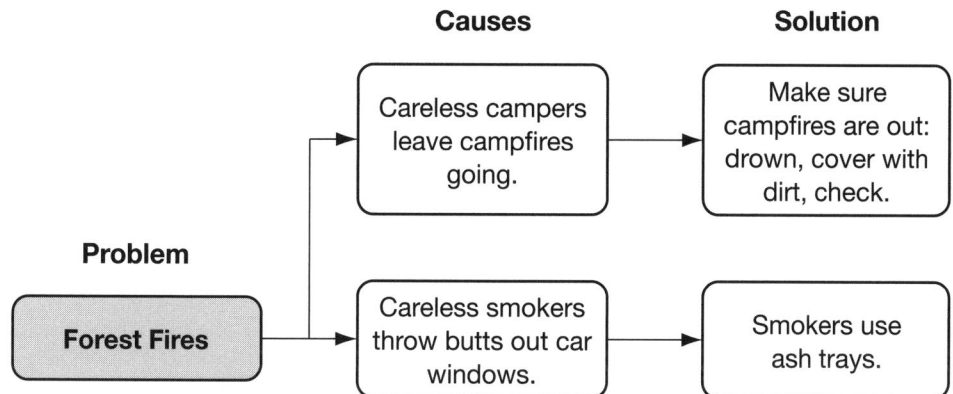

Name: _____ Date: _____

In pairs, write your own paragraph using this graphic organizer. Remember that your topic sentence must indicate a problem.

Bullying

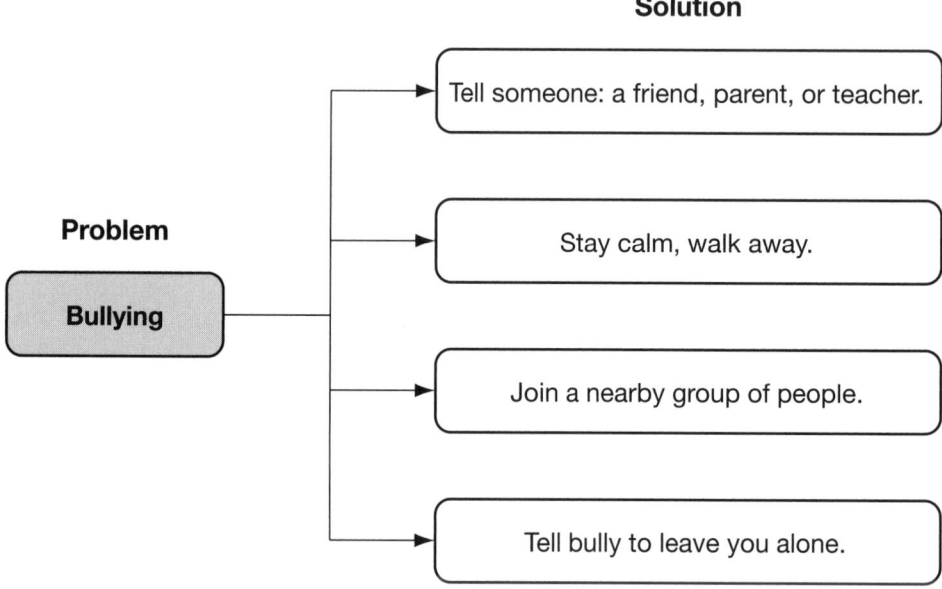

Name: _____ Date: _____

Compare your paragraph against this one.

Bullying

The problem of schoolyard bullying can be a concern for students. However, if you are being bullied, there are several actions you can take. Tell someone: a friend you can trust, your parents, or, if you are at school, a teacher. Also, try to stay calm and walk away from the bully if that is possible. Another solution might be to join a group of people that are nearby. Bullies like to pick on people who are by themselves. Another way this problem can be solved is to stand up straight, look the bully in the eye, and say in a firm voice, "Leave me alone." Bullies do not expect this reaction, and that might be enough to make them stop. Everyone needs to work together to prevent bullying.

Name: _____   Date: _____

Read and Discuss

The Human Threat

Humans have directly or indirectly contributed to many of the problems facing the world's ecosystems and their futures. Many of these changes are the result of human industry and misuse of the environment. Much of this misuse occurred as the human population grew dramatically following the beginning of the Industrial Revolution. Innovations in agriculture and technology enabled people to produce more food than ever before and to move into regions that had been sparsely settled. These human advances helped foster a period of enormous human population growth that continues today. Since 1961, the world's population has doubled, from 3 billion people to more than 6 billion. Estimates for future population growth predict that there will be 8 billon people on Earth by the year 2027.

As the world's population continues to grow, so does the strain upon Earth's resources. The degradation of Earth's ecosystems is expected to accelerate over the next fifty years if misuse continues. Many of the same problems, such as deforestation, desertification, and pollution, will continue on a broader scale as populations and industries continue to grow in developing nations.

There are steps that can be taken to slow or even reverse environmental degradation over the next fifty years. Governments and international organizations must encourage citizens and businesses to conserve the world's resources. The use of carbon-producing fossil fuels to generate energy must eventually be phased out in favour of more sustainable energy sources, such as solar, wind, and water power or hydroelectricity. Landowners must be encouraged to manage their property in ways that protect and enhance ecosystem services such as forests and freshwater supplies. Farms and factories must begin looking for ways to be productive without harming the environment. Exploitation of ocean resources and freshwater supplies must be managed responsibly. Unless these changes take place soon, Earth's growing human population faces an uncertain future.

Porterfield, *Looking at the Human Impact on the Environment with Graphic Organizers, Using Graphic Organizers to Study the Living Environment* (New York: Publishing Group), 2006, 411–42.

Name: _____ Date: _____

Read and Discuss

Underground Mining

Underground mining does not destroy large areas of land on the surface. It causes other problems, however. The groundwater that flows through the rocks can be polluted by the mining, and this can pollute water far away from a mine. As well, underground mining is very expensive. It costs a lot of money to build underground tunnels and to move equipment to them. Underground mining is also dangerous. Harmful gases can build up in the tunnels and cause explosions. Workers in many underground mines must wear breathing equipment to protect themselves from breathing in harmful dust and gases.

S. Doyle et al., *B.C. Science Probe 5* (Toronto: Nelson), 2006, 209.

TEACHING QUESTION AND ANSWER STRUCTURES

6

DEFINING THE STRUCTURE

The question and answer structure is one of the easiest for students to identify. In this structure, *a question is posed about a topic, event, concept, or idea and then answered*. Often the question is highlighted in some way or included as a heading. The answer directly follows the question and can be one or more paragraphs. This structure has become increasingly common in **grades 4 to 6** and **grades 7 and 8** texts and juvenile non-fiction books. In fact, books for this lower age group are often designed in a question and answer format, with questions as headings and answers below. In more advanced informational texts, the question can be embedded within the text. In these cases, students have to search for the question in order to identify the answer.

Other structures are often used in the development of the question and answer structure. For example, for the question, "What caused World War I?" the answer could be expressed as a cause and effect structure. For the question, "How do you make a kaleidoscope?" a sequence structure might be suitable.

Some books are set up entirely in a question and answer format. For example:

- **Scholastic Book Question and Answer Series**—Titles include *Do Stars Have Points?* (1998) and *Why Do Volcanoes Blow Their Tops?* (1999)—both written by Melvin and Gilda Berger (New York: Scholastic).
- *I Wonder Why Trees Have Leaves and Other Questions About Plants* (1997) by Andrew Charman (New York: Larousse Kingfisher Chambers).

Paragraph Features

Topic Sentence

The topic sentence can be in the form of a question. For example, if the question is, "How do people live and work in communities in Peru?" the reader can assume that the topic of the paragraph will be the people in Peru, particularly how they live and work. In more advanced texts, where the question is embedded in the opening paragraph, the topic sentence would just indicate the subject of the paragraph. (See Figure 6.5, page 145, for an example.)

Clincher Sentence

There may not be a clincher sentence for this structure. If there is one, it will likely be found at the end of the answer, summing up the information given in the paragraph.

Signal Words

Signal words for this structure are often found in the question. They include the 5 Ws (**who, why, when, where,** and **what**). There are also a few signal words that might be found in the answer (e.g., **as a result of**).

Format of Graphic Organizers

The format for question and answer graphic organizers will depend on the type of question asked and how the answer is developed. Figure 6.1 outlines typical examples.

SIGNAL WORDS FOR QUESTION AND ANSWER STRUCTURES	
how	how many
why	where
when	as a result of
who	question
what	answer

Question	Text Structure
"What is the life cycle of a frog?"	Sequence organizer
"What is the difference between the landforms in the Cordillera and the St. Lawrence/Great Lakes Lowlands?"	Compare and contrast organizer
"How does algae growth affect our lakes?"	Cause and effect organizer
"Why do stars twinkle?"	Enumerative organizer

FIGURE 6.1

Grades 4 to 8 Classrooms

For **grades 4 to 6** students, most question and answer paragraphs will be easily recognizable. In some examples, the question is identified by font size, style (bold or italic), or colour (or a combination of these characteristics). The paragraph that answers the question usually follows. Sometimes the answer is explained in more than one paragraph so that students have to read the text carefully to find all its elements. In other examples, the topic sentence is the question. When the question is embedded within the paragraph, students may find it more difficult to determine the answer.

Similar examples and challenges apply for **grades 7 and 8** students. However, more sophisticated vocabulary is often found in textbooks at this level, and more complex concepts are discussed.

To introduce the structure at either level, start with examples that have the questions highlighted in bold and/or in a larger font, followed by one-paragraph answers. Once students understand this one-paragraph format, they can go on to examples where the answer is developed in more than one paragraph. Next, introduce them to examples where the question is the topic sentence of the paragraph. Finally, explore question and answer structures in which the question is embedded within the opening paragraph. (See Figures 6.3 to 6.8 for specific examples.)

Additional Instructional Support

For English Language Learners (ELL) and special education students, try using single sentences, rather than paragraphs, as answers. For example, begin by giving students a few questions and have them answer each in one sentence. Then present students with a number of answers and see if they can create a question for each one. Use material with which students are familiar so they can concentrate on the structure and not on the vocabulary. Once they can create questions for answers and answers for questions, ask students to work in small groups to develop their own questions and answers. Ask them to write the questions in large, bold letters with the one-sentence answers below. After students have had many opportunities to work with questions and one-sentence answers, challenge them to write more complex answers of two or three sentences.

INTRODUCING THE STRUCTURE

As part of this introduction, you might wish to review any other text structures students have already been taught.

Step 1: Start by asking students what they would expect to see in a question and answer structure. If they have studied other text structures, they will probably be able to tell you that a question and then the answer will be given.

Step 2: Playing the game "Twenty Questions" (see page 153) before introducing the model paragraphs helps students understand the need for questions that elicit specific answers and develops their questioning skills.

EXAMINING DIFFERENT MODEL PARAGRAPHS

Introduce the Models

Step 1: Examine each format for this structure separately before introducing students to the graphic organizers. Figure 6.2 summarizes the question and answer paragraphs that follow.

Format	Example
(a) The question is highlighted and separate from the answer.	Figure 6.3 and Figure 6.4
(b) The question is the topic sentence, and the answer is explained in the rest of the paragraph (or paragraphs).	Figure 6.5 and Figure 6.6
(c) The question is embedded in the first paragraph, with its answer developed in one or more paragraphs.	Figure 6.7 and Figure 6.8

FIGURE 6.2

(a) The Question Is Highlighted and Separate

Step 2: Show students examples of the simplest format, where the question is clearly stated and is written in a larger and/or bolded font. The answer follows in the paragraph below.

Why Do People Visit Manitoba? ← question

With its many campgrounds, parks, lakes, and rivers, Manitoba offers many fun outdoor activities. Visitors come to Manitoba to enjoy bird watching, fishing, canoeing, white-water rafting, and hiking. Others come to see the province's many historic sites and to visit its lively cities and pleasant farming communities. Ukrainian, Icelandic, Mennonite, and other traditions have been preserved in these rural communities.

answer

W. Mathieu, *Manitoba* (InfoCanada: Provinces and Territories series)(Toronto: Nelson), 2004, 44.

FIGURE 6.3   BLM 6.1

Step 3: For this example, have students determine why people come to Manitoba (e.g., bird watching, fishing, canoeing, white-water rafting, hiking, seeing historic sites, visiting cities and farming communities).

Step 4: Ask them how the question helped them as readers (e.g., they focused on finding the answer to one question and ignored other details).

Step 5: Using another example, where the answer is developed in more than one paragraph (see Figure 6.4, BLM 6.2), ask students what details they might expect to find in the answer to the question. After they have read the answer, ask them to circle the sentence(s) in which they found the answer (first sentence of the second paragraph shown in this paragraph).

question ──────────▶

Is Soil the Same Thickness Everywhere?

As bedrock is weathered, small rocks break off, deepening the subsoil. The subsoil is also being weathered by plant roots and small burrowing animals, such as moles and worms, which bring humus down into the subsoil. As a result, the top of the subsoil slowly becomes topsoil. This process takes time—thousands of years.

answer

Depending on how long the soil has had to form, how much material was left by the glaciers, and the amount of erosion that has occurred, the soil has different thicknesses in different parts of the country. In southern Ontario, where great trees and countless animals have lived, died, and contributed their bodies to soil humus for 10 000 years, soil layers tend to be deeper. In northern Ontario, where the glacier of the last Ice Age lasted much later, there has been less time for soil to form. It is also cooler in the north, so plants grow more slowly and there is less biological weathering. Near the glaciers of the Columbia Icefield in the Canadian Rockies, little pine trees can be seen growing in rocky soil that is just a few centimetres deep. There has been little time there for soil formation.

T. Gibb, A. Hirsch, D. White, S. White, J. Wiese, B. Ritter, *Science Technology 7* (Scarborough, Ont.: Nelson), 2000, 211.

FIGURE 6.4 BLM 6.2

(b) The Question Is the Topic Sentence

Step 6: Show students a few examples where the question is the topic sentence (see Figures 6.5 and 6.6).

Step 7: Ask questions such as the following:

What sentence contains the answer?

- For Figure 6.5, the second sentence: "It travels through blood vessels."
- For Figure 6.6, the second sentence: "A culture is a way of life shared by a group of people and is composed of a number of things, such as the way people obtain their food, the way they bring up their children, and the values they believe in."

What is the function of the other sentences in the answer paragraph?

- For Figure 6.5, they give additional information: what blood vessels are and the two types of blood vessels.
- For Figure 6.6, they explain that cultures change over time, and that your culture today is different from when our grandparents were young.

Your Blood

How does your blood get to where it's going? It travels through blood vessels. Blood vessels are hollow tubes that contain your blood. Your blood moves through your body in these blood vessels. Two types of blood vessels are arteries and veins.

question

answer

S. Doyle et al., *BC Science Probe 5* (Toronto: Nelson), 2006, 105.

FIGURE 6.5 BLM 6.3

Culture

What is a culture? A culture is a way of life shared by a group of people and is composed of a number of things, such as the way people obtain their food, the way they bring up their children, and the values they believe in. Cultures change over time. Imagine the way things were when your grandparents were your age. Think about how your culture has changed since then.

question

answer

G. Draper et al., *Human Geography* 8 (Toronto: Gage Learning), 2000, 247.

FIGURE 6.6 BLM 6.4

(c) The Question Embedded in the First Paragraph

Step 8: Introduce the question and answer structure where the question is embedded within the paragraph. (See Figures 6.7 and 6.8.) Ask students to do the following:

Indicate the part of the paragraph in which the question is found.
- For Figures 6.7 and 6.8, the question is found in the middle. Note that, for Figure 6.8, there is more than one question but only one answer.

Find the answer to the question. For example:
- For Figure 6.7, it is that, in fall, trees stop making chlorophyll, so green disappears from the leaves, and other colours are evident.
- For Figure 6.8, it is because of social, economic, or political factors.

Autumn Colours

When the summertime greens of deciduous leaves turn to the reds, yellows, oranges, and purples of fall, you know that winter is coming. <u>Have you ever wondered where the bright autumn colours come from?</u> The yellows and oranges are actually in the leaves all summer long, but they are hidden by the stronger green colour of chlorophyll. When fall comes, leaves stop making chlorophyll. Soon afterward, the green colour disappears and the other colours take over.

P. Hickman, *The Kids Canadian Tree Book* (Toronto: Kids Can Press),1995, 10.

FIGURE 6.7 BLM 6.5

question →

answer

The Boat People

There have been many news stories about boatloads of people who have endured terrible travelling conditions in order to arrive on the shores of Canada or some other country. <u>Why do people take such risks? Why are they so desperate to risk everything to find a new start? Why do they feel they have no choice except to leave their homes for a new country?</u>

In general, people move because of social, economic, or political factors. Usually, more than one factor influences their decision.

G. Draper, et al., *Human Geography 8* (Toronto: Gage Learning), 2000, 211.

FIGURE 6.8 BLM 6.6

questions →

answer

Text Structures: Teaching Patterns in Reading and Writing

Share and Discuss

Step 9: As a class, discuss the differences between the different types of models. Challenge students to explain how they determined the answer and how they identified the question in each one.

Step 10: While signal words are not as frequently used in question and answer paragraphs as they are in some structures, students should still be aware of them and how they function in the structure (e.g., **why** or **what** is sometimes part of the question). Discuss the use of signal words in the models students have studied, and compile a class list.

DEVELOPING A GRAPHIC ORGANIZER

Introduce the Model

Step 1: Introduce students to another question and answer paragraph.

Figure 6.9, "Ravens and Crows," is a question and answer example where the question is not part of the paragraph. A compare and contrast structure is used to answer the question. The paragraph elements are highlighted with signal words circled.

> Alternatively, before giving students the model paragraph, you could first give them the graphic organizer and have them identify its structure, and then predict the structure of the paragraph.

Ravens and Crows

Question: How do you know whether you are looking at a raven or a crow?

Ravens and crows are both black in colour, but there are many differences that will help you tell them apart. One difference is that crows are smaller than ravens. Also, if you take a close look, crows have smooth feathers on their throats compared to ravens' shaggy rough-looking feathers. Another difference is that crows caw whereas ravens croak. In addition, crows usually live in flat areas and are usually found in flocks. Ravens, on the other hand, live alone. Even though at first glance they look the same, the raven and crow definitely have many differences.   ← topic sentence

signal words

← clincher sentence

Adapted from J. Diehl and D. Plumb, *What's the Difference?* (Toronto: Annick Press), 2000, 17.

FIGURE 6.9 BLM 6.7

Step 2: Introduce the paragraph's organizer and have students compare its organization to that of the paragraph. The compare and contrast format in Figure 6.10 reflects the organization of the previous paragraph.

Explain that there is not a specific organizer for this structure as there has been for other structures. The format of the organizer depends on the nature of the answer. (See Figures 6.11 and 6.12 for two examples.)

RAVENS AND CROWS

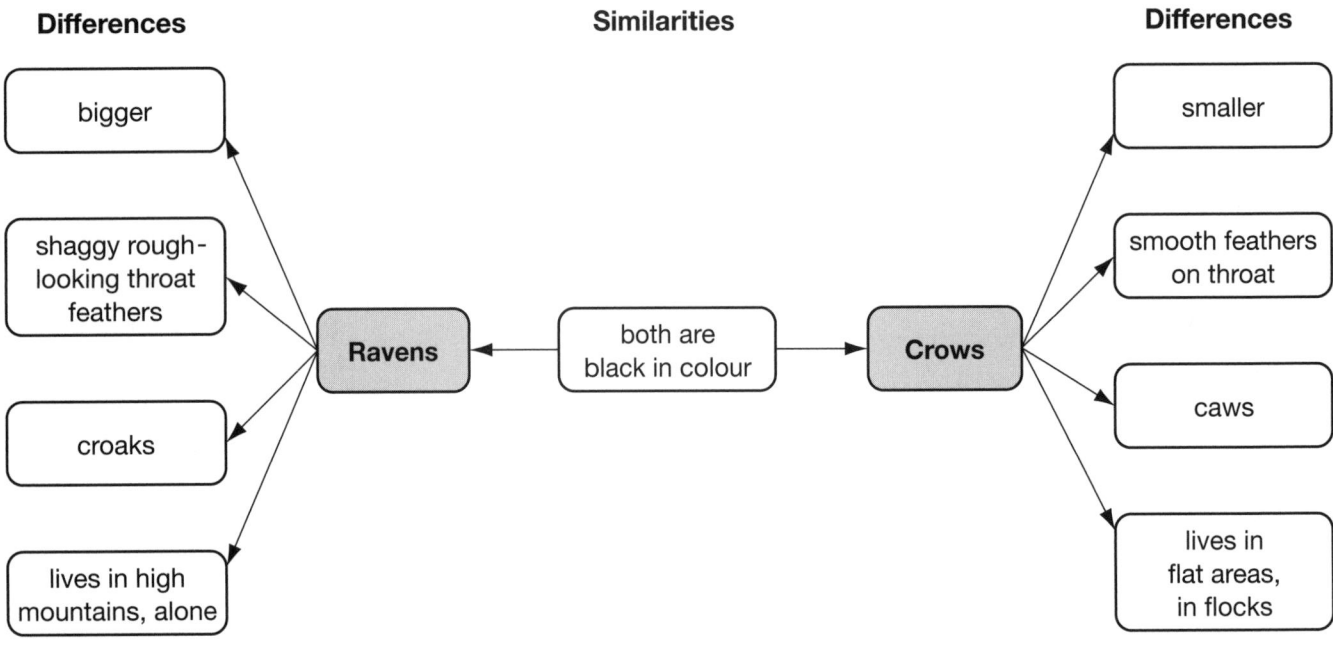

FIGURE 6.10 BLM 6.8

WHAT RULES WOULD YOU FOLLOW TO KEEP SAFE AT HOME?

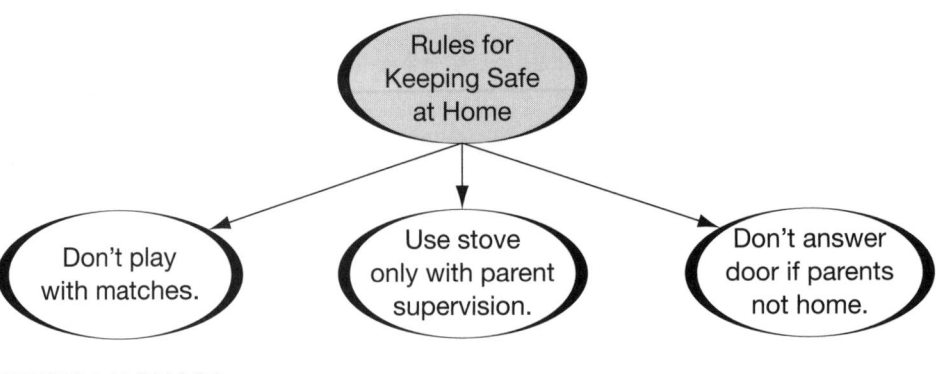

FIGURE 6.11 BLM 6.9

Text Structures: Teaching Patterns in Reading and Writing

WHAT CAUSED THE WAR OF 1812?

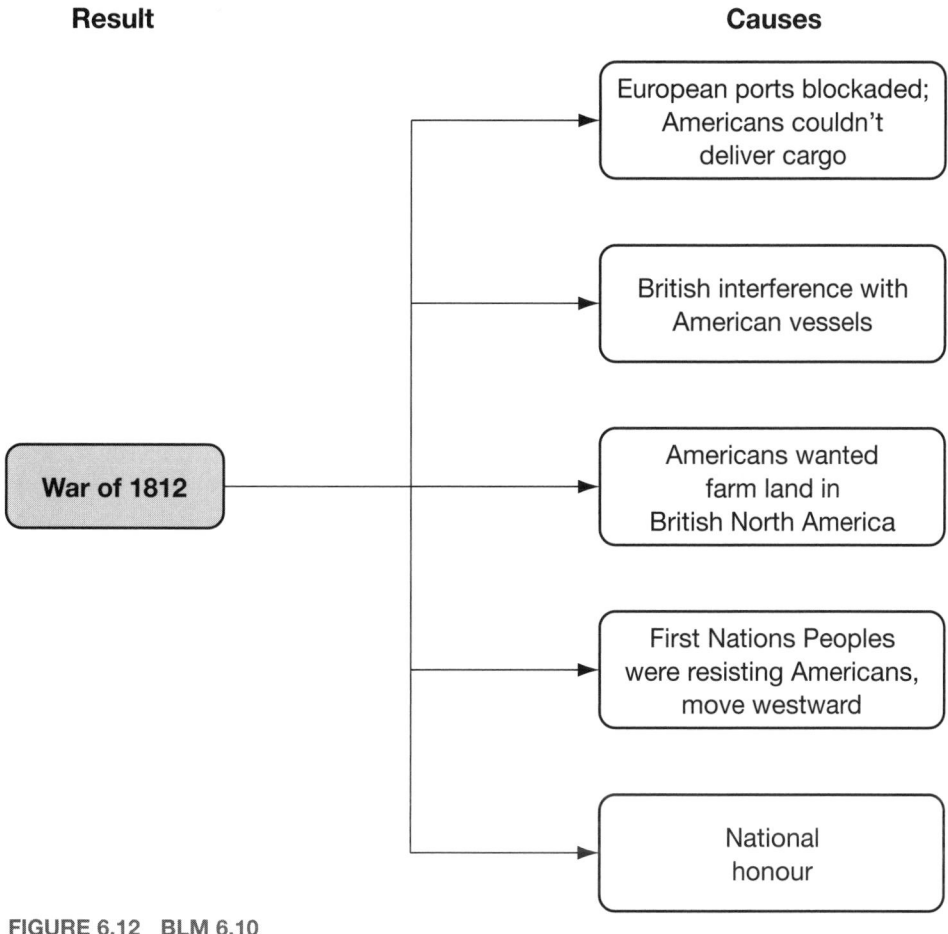

FIGURE 6.12   BLM 6.10

Create the Graphic Organizer

Step 3: Give students a different question and answer paragraph, and ask them to create an organizer from it. For example, "Becoming a Medieval Knight" in Figure 6.13 uses a sequence structure. Sequence signal words are circled. (If students have not studied this structure, create another paragraph using a structure with which they are familiar.) See BLMs 6.15 to 6.18 for other examples of question and answer paragraphs.

Becoming a Medieval Knight

Question: [What] were the steps to becoming a knight in medieval times?

topic sentence ⟶

signal words

There were three stages a boy had to go through to become a knight. [To begin with,] he had to leave home when he was 7 years old to live in a neighbouring castle. At the castle, he worked as a page, helping the lord dress and put on armour. He also learned manners from the lady of the castle and played games that would train him to become a knight, such as wrestling, sword practice with wooden swords, and small shield and lance practice. [After that,] when the boy was 14, he became a squire, a knight's personal servant. He would bring the knight his lances, swords, armour, or horse and accompany him into battle. Like the knights, squires participated in tournaments using real weapons to gain practice in fighting. [Finally,] when the squire was 21, he was "dubbed" a knight by his lord. It was a long and difficult process to become a knight.

clincher sentence ⟶

FIGURE 6.13 BLM 6.11

Identify Paragraph Elements

Step 4: Have students identify the answer to the question posed in the paragraph. In Figure 6.13, the answer is developed in more than one sentence, which is typical of most question and answer paragraphs.

Step 5: Encourage students to see that the question and answer paragraphs—even if the question is separate from the paragraph—will still have topic sentences, signal words that could indicate more than one structure, and sometimes clincher sentences. Ask them to highlight each element and be able to defend their choices. Students can work in pairs to identify the paragraph elements and the structure of the paragraph as well as to create the organizer.

Share and Discuss

Step 6: Complete a class organizer on an overhead transparency using descriptive feedback from students. Have them compare their own organizers with the class example, and discuss any differences between them. An example of an organizer based on "Becoming a Medieval Knight" is shown in Figure 6.14.

WHAT WERE THE STEPS TO BECOMING A KNIGHT IN MEDIEVAL TIMES?

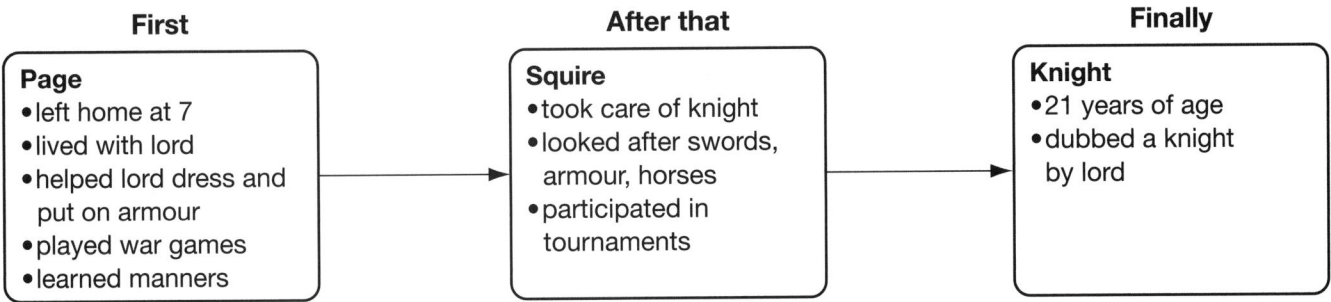

FIGURE 6.14   BLM 6.12

WRITING A QUESTION AND ANSWER PARAGRAPH

Use a Graphic Organizer

Step 1: Have pairs of students use the notes from a completed organizer to write a question and answer paragraph. See Figure 6.15 for one example of an organizer that indicates a problem and solution structure. (Figure 6.16 is a paragraph based on this organizer.)

SPACE JUNK

What are some solutions to the space junk problem?

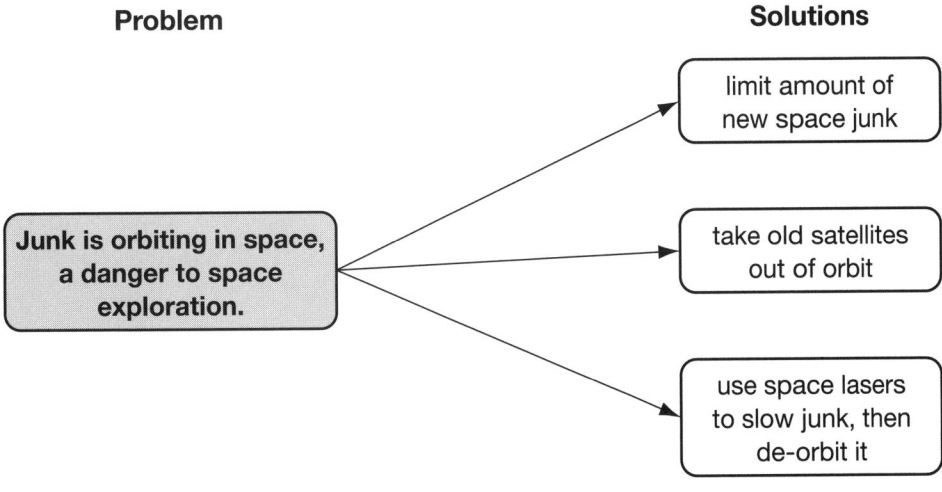

FIGURE 6.15   BLM 6.13

Space Junk

Question: What are some solutions to the space junk problem?

topic sentence → One of the problems of space exploration is the amount of junk that is left up in space. Items such as telescopes, old satellites, and parts of spacecraft are orbiting Earth and pose serious threats to space exploration. Even small pieces of junk can do serious damage to spacecraft due to the speed at which the junk travels. Several solutions to this problem have been suggested. The first solution is to limit the amount of space junk in the first place. This solution doesn't deal with the space junk already orbiting Earth, but it would prevent more from accumulating. The second solution would be to take satellites out of orbit when they are no longer needed instead of leaving them up in space. This would help limit the amount of new space junk but would not deal with the junk that is presently there. Another solution that has been suggested is to use space lasers to slow the junk down and then de-orbit it. However, much more research needs to be

clincher sentence → done before this becomes a possible solution. Due to the danger of space junk to space exploration, research to decrease the amount of junk in space must continue until more feasible solutions are found.

signal words

FIGURE 6.16   BLM 6.14

Share and Discuss

Step 2: Distribute paragraphs based on the organizer in Figure 6.15. Alternatively, ask volunteers to share their work with the class. After each example, discuss whether

- the paragraph has a suitable topic sentence
- the paragraph answers the question
- the signal words are appropriate for the structure used
- the clincher sentence sums up the paragraph

COMPOSING THEIR OWN PARAGRAPHS

Step 1: Now challenge students to write a question and answer paragraph. (They can work in pairs to do this assignment.) Remind them that their paragraphs should have a topic sentence and appropriate signal words.

Step 2: Students can begin by brainstorming questions that can only be answered by a detailed paragraph—not a "yes" or "no," or simple answers. For example, "When was World War II?" can be answered briefly with a date: "World War II was from 1939 to 1945." However, "What were the causes of World War II?" requires a much more detailed answer.

Step 3: The final challenge is to have students work independently to create a question and answer paragraph.

Share and Discuss

Step 4: Invite students to share their paragraphs with a partner or members of a group. Have them discuss whether the question and answer paragraphs have the necessary elements and if the question is one that requires a detailed answer.

Step 5: After students have a thorough understanding of the structure, ask them to search for good examples in their textbooks and library books. Encourage them to share their findings with the class.

DIFFERENTIATED INSTRUCTION

If you find that some students have difficulty understanding the question and answer structure or composing strong enough questions, you might want to consider the following activities. Each one allows students to explore this structure without doing any writing.

Twenty Questions

1. This game should be familiar to most students. One student (the player) thinks of a person, place, or thing, and the other students try to guess what it is by asking a maximum of twenty questions. Only "yes" or "no" answers are allowed. The student who guesses the correct answer gets to think of the next item. If there is no correct answer by the twentieth question, the player gets another turn to think of an item.

2. When playing the game, students will likely realize that they must ask questions that are going to give them the most information. For example, the question "Is it a car?" only eliminates one item (car); while "Does it have wheels?" could take in a great number of items (car, bike, truck, wagon, etc.).

What Is the Question?

1. In this activity, the answer to a question is given and students must come up with the question that was asked. Begin with a simple answer and increase the complexity as students become more confident. For example, for the answer "It rained during the night" some possible questions might include the following:

   • What happened during the night?
   • Why was there so much water on the road?

   For the answer "She is playing soccer" the question might be
   • What is she doing?
   • Why is she not watching the movie with us?
   • Why is she late for dinner?

   For a more complex answer, students will have to understand the nature of the topic in order to suggest suitable questions. See Figure 6.17 for an example.

Answer	Questions
The Canadian Shield is the largest geographic region in Canada. It covers a large section of Quebec and Ontario and smaller parts of Labrador, Manitoba, Saskatchewan, Alberta, the Northwest Territories, and Nunavut. This region is very large and is covered with many lakes and forests.	Where would you find the Canadian Shield? How would you describe the Canadian Shield?

FIGURE 6.17

2. This game can also be played in math class. For example, for an answer of "6 km," questions could vary depending on the topic being studied. Here are some examples:

- How far did Jasmeet run if she ran 1 km on Monday, 2 km on Wednesday, and 3 km on Friday?
- How many kilometres are there in 6000 m?

Encourage students to think of as many questions as they can for each answer.

3. The activity can be made more competitive by awarding one point to any student or group that suggests a question that makes sense with the answer, and two points to the student or group that provides the *strongest* question. For example, for the answer, "The day was cold and rainy," award one point for a question such as "What was it like yesterday?" and two points for "Why did the team not play soccer yesterday?"

SUGGESTED CROSS-CURRICULAR TOPICS

Any curriculum topic will fit with the question and answer structure. Some suggestions of questions for this structure are listed below.

Social Studies

- Why was Laura Secord considered a hero in the War of 1812?
- Who was Tecumseh, and why was he important?
- What are some of the challenges and opportunities that migration presents to individuals in Canada?
- What are the different kinds of land use in Canada?
- How can people affect the environment in a positive way? How can they affect it in a negative way?
- What are the main factors contributing to the settlement and development of the Prairie Provinces?
- What are some of Canada's economic and political links with the United States?
- What are the different levels of government in Canada?
- How are the Cordillera and Canadian Shield regions similar? How are they different?
- What did the early settlers learn from First Nations that helped them adapt to their new environment?

Science

- What are the main requirements of plant life?
- What are the main systems in our bodies, and how do they work?
- What are the principles of flight?
- How can light and sound be produced and transmitted?
- What is erosion?
- What is space junk, and why is it a problem?
- How are rocks and minerals different?

Math

- What is the difference between a fraction and a decimal?
- Is a square a rectangle?
- What is theoretical probability?
- What is the relationship between area and perimeter?
- How do you subtract 24 from 313?
- What is the relationship between percent, ratio, fractions, and decimals?

Arts

- How do the different types of musical instruments create sound?
- What are the elements of design that should be considered when creating a piece of art?
- What is a tableau?

Physical Education and Health

- Why is it important to participate in physical activity each day?
- What are some safety rules you should follow at school? at home?
- What are the effects of under-eating on your health and well-being?
- What are some possible negative consequences of substance abuse?

Language Arts

- How do you put voice into your writing?
- What are some important characteristics of persuasive writing?
- What are some themes that are found in literary works?

QUESTION AND ANSWER STRUCTURES IN THE CONTENT AREAS

Blackline masters 6.15 to 6.17 are some examples of question and answer paragraphs taken from textbooks and nonfiction books:

- **Question Is Separate or Bolded** (BLM 6.15)—This is a **grade 4 to 6** basic question and answer format paragraph. The question is easy to identify since it follows a large "Q" and is in boldfaced capital letters. I would introduce this basic format first to my students before examining more complex structures. The question is obvious, and the answer fairly short.
- **Question Is the Topic Sentence** (BLM 6.16)—This paragraph comes from a **grade 8** textbook. Because it is not separate from the paragraph, the question is not as obvious to the reader as in the basic example. Students should be reminded to watch for the 5 Ws if they have difficulty locating the question. The answer is developed in the remainder of the paragraph.
- **Question Is Embedded within the Paragraph** (BLM 6.17)—In this **grade 5** textbook paragraph, students will have to read carefully to find the question embedded within the paragraph before they can look for the answer.

LINKING ASSESSMENT TO LEARNING

The primary focus for the assessment of the question and answer structure will be on whether students can ask strong questions that elicit detailed answers and then write effective answers to the questions, using correctly formed paragraphs.

Figures 6.18 and 6.19 show typical **grade 4** examples for this structure.

In Figure 6.18, the student has asked a good question that cannot be answered with a "yes" or "no" response. Unfortunately, this student develops the answer in several sentences instead of showing an understanding of proper paragraph structure. The reasons given are simple, and there are no supporting details.

The student example in Figure 6.19 does not answer the question that has been asked. The answer given deals with the effects of gravity. (A better question for this paragraph might be, "How does gravity affect us?") The student shows a basic understanding of the question and answer structure but lacks the scientific knowledge common to most **grade 4** students to correctly answer the question.

Traits "are the characteristics or qualities that define good writing" (Trehearne, 2006, 230). These include
- ideas presented
- word choice
- voice (the personality of the writer)
- language conventions (grammar, spelling, etc)
- sentence fluency (using sentences that make sense and vary in length and structure)

Why do people have jobs?

People have jobs because they need money.

People have to buy food.

People get jobs to help people.

FIGURE 6.18

These are two typical grade 4 examples of the question and answer structure. Note that spelling and other errors have not been corrected.

Why does gravity pull down?

Gravity pulls down so that we are able to walk on the ground instead of floating up to the ceiling. If we didn't have gravity, we would fly around and not be able to stay on the ground. Objects like bikes would fly around too and might hit us. We are lucky there is gravity.

FIGURE 6.19

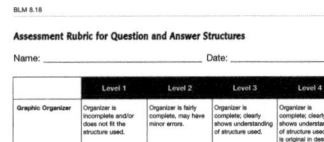

Assessment Checklists and Rubrics

The assessment checklists for question and answer structures can be found on pages 247–248 (BLM 8.16 and 8.17). Figures 6.20 and 6.21 show examples of typical **grade 4** and **grade 6** student responses. The assessment rubric for Chapter 6 question and answer structures (BLM 8.18) can be found on page 249.

GRADE 4 STUDENT SELF-ASSESSMENT

(Below are some grade 4 assessments of their own writing.)

The weaknesses in my question and answer paragraph include:
I did not have a very long paragraph
I like my topic (hockey).

(This student is not looking at the text structure, but at length and topic. I would sit down with him and ask him questions to find out if he could verbalize the important parts of a question and answer paragraph.)

I had a good question and I had a good clincher and topic and finally I gave good reasons.

(This student struggled with the cause and effect structure, and she is saying that she now understands how to give detail to explain things. I would ask her what she meant by "good" question and clincher and topic sentences. But I am thrilled that, at Grade 4, she has realized what she has learned and how she has improved in her writing.)

FIGURE 6.20

    Text Structures: Teaching Patterns in Reading and Writing

(Below are some grade 6 assessments of their peers' writing.)

He wrote a good question but there wasn't much detail. A little more detail would help. His clincher was ok and his topic sentence was the question.

(This peer editor understands what is needed in a question and answer paragraph.)

It was well done and it was really good.

(A conference would definitely be needed with this student to find out why she felt it was well done and really good. She gives no indication of the criteria she used.)

FIGURE 6.21

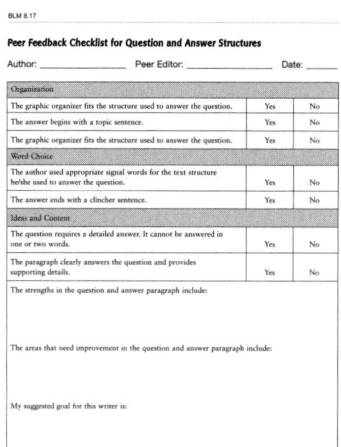

Identifying Text Structures: Reading Like a Writer

When students are familiar with writing the text structure, it is important that they make the connection between what they have learned and what they read. Having written paragraphs using the question and answer structure, they should now be able to identify the structure when they encounter it in their textbooks and library books. The tool below (Figure 6.22) can be used to track their progress in this area.

Anecdotal Records

Keeping anecdotal records from teacher–student conferences, as well as samples of students' work and marks from various assignments, helps track students' progress over the year. When students turn in question and answer structure assignments, most marks will be for organization and ideas. However, marks could also be given for language conventions and effective use of vocabulary if those traits have been discussed earlier in the year.

BLM 8.23

Checklist for Identifying Text Structure Criteria

Name: _____ Date: _____

	Sequence	Enumerative	Compare and Contrast	Cause and Effect	Problem and Solution	Question and Answer	Description
Is able to identify the structure when it is in its basic form in an individual paragraph.							
Is able to identify the characteristics of the structures when reading textbooks and trade books (signal words, topic sentence, clincher sentence, etc.).							
Is able to identify the structure when reading textbooks or trade books even though it is not in its basic form (bullets used instead of signal words, no clincher sentence, etc.).							

Comments

FIGURE 6.22   BLM 8.23

Blackline Masters

Name: _____ Date: _____

Read the following text. How does the question being bold and separate from the rest of the text help you as readers? Use a double underline to answer the question.

Why Do People Visit Manitoba?

With its many campgrounds, parks, lakes, and rivers, Manitoba offers many fun outdoor activities. Visitors come to Manitoba to enjoy bird watching, fishing, canoeing, white-water rafting, and hiking. Others come to see the province's many historic sites and to visit its lively cities and pleasant farming communities. Ukrainian, Icelandic, Mennonite, and other traditions have been preserved in these rural communities.

W. Mathieu, *Manitoba* (InfoCanada: Provinces and Territories series) (Toronto: Nelson), 2004, 44.

Name: _____ Date: _____

Read the following text. Where do you find the answer to the question?

Is Soil the Same Thickness Everywhere?

As bedrock is weathered, small rocks break off, deepening the subsoil. The subsoil is also being weathered by plant roots and small burrowing animals, such as moles and worms, which bring humus down into the subsoil. As a result, the top of the subsoil slowly becomes topsoil. This process takes time—thousands of years.

Depending on how long the soil has had to form, how much material was left by the glaciers, and the amount of erosion that has occurred, the soil has different thicknesses in different parts of the country. In southern Ontario, where great trees and countless animals have lived, died, and contributed their bodies to soil humus for 10 000 years, soil layers tend to be deeper. In northern Ontario, where the glacier of the last Ice Age lasted much later, there has been less time for soil to form. It is also cooler in the north, so plants grow more slowly and there is less biological weathering. Near the glaciers of the Columbia Icefield in the Canadian Rockies, little pine trees can be seen growing in rocky soil that is just a few centimetres deep. There has been little time there for soil formation.

T. Gibb, A. Hirsch, D. White, S. White, J. Wiese, B. Ritter, *Science Technology 7* (Scarborough, Ont.: Nelson) 2000, 211.

Name: _____ Date: _____

Read the following text. Where is the question in this paragraph? What sentence has the answer? What is the purpose of the other sentences?

Your Blood

How does your blood get to where it's going? It travels through blood vessels. Blood vessels are hollow tubes that contain your blood. Your blood moves through your body in these blood vessels. Two types of blood vessels are arteries and veins.

S. Doyle et al., *BC Science Probe 5* (Toronto: Nelson), 2006, 105.

Name: _____ Date: _____

Read the following text. Where is the question in this paragraph? What sentence has the answer? What is the purpose of the other sentences?

Culture

What is a culture? A culture is a way of life shared by a group of people and is composed of a number of things, such as the way people obtain their food, the way they bring up their children, and the values they believe in. Cultures change over time. Imagine the way things were when your grandparents were your age. Think about how your culture has changed since then.

G. Draper et al., *Human Geography 8* (Toronto: Gage Learning), 2000, 247.

Name: _____ Date: _____

Read the following text. Where is the question in this paragraph? Find the answer to the question.

Autumn Colours

When the summertime greens of deciduous leaves turn to the reds, yellows, oranges, and purples of fall, you know that winter is coming. Have you ever wondered where the bright autumn colours come from? The yellows and oranges are actually in the leaves all summer long, but they are hidden by the stronger green colour of chlorophyll. When fall comes, leaves stop making chlorophyll. Soon afterward the green colour disappears and the other colours take over.

P. Hickman, *The Kids Canadian Tree Book* (Toronto: Kids Can Press),1995, 10.

Name: _____ Date: _____

Read the following text. Note that there is more than one question but only one answer. Find the answer to the question.

The Boat People

There have been many news stories about boatloads of people who have endured terrible travelling conditions in order to arrive on the shores of Canada or some other country. Why do people take such risks? Why are they so desperate to risk everything to find a new start? Why do they feel they have no choice except to leave their homes for a new country?

In general, people move because of social, economic, or political factors. Usually, more than one factor influences their decision.

G. Draper, et al., *Human Geography 8* (Toronto: Gage Learning), 2000, 211.

Name: _____ Date: _____

Read the paragraph. Underline the topic and clincher sentences, circle the compare and contrast signal words, and put a box around the question and answer signal words.

Ravens and Crows

Question: How do you know whether you are looking at a raven or a crow?

Ravens and crows are both black in colour, but there are many differences that will help you tell them apart. One difference is that crows are smaller than ravens. Also, if you take a close look, crows have smooth feathers on their throats compared to ravens' shaggy rough-looking feathers. Another difference is that crows caw, whereas ravens croak. In addition, crows usually live in flat areas and are usually found in flocks. Ravens, on the other hand, live alone. Even though at first glance they look the same, the raven and crow definitely have many differences.

Adapted from J. Diehl and D. Plumb, *What's the Difference?* (Toronto: Annick Press), 2000, 17.

Name: _____ Date: _____

In pairs, review this graphic organizer for the paragraph, "Ravens and Crows."
Compare its organization with that of the paragraph. What do you notice?

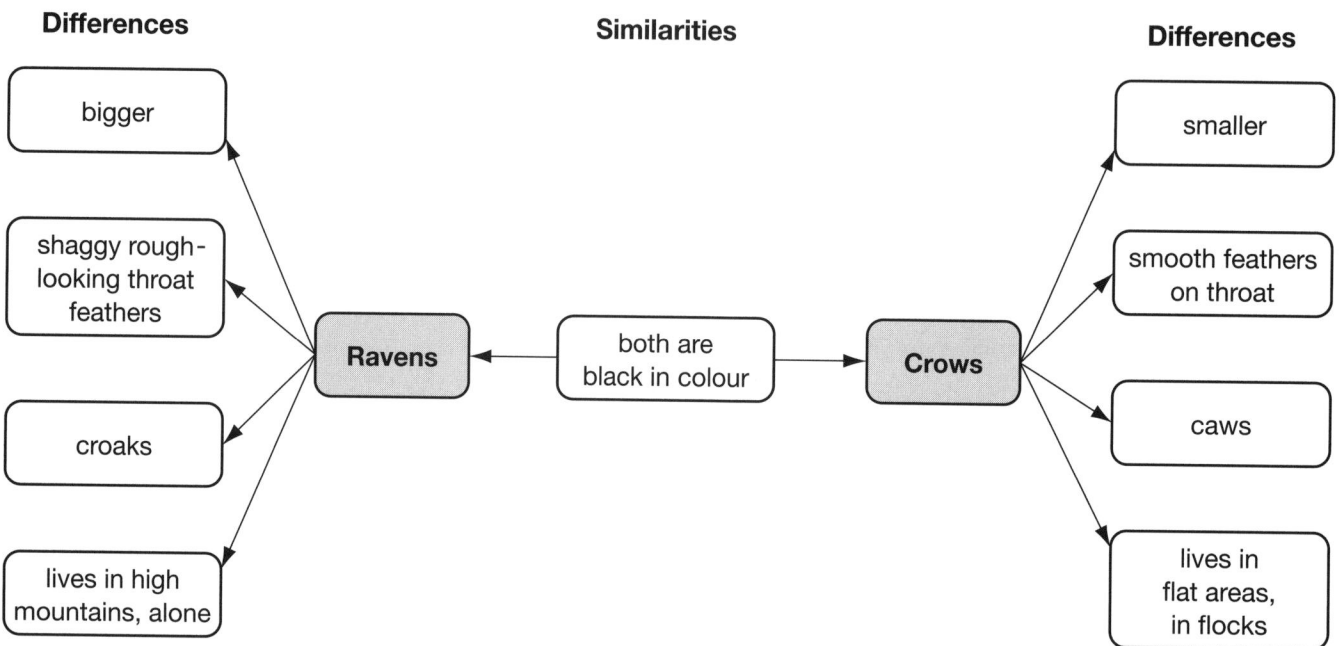

Name: _____ Date: _____

What do you notice about the format of this organizer?

What rules would you follow to keep safe at home?

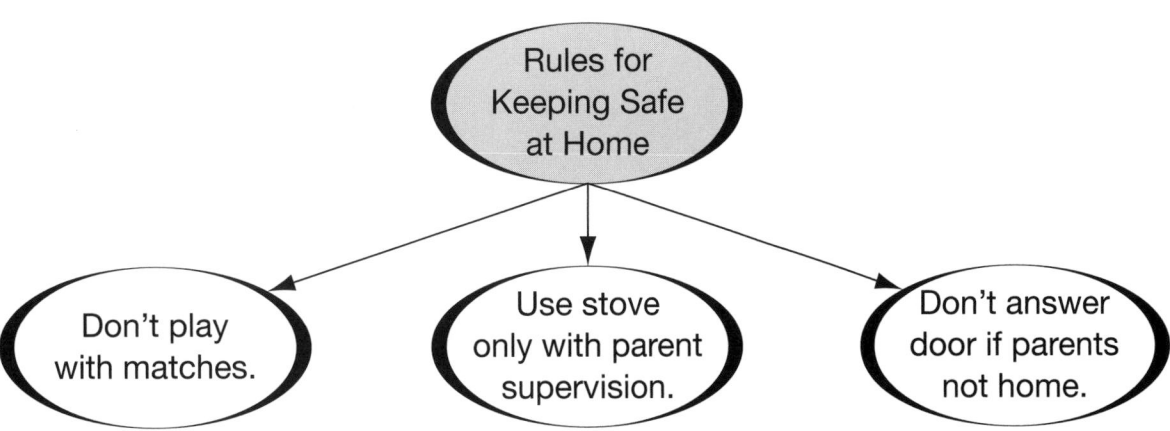

Name: _____ Date: _____

Read and Discuss.

What Caused the War of 1812?

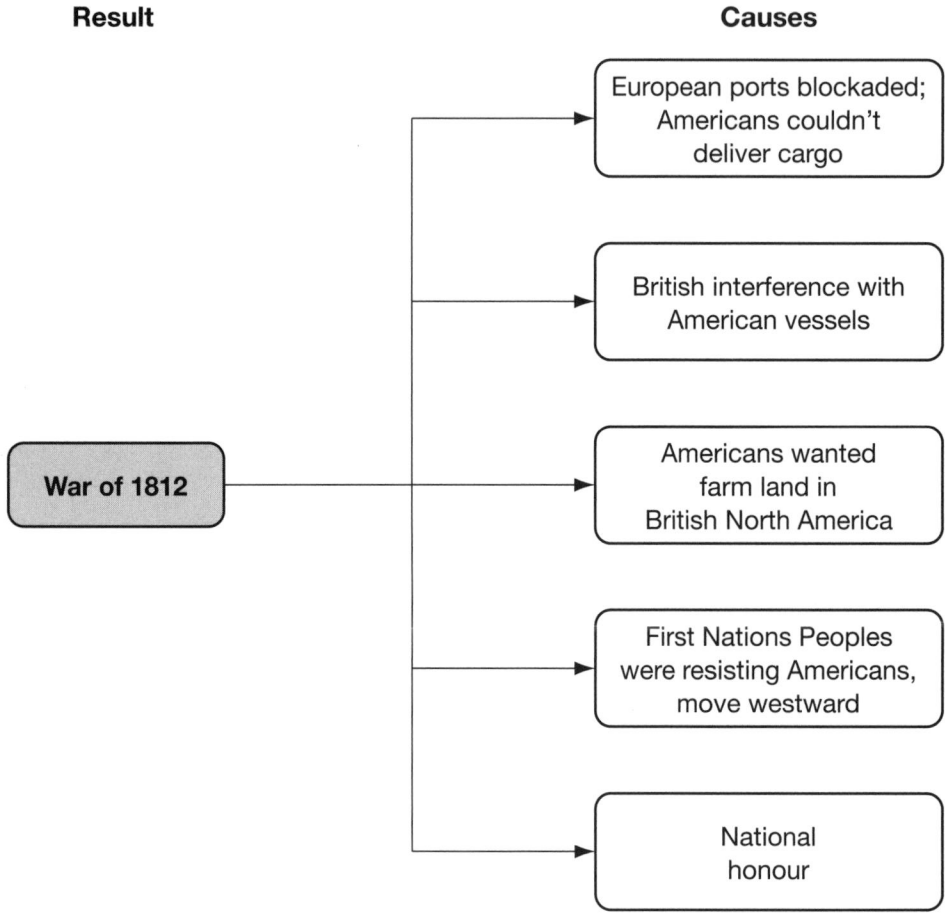

Result

Causes

European ports blockaded;
Americans couldn't
deliver cargo

British interference with
American vessels

War of 1812

Americans wanted
farm land in
British North America

First Nations Peoples
were resisting Americans,
move westward

National
honour

Name: _____ Date: _____

In pairs, answer the question. Underline the topic sentence, the clincher sentence, and identify the signal words. Remember that the signal words could indicate more than one structure.

Becoming a Medieval Knight

Question: What were the steps to becoming a knight in medieval times?

There were three stages a boy had to go through to become a knight. To begin with, he had to leave home when he was 7 years old to live in a neighbouring castle. At the castle, he worked as a page, helping the lord dress and put on armour. He also learned manners from the lady of the castle and played games that would train him to become a knight, such as wrestling, sword practice with wooden swords, and small shield and lance practice. After that, when the boy was 14, he became a squire, a knight's personal servant. He would bring the knight his lances, swords, armour, or horse and accompany him into battle. Like the knights, squires participated in tournaments using real weapons to gain practice in fighting. Finally, when the squire was 21, he was "dubbed" a knight by his lord. It was a long and difficult process to become a knight.

Name: _____ Date: _____

Make your own graphic organizer for the "Becoming a Medieval Knight" paragraph. Remember to use point form, not full sentences, to fill in the organizer.

Becoming a Medieval Knight

What were the steps to becoming a knight in medieval times?

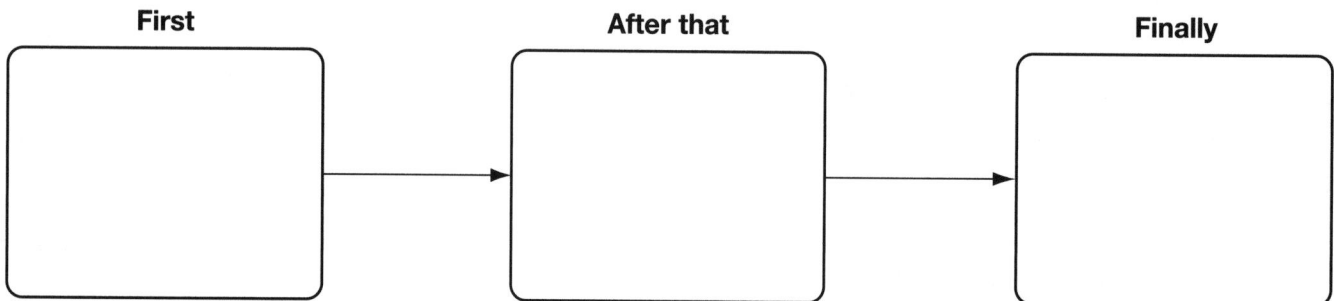

First   After that   Finally

Name: _____ Date: _____

In pairs, write a question and answer paragraph using the notes from a completed organizer.

Space Junk

What are some solutions to the space junk problem?

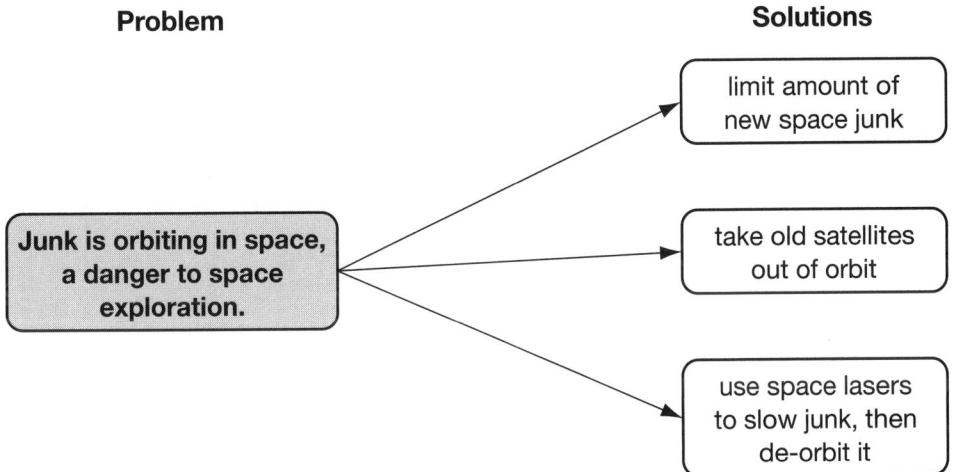

Name: _____ Date: _____

Share and Discuss

Does the paragraph have a suitable topic sentence?
Does it answer the question? Are the signal words appropriate for the structure used?
Does the clincher sentence sum up the paragraph?

Space Junk

Question: What are some solutions to the space junk problem?

One of the problems of space exploration is the amount of junk that is left up in space. Items such as telescopes, old satellites, and parts of spacecraft are orbiting Earth and pose serious threats to space exploration. Even small pieces of junk can do serious damage to spacecraft due to the speed at which the junk travels. Several solutions to this problem have been suggested. The first solution is to limit the amount of space junk in the first place. This solution doesn't deal with the space junk already orbiting Earth, but it would prevent more from accumulating. The second solution would be to take satellites out of orbit when they are no longer needed instead of leaving them up in space. This would help limit the amount of new space junk but would not deal with the junk that is presently there. Another solution that has been suggested is to use space lasers to slow the junk down and then de-orbit it. However, much more research needs to be done before this becomes a possible solution. Due to the danger of space junk to space exploration, research to decrease the amount of junk in space must continue until more feasible solutions are found.

Name: _____ Date: _____

The Nervous System

Question: What Parts of the Body Make Up the Nervous System?

The nerves, spinal cord, and brain make up the nervous system. The spinal cord and brain form the central nervous system, while a network of nerves running throughout the body forms the peripheral nervous system.

S. Bruno, *The Human Body* (Milwaukee: Gareth Stevens Publishing), 2002, 8.

Name: _____ Date: _____

Canada Census

How are all the people in a country counted? Every five years, governments collect information about the number of people living in their region. Every 10 years a more detailed census is carried out: people are hired to conduct door-to-door surveys in their neighbourhoods, collecting information about age, ethnic background, language, family size, and other facts. Statistics Canada is the branch of government responsible for the Canadian census.

G. Draper, L. French, and Andrea Craig, *Human Geography 8* (Toronto: Gage Learning), 2000, 6.

Name: _____ Date: _____

Nature's Resources

Soil, water, plants, air and the sun are resources that nature provides us. Can you imagine what your life would be like without each of these resources? Not only would you be cold and hungry, you wouldn't be able to stay alive. These resources make Earth the only planet that we know of in the Universe where humans can survive.

S. Doyle et al., *B.C. Science Probe 5* (Toronto: Nelson), 2006, 159.

Name: _____ Date: _____

The Northern Lights

You see ghostly green and pink in the sky. You have no clue what it is. It's the northern lights. What causes the northern lights? Well, the northern lights are caused when charged particles called electrons collide with atoms. The energy from the electrons is transferred to the atoms causing light. The northern lights are also known as the Aurora Borealis. Do me a favour. Next time you see them, don't get scared and run off. Stop and enjoy the world's most incredible light show.

TEACHING DESCRIPTION STRUCTURES

7

DEFINING THE STRUCTURE

The description structure is a widely used pattern commonly found in student texts and trade books. In this structure, *the main topic is developed by describing its characteristics or attributes.* Descriptive language helps the reader form vivid images, making the topic more comprehensible.

The three forms of description that students are likely to encounter and use are discussed below. They are:

- one-paragraph descriptions
- description reports
- five-paragraph description mini-essays

One-Paragraph Description

This form is similar to the majority of examples in the preceding chapters where one paragraph develops the structure (i.e., a description of an object, person, animal, or event). "The Moon" is a good example of a one-paragraph description. A marked up example is shown in Figure 7.4 (page 184).

In these paragraphs, students should be encouraged to use a variety of effective adjectives and adverbs as well as language that appeals to the reader's senses (i.e., describing how something smells, feels, sounds, looks, and tastes). Introducing the language conventions of similes and metaphors would also help students add description to their writing.

It would be beneficial as an introduction to this structure to show students a few examples of vivid description paragraphs and discuss what makes them effective. For example, have students pick out the descriptive words, similes, metaphors, and words that appeal to the senses.

Mini-lessons on replacing overused words—such as *good, neat, went, bad, pretty, big, sad, happy, get,* and *said*—would also be helpful to students. They could brainstorm replacement words and post the lists around the classroom so they can refer to them as they write. For example, for the word *bad* the list might contain the words *evil, wicked, contaminated, substandard, horrible, atrocious, deplorable,* and *rotten.*

Description Reports

The second form is a more developed version of the structure: a description report. These examples are just longer versions of the description paragraph; they are made up of two or three description paragraphs on one topic. Each paragraph contains a topic and a clincher sentence. BLM 7.12, "The Beaver" is a good example of a simple report. A marked up example is shown in Figure 7.10 (page 189).

Five-Paragraph Description Mini-Essays

When students have become more confident and competent using the longer report format, it is time to introduce them to the third form: the five-paragraph mini-essay. This form is similar to the basic expository essay of five paragraphs that is studied in later grades. It has three main parts:

- A topic paragraph (or sometimes just the topic sentence) acts like a thesis statement. It indicates the three subtopics that will be developed in the subsequent paragraphs.
- The body of the essay contains three paragraphs, one for each subtopic.
- A concluding summary paragraph (the clincher) sums up the important facts of the essay.

BLM 7.14, "Types of Rocks," is an example of this type of essay. Figure 7.14 (page 192) shows the highlighted mini-essay paragraph elements.

Paragraph, Report, and Mini-Essay Features

Topic Sentence

The topic sentence for the one paragraph structure indicates the main topic that will be described in some fashion (e.g., "The Moon is a natural satellite that orbits Earth"). In a description mini-essay, there would be a topic sentence for each of the subtopic paragraphs. For example, if the subject of the essay were hurricanes, the subtopics might be:

- how hurricanes are created
- the dangers of hurricanes
- how to decrease the damage caused by hurricanes

In a complete expository essay, there would be a thesis statement in the first paragraph instead of a topic sentence.

Clincher Sentence

The clincher sentence sums up the ideas in the paragraph. In a report of more than two paragraphs, each paragraph might have its own clincher sentence. In a mini-essay, there would be a clincher paragraph instead of a clincher sentence.

Signal Words

The description structure does not have specific signal words of its own, although it often contains sensory language. However, adjectives, adverbs, and, of course, nouns relating to the topic will be part of the description. Students are also likely to find other structures and their signal words within this structure. (See Figure 7.16, BLM 7.16, (pages 193–194) "Hurricanes," for an example.)

Distinguishing Between Description Structures

I use three different organizers to distinguish between the description paragraph, the description report and the five-paragraph mini-essay. For the description paragraph, I use an organizer with one main topic box (BLM 7.1). All the information about the topic of the paragraph is written on lines coming out from the box.

For the report, the organizer indicates that there are subtopics. There is a main topic box and several smaller boxes to indicate the subtopics (see BLM 7.2). The spaces under the subtopic boxes can be used to add information (jot notes) about each subtopic. The mini-essay's organizer is similar to the report's except its five paragraphs are indicated (see BLM 7.4).

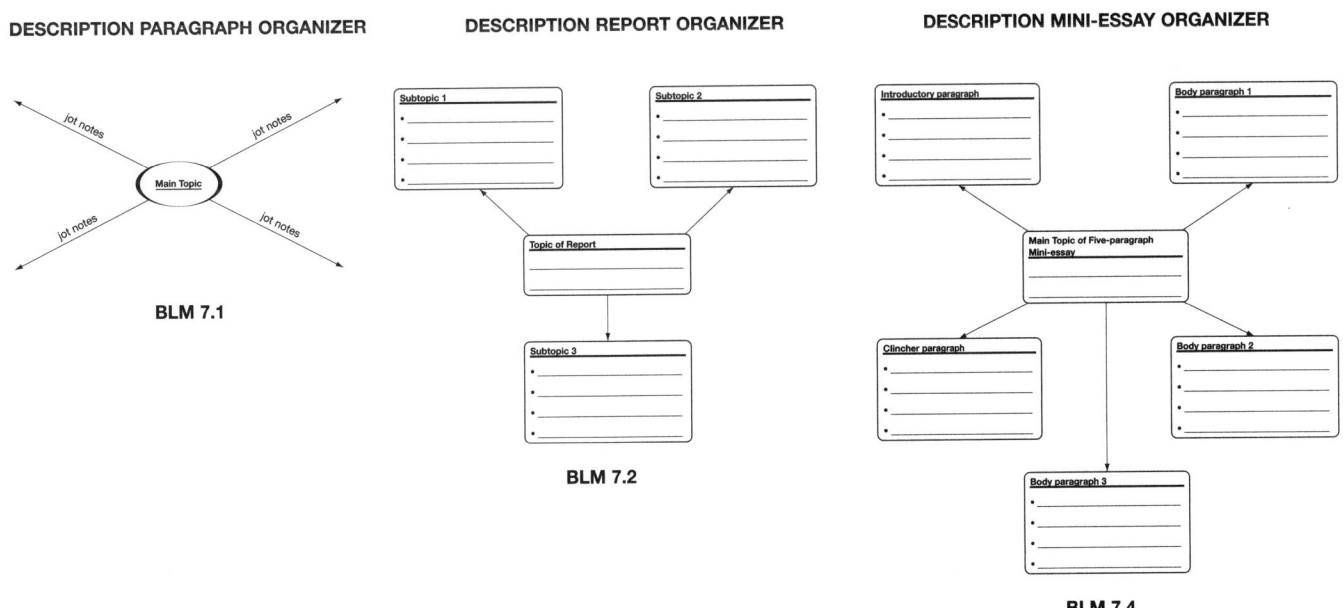

FIGURE 7.1 BLMs 7.1, 7.2, AND 7.4

For **grades 4 and 5** students, it would be excellent if they could write a three-paragraph description report that includes a topic and clincher sentence for each paragraph. However, I would still recommend exposing them to the five-paragraph format of the mini-essay, with topic and clincher paragraphs. I do not expect most **grades 4 and 5** students to be able to write this type of description, but there will certainly be some among them who are capable of handling it. Using different complexities of organizers might also help students who are struggling with the concept of the essay form. These students first could be given a simple organizer (see Figure 7.1, BLM 7.2). They could then use a second organizer (BLM 7.3) to turn their jot notes into sentences.

Grades 7 and 8 and advanced **grades 4 to 6** students could use an organizer similar to Figure 7.1, BLM 7.4 and then use an outline organizer (BLM 7.5) that leads them through a very basic five-paragraph mini-essay.

The majority of **grades 7 and 8** students should be able to handle the five-paragraph mini-essay form with topic and clincher paragraphs. Once again, providing a more detailed outline organizer to students who are struggling with this format will help guide them in writing their essays. Creating a class essay as a guided writing activity is also a helpful teaching strategy.

Additional Instructional Support

I would not expect my special needs students to write descriptive reports of more than two or three paragraphs, nor would I expect each paragraph to be longer than three sentences. I like to use easy-to-follow organizers to help students gain an understanding of the structure. For example, students could use one organizer for each paragraph as shown in Figure 7.2, BLM 7.6.

jot notes   jot notes

Why the panda is endangered

jot notes

FIGURE 7.2 BLM 7.6

You could then give them a fill in the blanks organizer such as the one in Figure 7.3, to use after they have their jot notes. I would also have students work in a group to write another essay in a guided writing activity before asking them to work in pairs to attempt to write an essay.

Why the Panda Is Endangered

The panda is an endangered animal. It is endangered because _____. Another reason it is endangered is because _____ _____. The third reason it is endangered is because _____ _____. We must all work together to protect the panda from extinction.

FIGURE 7.3

INTRODUCING THE STRUCTURE AND EXAMINING A MODEL PARAGRAPH

Step 1: Introduce the structure by asking students to compare a description paragraph to others they have studied, such as those for the sequence and enumerative structures. "The Moon" in Figure 7.4, BLM 7.7, is one example.

- While all have topic and clincher sentences, in description paragraphs, there are no specific signal words.
- Another important difference is that description paragraphs can use other text structures in their development. Thus, a *compare and contrast* structure might be used to describe the dark and light sides of the moon; a *cause and effect* structure might serve to illustrate hurricanes; an *enumerative structure* might list the types of food that polar bears eat.

The Moon

topic sentence →

<u>The Moon is a natural satellite that orbits Earth.</u> Scientists have discovered that its soil is made up of [fine] sand and gravel. It has no atmosphere—which means the sky isn't [blue]—and therefore no sound because it is air that carries sound waves. Temperatures on the moon are [severe,] with [extremely hot] days (130° C) and [extremely cold] nights (–190° C). A [vast] number of craters is its best-known [surface] feature. These are holes on the Moon's surface. The [darkest] parts of the Moon are [lava-filled] craters called *maria*. It is these [surface] features that create the ["Man in the Moon" look.] <u>Taking about 27 days to orbit our planet, it is Earth's only moon.</u>

descriptive words

clincher sentence →

FIGURE 7.4 BLM 7.7

Share and Discuss

Step 2: As a class, discuss the similarities and differences between a model description paragraph and paragraphs of other text structures.

DEVELOPING A GRAPHIC ORGANIZER

Introduce the Model

Step 1: Introduce the graphic organizer that goes with the model paragraph (see Figure 7.5 below). Point out that this organizer only has one main idea. Its organization shows that there are no subtopics. Each jot note describes this central topic and radiates from the centre.

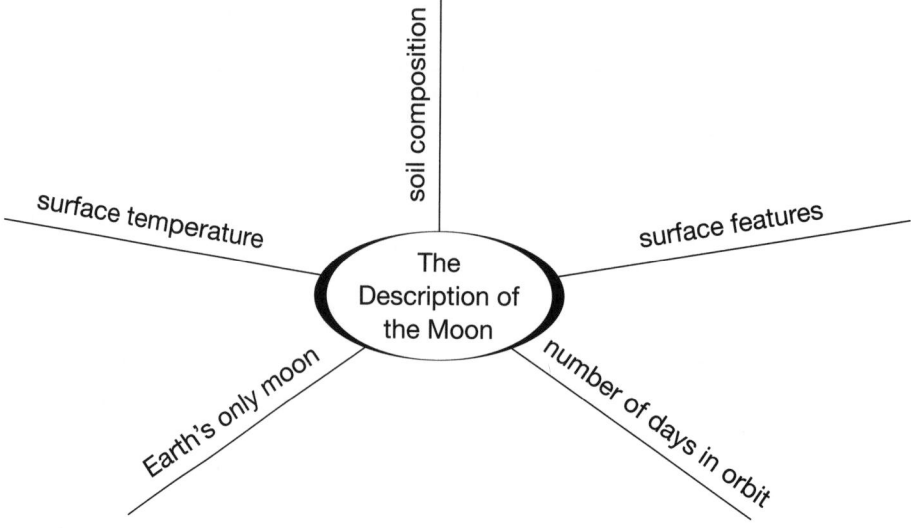

FIGURE 7.5 BLM 7.8

Text Structures: Teaching Patterns in Reading and Writing

Step 2: Ask students to read the paragraph again to look for descriptive words that describe the moon. For example:

- fine sand and gravel
- extremely hot days
- extremely cold nights
- darkest parts

Step 3: Introduce students to another description paragraph. Display it on an overhead transparency and have students follow along as you read the paragraph aloud. Ask them to identify the topic sentence and clincher sentence. Have them also identify descriptive words the author has used to help the reader visualize the subject. (See Figure 7.6, "The Polar Bear." Descriptive words are circled.)

The Polar Bear

The polar bear is one of the largest and strongest carnivores in the world. Its massive body measures 240 to 260 centimetres in length, and it can weigh up to 800 kilograms. Glossy guard hairs on its thick winter coat and a dense under-fur protect it from the harsh Arctic winter. The guard hairs repel water. Both layers of fur, along with the layer of fat that is under the fur, keep the bear warm in the cold temperatures. Its white colour serves as an excellent camouflage in the Arctic environment. Small bumps and cavities on its soles act like suction cups and help to prevent the bear from slipping on the ice. Its short, fairly straight, and sharply pointed claws aid it in catching and eating its food. All these characteristics make the polar bear well equipped for living in the harsh Arctic climate.

topic sentence

descriptive words

clincher sentence

FIGURE 7.6   BLM 7.9

Step 4: Next, show students the graphic organizer for the paragraph (see Figure 7.7, BLM 7.10). Once again, remind them that the organizer should have one section or topic with lines going out to show the jot-note information for the paragraph.

THE DESCRIPTION OF A POLAR BEAR

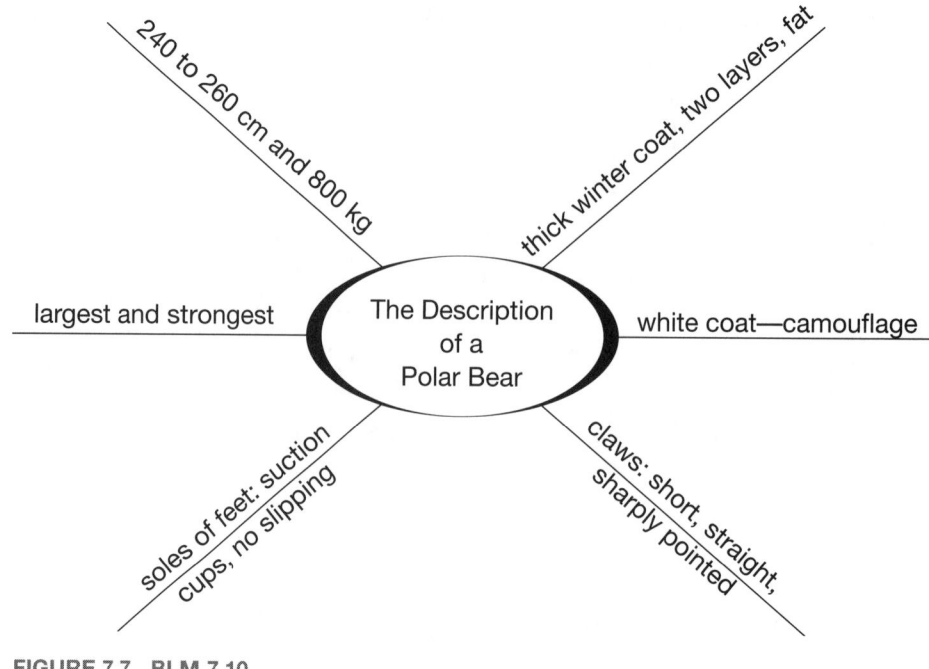

240 to 260 cm and 800 kg

thick winter coat, two layers, fat

largest and strongest

The Description of a Polar Bear

white coat—camouflage

soles of feet: suction cups, no slipping

claws: short, straight, sharply pointed

FIGURE 7.7   BLM 7.10

WRITING A DESCRIPTION PARAGRAPH

Create a Class Paragraph

Step 1: Work with students to write a class paragraph using the description structure. Ask them for suggestions about what to describe (it could be from a current topic of study, or you could choose a different topic that you know is a popular one). Use students' suggestions to develop an organizer for the paragraph.

Step 2: Write the topic in the centre of the blank organizer (e.g., Figure 7.8, BLM 7.11), using an overhead transparency or chart paper. Have students suggest ideas to include on the organizer, and record them on the lines radiating from the main idea. Five to six ideas should be enough for a description paragraph.

Step 3: Once students have provided enough ideas, show them how to take the ideas and write a paragraph. Guide them by asking questions such as the following:

- What would be a strong topic sentence for our paragraph?
- In what order do we want to put our ideas? Is there an order that would be best?
- What would be a strong clincher sentence?

DESCRIPTION PARAGRAPH ORGANIZER

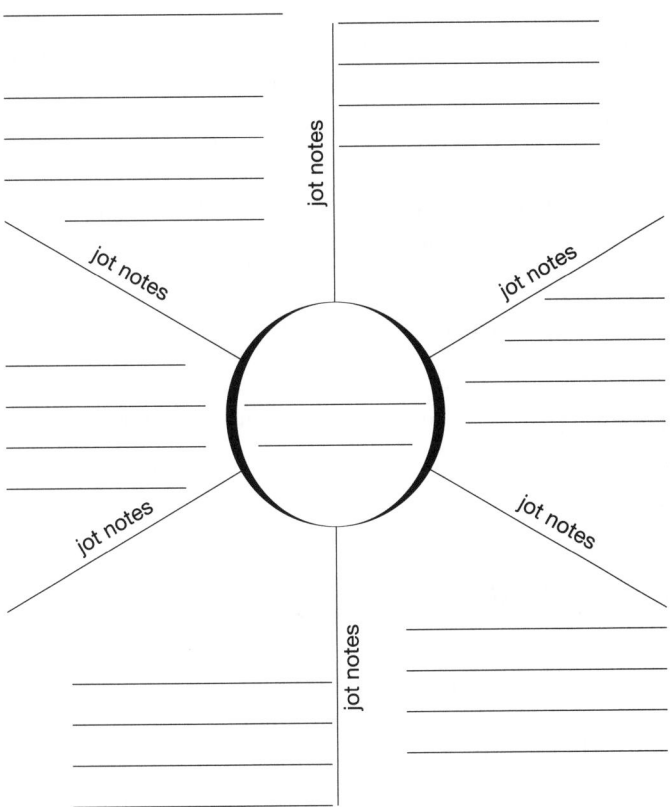

FIGURE 7.8   BLM 7.11

Share and Discuss

Step 4: When they have completed their first draft, ask students to look
back at the paragraph.

- Ask them if they think there are any words they could change to
help give readers a more vivid image in their minds.
- Suggest places where they might add adjectives or adverbs.
- Encourage them to think of a simile or metaphor that might give
a better picture.
- Challenge them to include sense words.
- Have them compare their first draft with their second one.

COMPOSING THEIR OWN PARAGRAPHS

Step 1: Divide students into pairs and have them choose their own topics
(or ask them to select one related to their studies). Have them first
make an organizer to outline their topics before writing their
paragraphs. When they have completed the paragraphs, ask them to
reread them and consider whether they have provided enough descriptive vocabulary to help the reader visualize what they are
writing about.

Share and Discuss

Step 2: Distribute description paragraphs along with their organizers to the class. After each example, discuss the following questions:

- Does the organizer reflect the paragraph's structure and information?
- Has the paragraph a suitable topic sentence?
- Does its descriptive language help the reader visualize the paragraph's topic?
- Does the clincher sentence reflect the topic sentence?

These questions could form the basis of a rubric that students can use to assess their paragraphs.

Step 3: When they are familiar with this structure, have students locate and share description paragraph examples from their textbooks or library books. (See *Description Structures in the Content Areas*, page 199.)

UNDERSTANDING THE ESSAY

Simple Description Reports

Step 1: When students understand the description structure using one paragraph, introduce them to a longer version: the description reports. (See Figure 7.9 for the types of text structures used in the example reports and mini-essays that follow.) Have students compare the report's paragraphs to the types of paragraphs they have read and created for the description structure. They should see that the report has more than one paragraph, and that each paragraph has its own topic and clincher sentences. (See Figure 7.10, BLM 7.12, "The Beaver," for an example. The topic and clincher sentences are underlined.)

Essay Title and Figure Number	Type of Text Structure
"The Beaver" Figure 7.10	Description
"Types of Rocks" Figure 7.14	Enumerative
"Hurricanes" Figure 7.16	2nd Paragraph: Sequence 3rd Paragraph: Cause and Effect 4th Paragraph: Problem and Solution

FIGURE 7.9

The Beaver

The beaver's watery home is unique for a member of the rodent family. Found in rivers, streams, dammed-up swamps, and freshwater lakes near woodlands, the beaver lodge is made of sticks and twigs that are packed together with mud and stones. Its entrance is under the water. As the weather becomes cold, the outside of the lodge is plastered with mud. Bank beavers burrow dens beside streams and lakes. No wonder these animals are considered "creative architects."

topic sentence

clincher sentence

With two layers of fur to keep them warm and dry, the beaver is well adapted to a life in and near water. Its flat tail, which resembles a paddle, acts like a rudder as it swims. On land, the tail helps prop the beaver up when sitting or standing upright. Besides the tail, the beaver's most unusual feature is its two huge front teeth. With them, it can gnaw down trees as large as 30 centimetres in diameter. All these characteristics make its appearance unique in the animal world.

topic sentence

clincher sentence

Like most rodents, a beaver is a herbivore or plant eater. It eats the bark, twigs, branches, and leaves of trees. Aspen, poplar, birch, and willows are their favourite foods. But they also eat water plants, especially the roots and tender sprouts of water lilies. A beaver works constantly to find and store its food. That is why "as busy as a beaver" best describes this fascinating mammal.

topic sentence

clincher sentence

FIGURE 7.10 BLM 7.12

Introduce the Graphic Organizer

Step 2: Show students the report's organizer (see Figure 7.11). Each circled topic coming out from the main idea indicates a subtopic, and therefore, a separate paragraph. By using a graphic organizer, students should be able to identify the relationship between the number of subtopics in the organizer and the number of paragraphs in the report. It is important for students to make this connection: the number of sections in the organizer should *always* equal the number of paragraphs in a report.

DESCRIPTION REPORT ORGANIZER—THREE PARTS

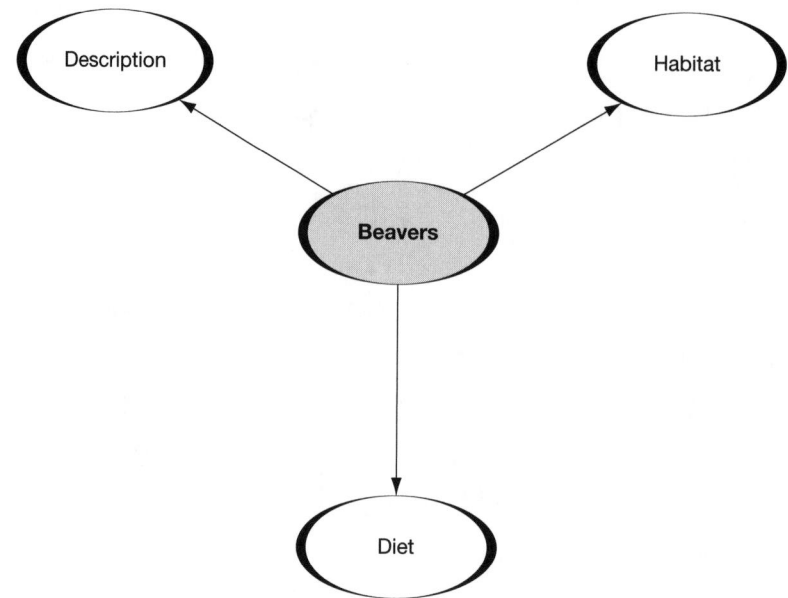

FIGURE 7.11 BLM 7.13

Step 3: To prompt students, ask questions such as the following:

If I had three paragraphs, how many parts to my organizer would there be? (Three parts.)

If I had six parts to my organizer, how many paragraphs must I have? (Six paragraphs.)

Continue asking these questions until every student is able to verbalize the fact that the number of parts in the organizer and the number of paragraphs in the report should be equal. (See Figures 7.12 and 7.13 for typical organizers.)

SIMPLIFIED DESCRIPTION ORGANIZER—THREE PARTS

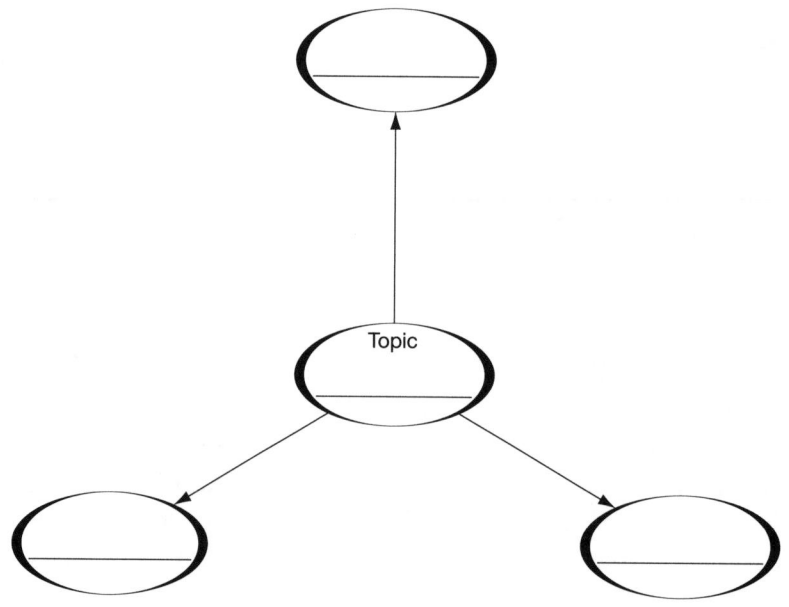

FIGURE 7.12

Text Structures: Teaching Patterns in Reading and Writing

SIMPLIFIED DESCRIPTION ORGANIZER—SIX PARTS

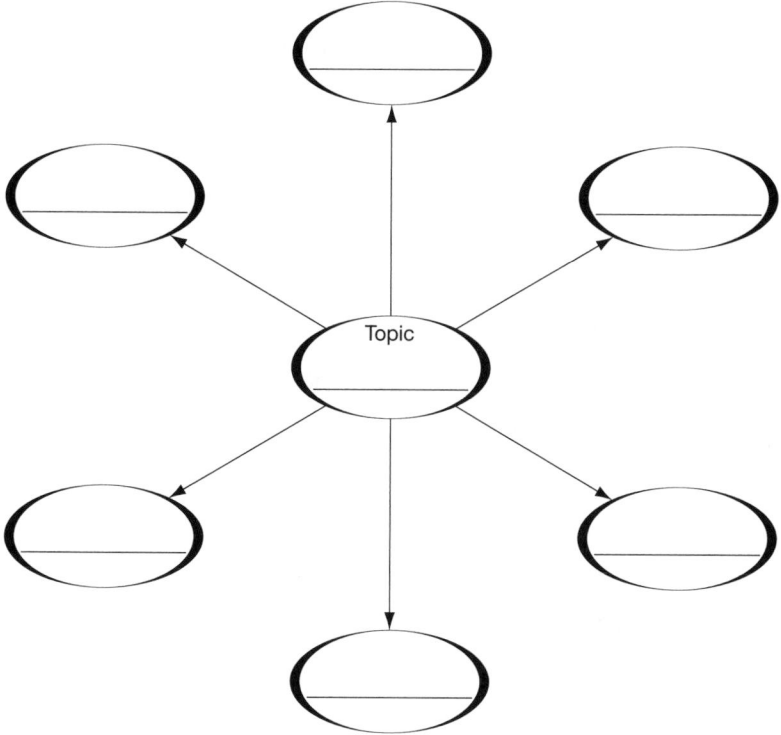

FIGURE 7.13

The Five-Paragraph Description Mini-Essay

Once students are able to put three paragraphs together on one topic, they are ready to do a five-paragraph mini-essay that is a simplified version of the basic expository essay. In this form, the first paragraph acts like a thesis statement and indicates the topic and the subtopics of the essay. The next three paragraphs discuss each of the subtopics. The last paragraph is the "clincher paragraph," and sums up the statements of the previous paragraphs.

Step 4: Figure 7.14, "Types of Rocks," is an example of a five-paragraph description mini-essay that uses an enumerative structure. (The topic is discussed in a sequence, but the order is arbitrary.) Similar to the question and answer structure, a five-paragraph description mini-essay can, and often does, contain more than one text structure. For this reason, I like to introduce the five-paragraph model mini-essay that uses a single structure, before exploring more complex, multi-structure models. (Note that, in Figure 7.14, enumerative signal words are circled and topic sentences are underlined. The last paragraph serves as the "clincher." The organizer is shown in Figure 7.15.)

Types of Rocks

topic sentence
of mini-essay

Rocks are classified into three different groups according to the way in which they were formed. They are igneous, sedimentary, and metamorphic rocks. These rocks are all related to each other through the rock cycle.

topic sentence

The first group is the igneous rocks, often called "fire rocks." These rocks are usually very hard. They can be formed above or below ground. Below Earth's surface, igneous rocks are formed when magma enters an under-ground chamber, cools very slowly, and turns into rocks full of large crystals. Above ground they are formed by the cooling of melted material such as the lava from a volcano. Some of these "fire-formed" rocks are granite, feldspar, and mica.

signal words

topic sentence

The next group of rocks is called sedimentary rocks. For millions of years, pieces of earth have been broken down and worn away by wind and water. These small pieces settle at the bottom of rivers, lakes, and oceans along with dead plants and tiny animal skeletons. Many layers form on top of the previous ones, pressing down and creating pressure on the lower layers. As they are compressed and hardened, these layers become rock. This action requires a very long period of time. Sedimentary rocks are soft and easily broken. Sandstone, shale, and limestone are some common types.

topic sentence

The last group into which rocks are classified is the metamorphic group. These rocks are "changed rocks." They once belonged to one of the other two groups but were under tremendous pressure. These forces built up heat that caused the rocks to change their composition. Metamorphic rocks are usually shiny and smooth. Slate, quartzite, and marble are examples of "changed" rocks.

clincher paragraph

All of these groups of rocks have played an important role in the development of Earth's crust. Over time, each type of rock changes to another as part of the never-ending rock cycle.

FIGURE 7.14   BLM 7.14

Text Structures: Teaching Patterns in Reading and Writing

"TYPES OF ROCKS" ORGANIZER

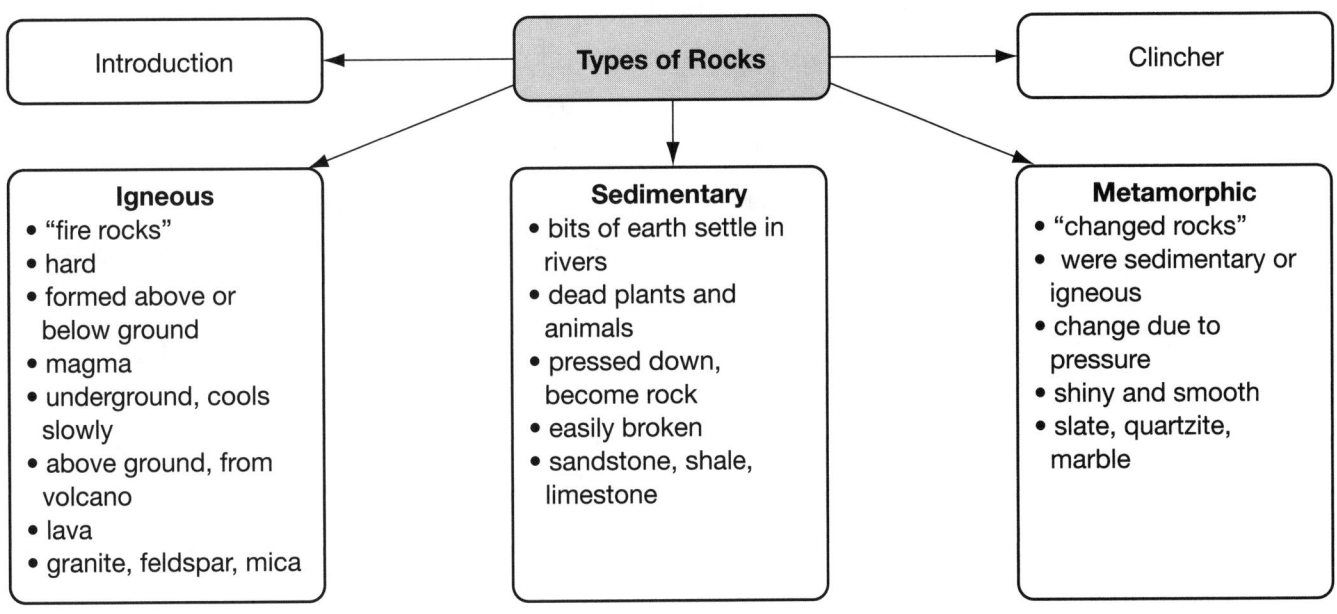

FIGURE 7.15 BLM 7.15

Multi-Text Structure Description Mini-Essays

Step 5: The next step in understanding the five-paragraph description mini-essay is to study an example with more than one text structure. The essay that follows ("Hurricanes," Figure 7.16, BLM 7.16) includes three text structures, even though the overall structure is description. (The signal words for each structure have been circled; topic sentences are underlined; clincher sentences are double-underlined, and clincher paragraphs are shaded.) Be sure to have students note that there is a topic and clincher sentence for *each* paragraph.

Hurricanes

Hurricanes are large, powerful storms that begin over the ocean. They leave destruction and death in their wake. <u>Many people are studying methods to decrease the problems hurricanes cause.</u>　　← topic sentence of mini-essay

<u>A hurricane forms over warm ocean water.</u> Air that has been warmed by the ocean begins to rise in an upward spiral and this causes areas of low pressure underneath it. Then, cooler air from a high-pressure area rushes in to fill the space left by the warm air. Soon after, this cooler air warms and also begins to rise and spin. <u>This cycle continues until gradually it builds up to form a hurricane.</u>

← topic sentence

signal words

← clincher sentence

continued ⟶

topic sentence → <u>The effects of hurricanes are among the most extreme examples of natural disasters.</u> High winds, heavy rains, storm surges, and sliding mud all ⬚cause⬚ extensive damage. Heavy rain and storm surges often ⬚result⬚ in a great deal of flooding. The winds of a hurricane can tear up trees, wreck houses, crush vehicles, and snap power lines. People are forced to evacuate their homes and find temporary shelter. Mudslides

signal words

often ⬚result⬚ in washed out roads, railroads, and bridges ⬚so⬚ it

clincher sentence → is difficult for help to arrive. <u>Hurricanes cause incredible amounts of damage.</u>

topic sentence → <u>Hurricanes cannot be prevented, but many things are being attempted to decrease the problems they cause such as severe damage to property and loss of life.</u> ⬚One solution⬚ is to continue to improve the weather tracking systems. Radar and satellites in space are used to track and understand hurricanes better and to enable meteorologists to forecast them more accurately. ⬚Also,⬚ computers are being used to help create better warning systems. If people get enough warning, they can leave the risk areas in time and without panic, thereby saving lives. ⬚Another solution⬚ being used in Jamaica and Australia is to have stricter building codes so buildings

clincher sentence → can withstand much stronger winds. <u>It is hoped that all attempts to decrease the devastating damage and loss of life caused by hurricanes will be successful.</u>

clincher paragraph → Hurricanes are among the most dangerous storms in the world. They cause major damage and death whenever they

clincher sentence → occur. <u>People will continue to look for ways to prevent these storms from creating the havoc that they do now.</u>

FIGURE 7.16   BLM 7.16

Mini-Essay Organizers

Organizers for the five-paragraph mini-essay can take two forms:

- a simple organizer that shows jot notes of what will be covered in each paragraph (Figure 7.17)
- an organizer that shows the different text structures that will be used in each paragraph (Figure 7.18)

For more complex organizers, such as the organizer for "Hurricanes" in Figure 7.16, students might find it easier to create an organizer for each paragraph on a separate sheet of paper.

FIVE-PARAGRAPH MINI-ESSAY ORGANIZERS: ONE STRUCTURE

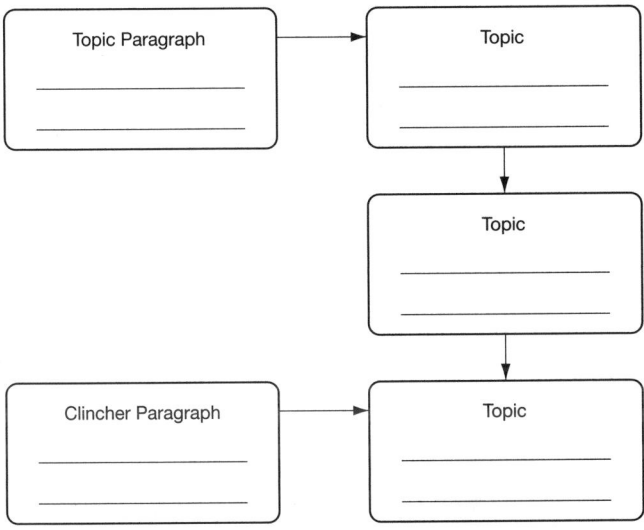

FIGURE 7.17 BLM 7.17

FIVE-PARAGRAPH MINI-ESSAY ORGANIZERS: MORE THAN ONE STRUCTURE

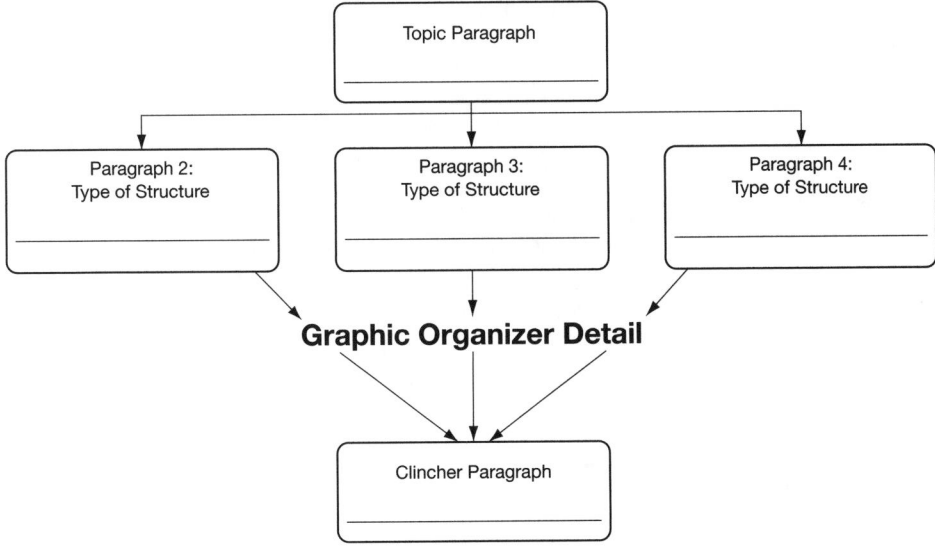

FIGURE 7.18 BLM 7.18

HURRICANE MINI-ESSAY ORGANIZER

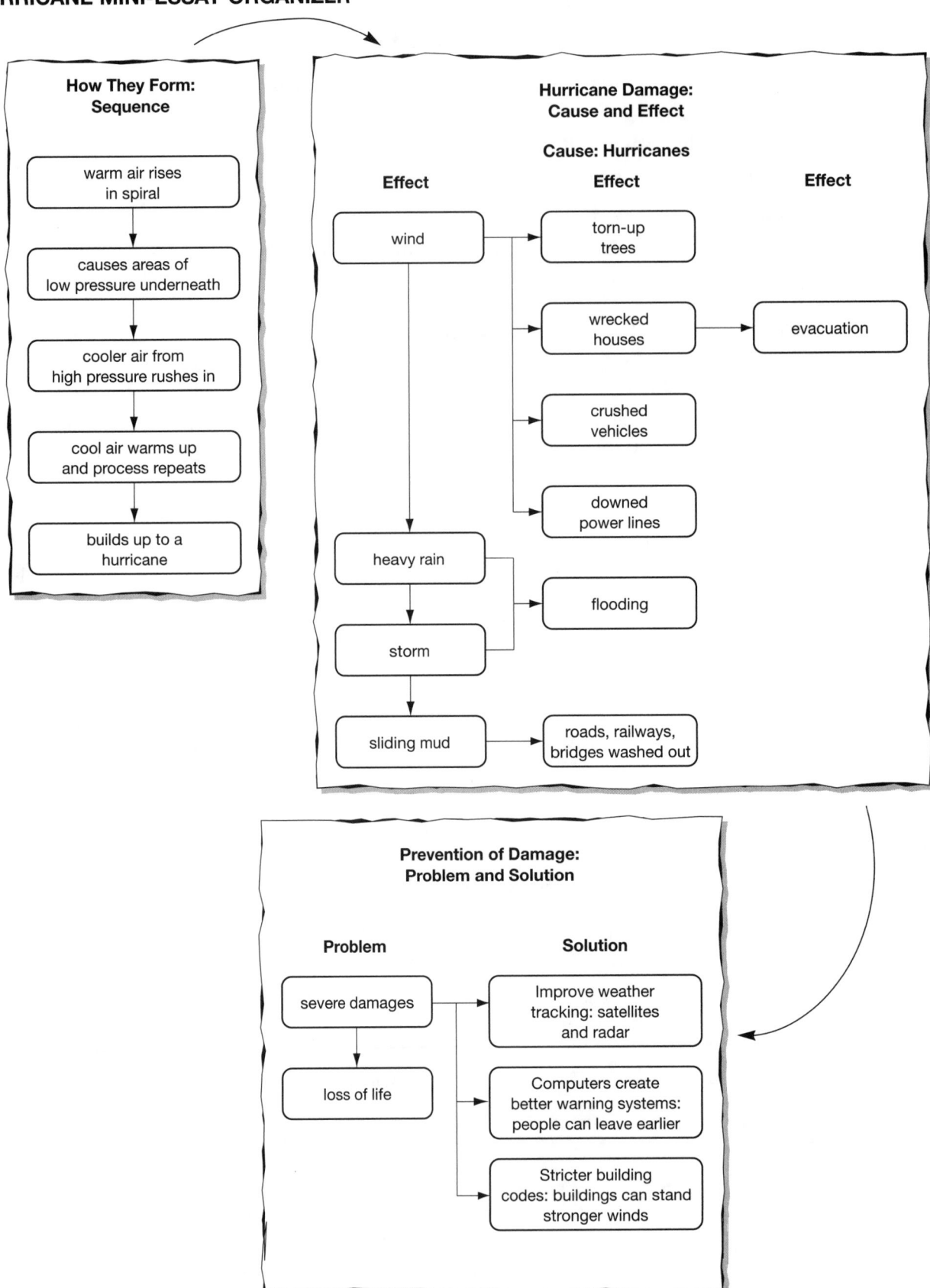

How They Form:
Sequence

- warm air rises in spiral
- causes areas of low pressure underneath
- cooler air from high pressure rushes in
- cool air warms up and process repeats
- builds up to a hurricane

Hurricane Damage:
Cause and Effect

Cause: Hurricanes

Effect	Effect	Effect
wind	torn-up trees	
	wrecked houses	evacuation
	crushed vehicles	
	downed power lines	
heavy rain	flooding	
storm		
sliding mud	roads, railways, bridges washed out	

Prevention of Damage:
Problem and Solution

Problem	Solution
severe damages	Improve weather tracking: satellites and radar
loss of life	Computers create better warning systems: people can leave earlier
	Stricter building codes: buildings can stand stronger winds

FIGURE 7.19   BLM 7.19

Text Structures: Teaching Patterns in Reading and Writing

WRITING THEIR OWN MINI-ESSAYS

Step 1: Have students work in pairs to create a mini-essay and share it with other students. As a class, discuss the strengths of the essays and the areas where improvement is needed.

Step 2: Next, have students write their own description mini-essays to share with the class.

Share and Discuss

Step 3: Encourage students to bring in examples of description paragraphs and mini-essays from textbooks and nonfiction books. (See *Description Structures in the Content Areas*, page 199, for some examples.)

DIFFERENTIATED INSTRUCTION

Class Essay

An activity that I have found very successful in helping students understand the five-paragraph mini-essay format, without requiring them to write the complete essay, is to write a class essay.

1. As a class, decide on a topic and three subtopics.

2. Work together to create a graphic organizer.

3. Divide the class into five groups. Each group is given one of the paragraphs to write, printing their finished paragraphs on chart paper. The five paragraphs are then put on display in the correct order.

With this activity, everyone contributes to creating the final mini-essay in its proper form, but no one has had to do the complete essay themselves. I have found that these essays are usually very strong, because each group concentrates only on one paragraph and can therefore focus on using rich vocabulary as well as using the correct format.

SUGGESTED CROSS-CURRICULAR TOPICS

Students will encounter many examples of description structures in both nonfiction trade books and textbooks. Three are included in the blackline master section at the end of this chapter. Students are often required to write descriptive passages in most subject areas. Many of these topics are listed on the following page.

Social Studies

- Countries and/or provinces
- Canada's peacekeeping role
- New France
- Biography of significant people in early Canada
- The Red River Rebellion
- The North West Rebellion
- The Winnipeg General Strike
- The War of 1812
- Medieval agricultural methods
- Medieval roles (e.g., peasant, king, noble, knight, priest)
- Natural resources
- Levels of government
- Current and historical political figures and their significance
- International organizations and their purposes (e.g., North Atlantic Treaty Organization, United Nations)

Science

- Animals
- Optical devices (e.g., kaleidoscopes, periscopes, telescopes)
- Floods, tornadoes
- The cell as basic unit of life
- Any of the body systems
- Constellations
- Planets
- Canadian contributions to space explorations (e.g., Canadarm)
- Astronauts

Arts

- Study of an artist, (e.g., painter, musician, actor)
- Description of an art technique

Physical Education and Health

- Dangers of smoking and taking illicit drugs
- Description of any game or activity
- Healthy eating

Language Arts

- Character study
- Description of a genre for fiction or nonfiction

DESCRIPTION STRUCTURES IN THE CONTENT AREAS

Blackline masters 7.20 to 7.22 are some examples of description structures in both nonfiction trade books and textbooks. Figure 7.20 lists some of their characteristics.

BLM	Example	Description
7.20	Description paragraph	The second sentence indicates the paragraph's topic. Note that the clincher sentence in this example is longer than students would write.
7.21	Three-paragraph report	This three-paragraph example is from a **grade 7** textbook. Topic sentences are evident, but clincher sentences are not.
7.22	Five-paragraph mini-essay	This is an example from a children's information website. The first paragraph is both an introduction and part of the fact-giving body of the essay. The fourth paragraph uses the enumerative structure.

FIGURE 7.20

LINKING ASSESSMENT TO LEARNING

If students are writing only one description paragraph, assessment is the same as it is for the other structures. In this case, the assessment checklists that have been discussed in previous chapters (peer feedback, self-assessment checklists and the assessment rubric for Chapter 7 description structures can be used). However, if the description structure comprises more than one paragraph (in a report or five-paragraph mini-essay), then the assessment checklists should be altered. They should include a section to determine whether students understand the alignment or match-up of the organizer to the essay's paragraphs. For example, if a student's organizer has four parts, does the mini-essay have four paragraphs? I have found that, when students work with organizers, they have little difficulty putting together a mini-essay with the proper number of paragraphs. The organizers are visual reminders of how many paragraphs are needed.

Student Self-Assessment Checklist for Description Report/Mini-Essay Structures

Name: _____ Date: _____

Organization		
My graphic organizer is complete and shows clear understanding of the structure(s) I have used.	Yes	No
Report/Mini-Essay		
I have a topic sentence for each paragraph.	Yes	No
I have a clincher sentence for each paragraph (report) or a clincher paragraph (mini-essay).	Yes	No
I have the same number of sections in my organizer as paragraphs in my mini-essay.	Yes	No
Word Choice		
I used _____ different signal words appropriate for structure(s) I have used. (number)		
Ideas and Content		
My topic sentence: • tells the reader the topic of the paragraph. • catches the reader's attention.	Yes Yes	No No
My clincher sentence ties the ideas of my paragraphs together.	Yes	No
The points in my paragraphs all link to the main idea, and there are supporting details.	Yes	No

The strengths in my description report/mini-essay include:

The areas that need improvement in my description report/mini-essay include:

My goal for future writing is:

Peer Feedback Checklist for Description Report/Mini-Essay Structures

Author: _____ Peer Editor: _____ Date: _____

Organization		
The graphic organizer is complete and shows clear understanding of the structure(s) used by the author.	Yes	No
Report/Mini-Essay		
There is a topic sentence for each paragraph.	Yes	No
There are clincher sentences for each paragraph (report) or a clincher paragraph (mini-essay).	Yes	No
There are the same number of sections in the organizer as paragraphs in the mini-essay.	Yes	No
Word Choice		
_____ different signal words were used (appropriate for structure(s) used). (number)		
Ideas and Content		
The topic sentence: • tells the reader the topic of the paragraph. • catches the reader's attention.	Yes Yes	No No
The clincher sentences tie the ideas of the paragraph together.	Yes	No
The points in the paragraphs all link to the main idea, and there are supporting details.	Yes	No

The strengths in the description report/mini-essay include:

The areas that need improvement in the description report/mini-essay include:

My suggested goal for this writer is:

Assessment Rubric for Description Report/Mini-Essay Structures

Name: _____ Date: _____

	Level 1	Level 2	Level 3	Level 4
Graphic Organizer	Organizer is incomplete and/or does not fit the structure.	Organizer is fairly complete, may have minor errors.	Organizer is complete; clearly shows understanding of structure.	Organizer is complete; clearly shows understanding of structure, and is original in design.
Alignment of Organizer to Paragraphs	No understandable divisions have been used.	Number of paragraphs is not equal to the number of sections in the organizer.	Number of paragraphs is equal to the number of sections in the organizer.	A topic paragraph and clincher paragraph are included in the organizer.
Text Structure Format Used	Proper use of topic and clincher sentences rarely evident.	Proper use of topic and clincher sentences evident in some of the paragraphs; signal words used if there is another structure involved.	Use of topic and clincher sentences evident in most of the paragraphs.	Use of topic and clincher sentences and signal words evident throughout the description report/mini-essay.
Body Sentences	Few points link to the main idea; there are no supporting details.	Some points link to the main idea; there are few supporting details.	All points link to the main idea; there are some supporting details.	All points link to the main idea and have supporting details.
Understanding of Description Format	Shows little understanding of description format.	Shows some understanding of description format.	Shows a considerable understanding of description format.	Shows a thorough understanding of the description format.

To move to the next level, I must ...

Assessment Checklists

Peer feedback and self-assessment checklists give students a chance to reflect on their own work and make changes to improve their paragraphs (see BLM 8.19 to 8.20, pages 250–251). Discussing the peer and self-assessment with students should help you assess their understanding of the structure and indicate where they need to go next.

Assessment Rubrics

When students write the description paragraph, report, or mini-essay that I will assess, I have them use the rubric for self-assessment so they have the opportunity to revise what they have written before they hand it in. I mark the student work using the same rubric. It quickly shows me who understands the criteria and who can apply it to their own work.

Identifying Text Structures: Reading Like a Writer

After students have had experience reading and writing description paragraphs, it is important that they make the connection between their classroom work and what they read. BLM 8.23 can be used to track their progress in this area.

BLM 8.23

Checklist for Identifying Text Structure Criteria

Name: _____   Date: _____

	Sequence	Enumerative	Compare and Contrast	Cause and Effect	Problem and Solution	Question and Answer	Description
Is able to identify the structure when it is in its basic form in an individual paragraph.							
Is able to identify the characteristics of the structures when reading textbooks and trade books (signal words, topic sentence, clincher sentence, etc.).							

FIGURE 7.21   BLM 8.23

Blackline Masters

Name: _____ Date: _____

Description Paragraph Organizer

This organizer is for your jot notes. **Remember:** jot notes are not sentences.

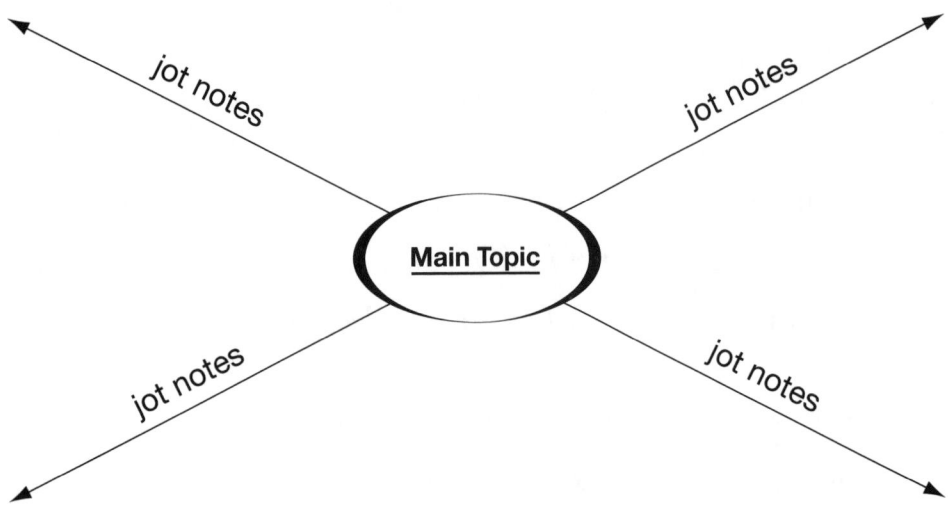

Name: _____ Date: _____

Description Report Organizer

This organizer is for your jot notes. **Remember:** jot notes are not sentences.

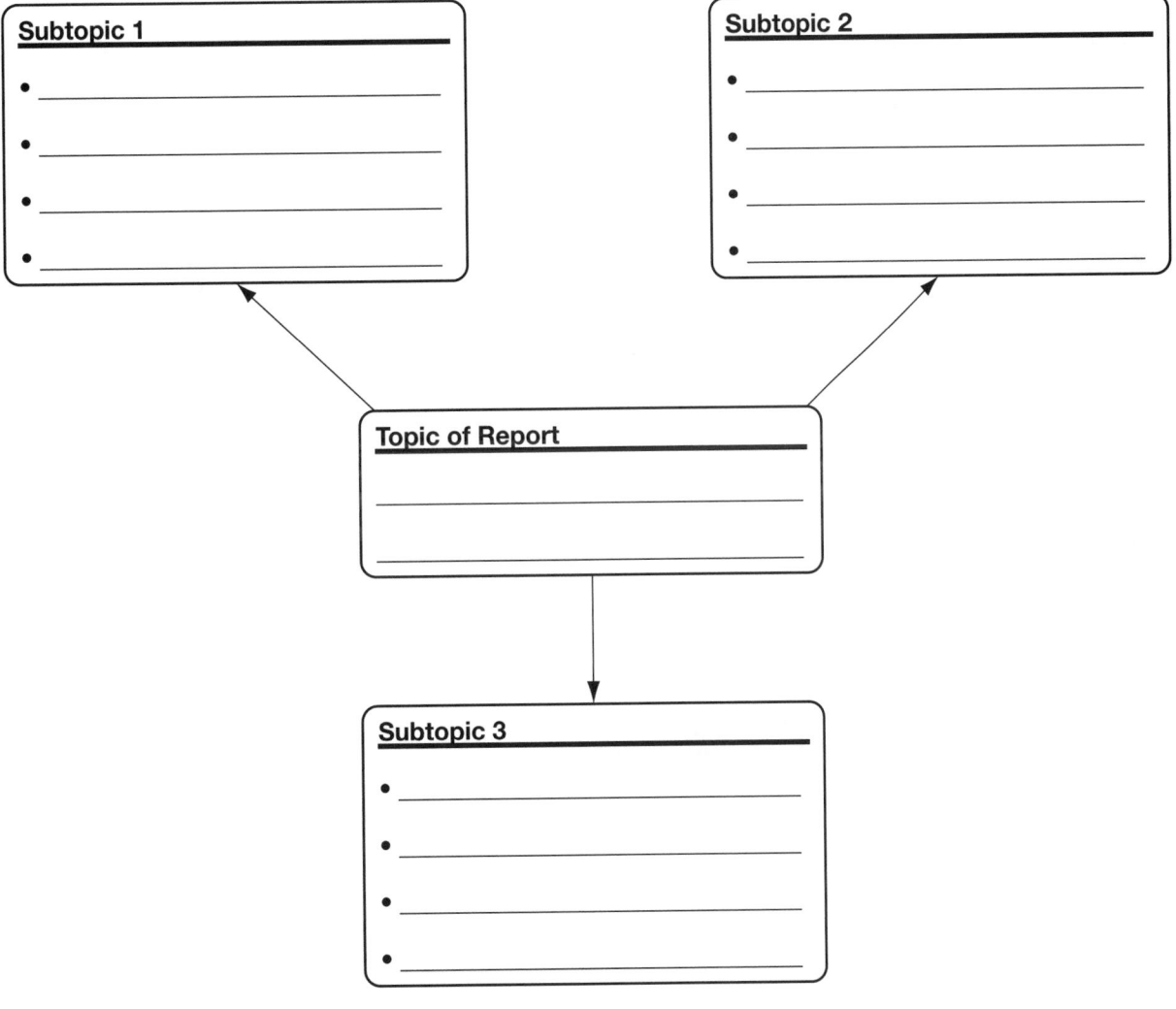

Name: _____ Date: _____

Report Outline Organizer

Paragraph 1	
Topic Sentence	
Sentence for Detail 1	
Sentence for Detail 2	
Sentence for Detail 3	
Clincher Sentence	

Paragraph 2	
Topic Sentence	
Sentence for Detail 1	
Sentence for Detail 2	
Sentence for Detail 3	
Clincher Sentence	

Paragraph 3	
Topic Sentence	
Sentence for Detail 1	
Sentence for Detail 2	
Sentence for Detail 3	
Clincher Sentence	

Name: _____ Date: _____

Mini-Essay Organizer

This organizer is for your jot notes. **Remember:** jot notes are not sentences.

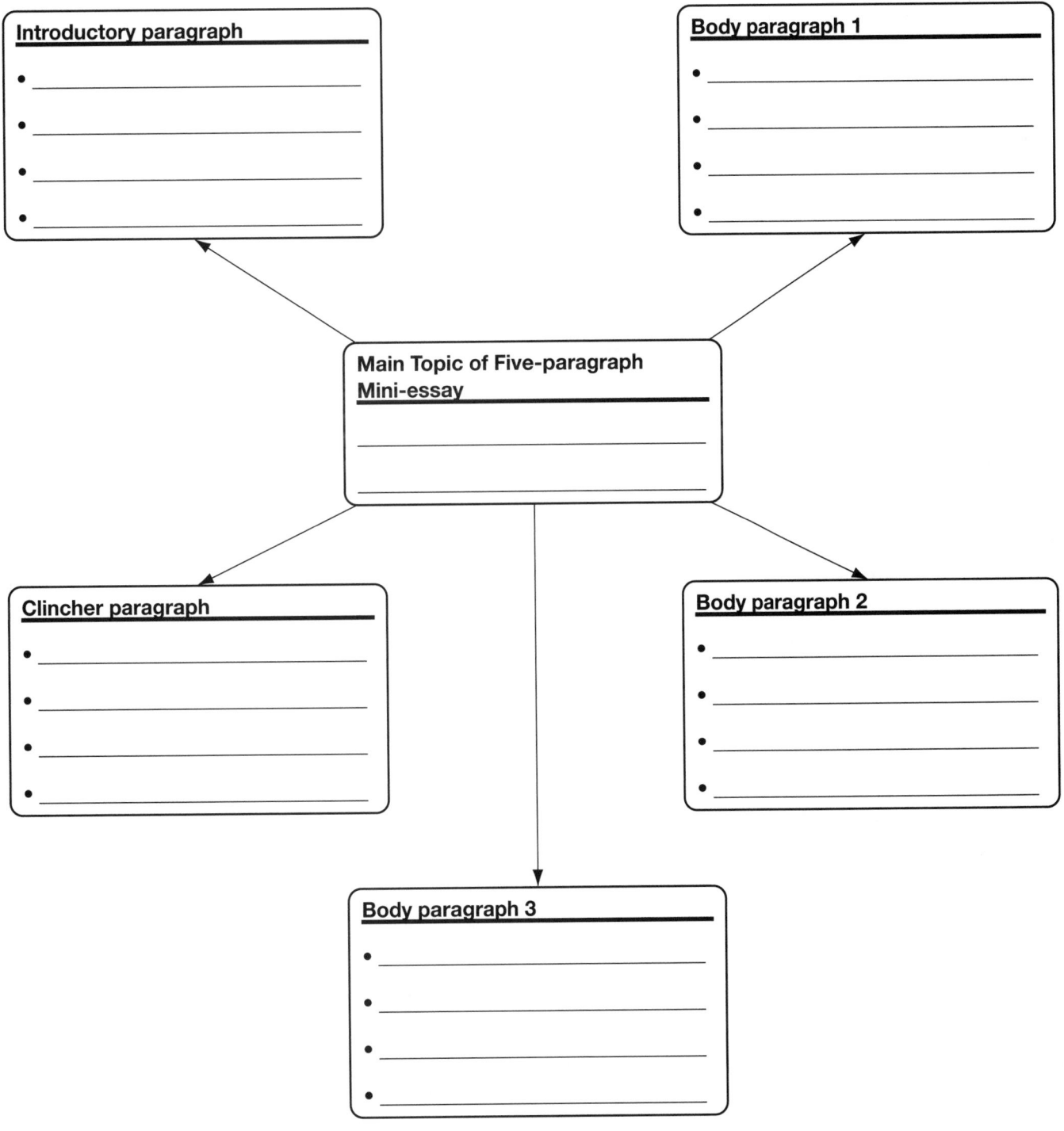

Introductory paragraph _____

- _____
- _____
- _____
- _____

Body paragraph 1 _____

- _____
- _____
- _____
- _____

Main Topic of Five-paragraph Mini-essay _____

_____
_____
_____

Clincher paragraph _____

- _____
- _____
- _____
- _____

Body paragraph 2 _____

- _____
- _____
- _____
- _____

Body paragraph 3 _____

- _____
- _____
- _____
- _____

Name: _____ Date: _____

Mini-Essay Outline Organizer

Topic Paragraph	
Topic Sentence	
Details for Paragraph 1 (usually two or three sentences telling what subtopics will be discussed)	

Body Paragraph 1	Discussion of Subtopic 1
Topic Sentence	
Sentence for Detail 1	
Sentence for Detail 2	
Sentence for Detail 3	
Clincher Sentence	

Body Paragraph 2	Discussion of Subtopic 2
Topic Sentence	
Sentence for Detail 1	
Sentence for Detail 2	
Sentence for Detail 3	
Clincher Sentence	

Name: _____ Date: _____

Body Paragraph 3	Discussion of Subtopic 3
Topic Sentence	
Sentence for Detail 1	
Sentence for Detail 2	
Sentence for Detail 3	
Clincher Sentence	

Clincher Paragraph	Sums up information given in paragraphs above (usually two to three sentences in length)

Name: _____ Date: _____

Use this graphic organizer to prepare your jot notes before writing your mini essay.

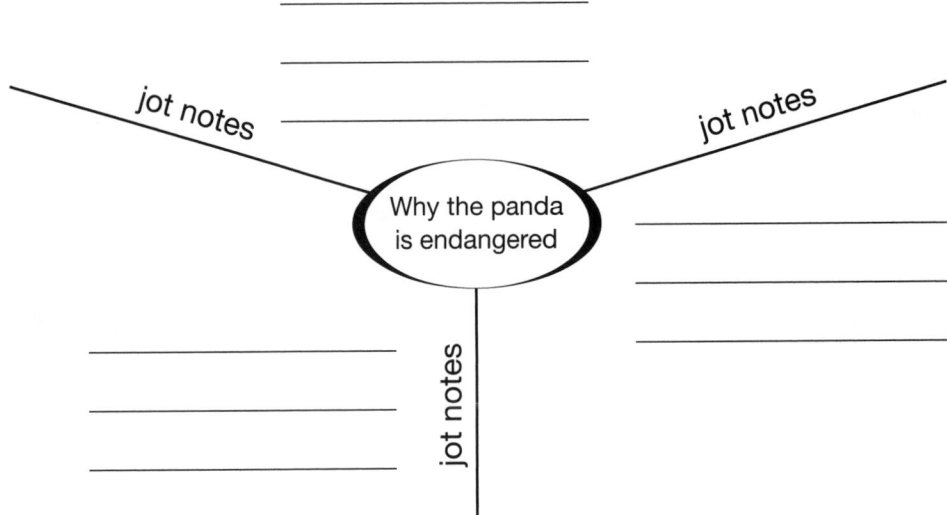

Name: _____ Date: _____

Examine this description paragraph. Think about the similarities and differences between a description paragraph and paragraphs of other text structures. Circle the descriptive words.

The Moon

The Moon is a natural satellite that orbits Earth. Scientists have discovered that its soil is made up of fine sand and gravel. It has no atmosphere—which means the sky isn't blue—and therefore no sound because it is air that carries sound waves. Temperatures on the moon are severe, with extremely hot days (130° C) and extremely cold nights (–190° C). A vast number of craters is its best-known surface feature. These are holes on the Moon's surface. The darkest parts of the Moon are lava-filled craters called *maria*. It is these surface features that create the "Man in the Moon" look. Taking about 27 days to orbit our planet, it is Earth's only moon.

Name: _____ Date: _____

Share and Discuss

The Moon

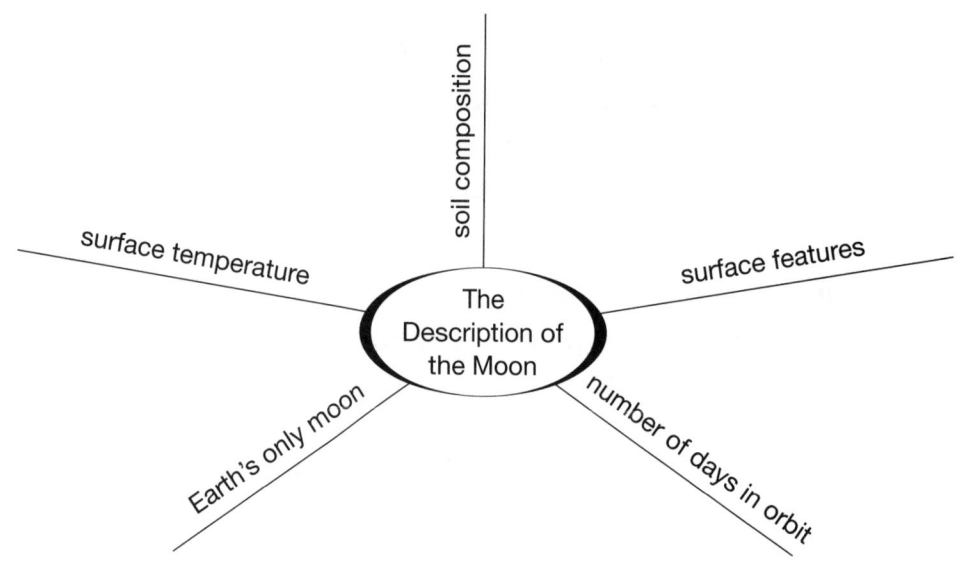

Name: _____ Date: _____

Read the paragraph below. Underline the topic and clincher sentences and circle the descriptive words.

The Polar Bear

   The polar bear is one of the largest and strongest carnivores in the world. Its massive body measures 240 to 260 centimetres in length, and it can weigh up to 800 kilograms. Glossy guard hairs on its thick winter coat and a dense under-fur protect it from the harsh Arctic winter. The guard hairs repel water. Both layers of fur, along with the layer of fat that is under the fur, keep the bear warm in the cold temperatures. Its white colour serves as an excellent camouflage in the Arctic environment. Small bumps and cavities on its soles act like suction cups and help to prevent the bear from slipping on the ice. Its short, fairly straight, and sharply pointed claws aid it in catching and eating its food. All these characteristics make the polar bear well equipped for living in the harsh Arctic climate.

Name: _____ Date: _____

Share and Discuss

The Polar Bear Graphic Organizer

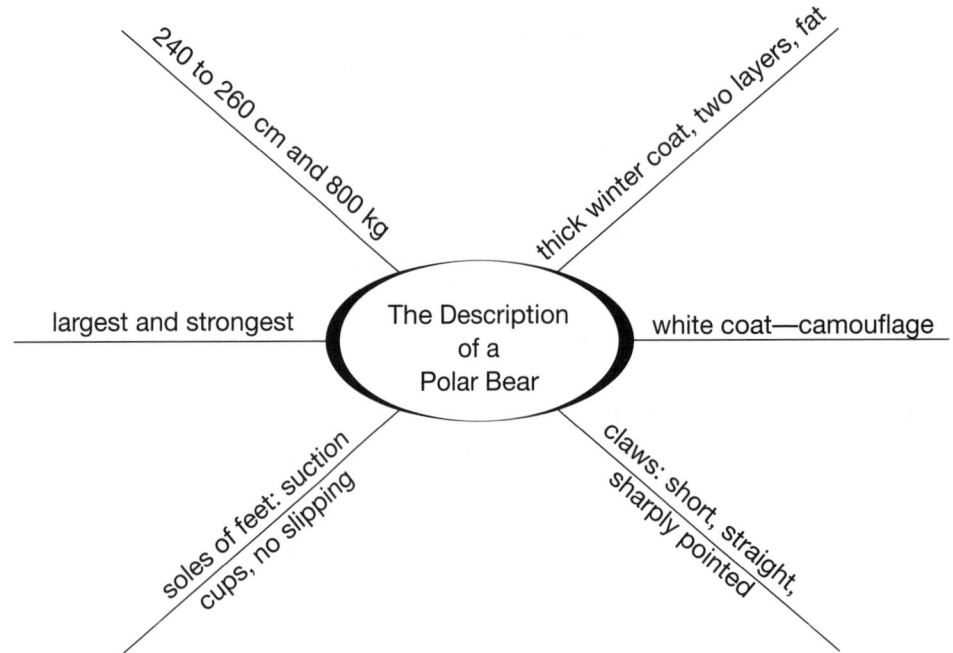

Name: _____ Date: _____

Share and Discuss

Write the topic in the centre of the organizer. Record ideas relating to your topic on the
lines radiating from the main idea.

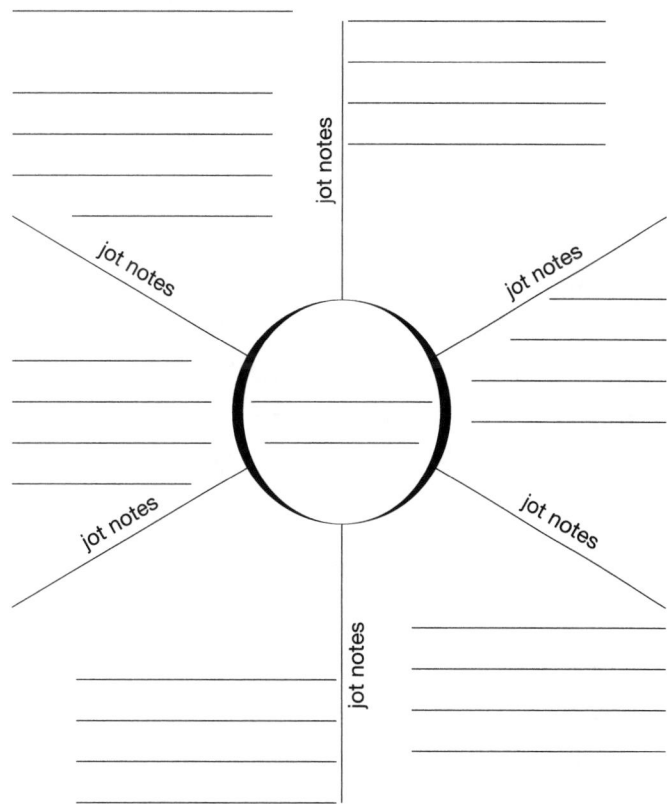

Name: _____ Date: _____

Read the following paragraph report. Underline the topic and clincher sentences, and circle the descriptive words. What text structures does this report use?

The Beaver

The beaver's watery home is unique for a member of the rodent family. Found in rivers, streams, dammed-up swamps, and freshwater lakes near woodlands, the beaver lodge is made of sticks and twigs that are packed together with mud and stones. Its entrance is under the water. As the weather becomes cold, the outside of the lodge is plastered with mud. Bank beavers burrow dens beside streams and lakes. No wonder these animals are considered "creative architects."

With two layers of fur to keep them warm and dry, the beaver is well adapted to a life in and near water. Its flat tail, which resembles a paddle, acts like a rudder as it swims. On land, the tail helps prop the beaver up when sitting or standing upright. Besides the tail, the beaver's most unusual feature is its two huge front teeth. With them, it can gnaw down trees as large as 30 centimetres in diameter. All these characteristics make its appearance unique in the animal world.

Like most rodents, a beaver is a herbivore or plant eater. It eats the bark, twigs, branches, and leaves of trees. Aspen, poplar, birch, and willows are their favourite foods. But they also eat water plants, especially the roots and tender sprouts of water lilies. A beaver works constantly to find and store its food. That is why "as busy as a beaver" best describes this fascinating mammal.

Name: _____ Date: _____

Share and Discuss

Compare this graphic organizer with the report on "The Beaver." What is the relationship between the subtopics in the organizer and the paragraphs in the report?

The Beaver Graphic Organizer

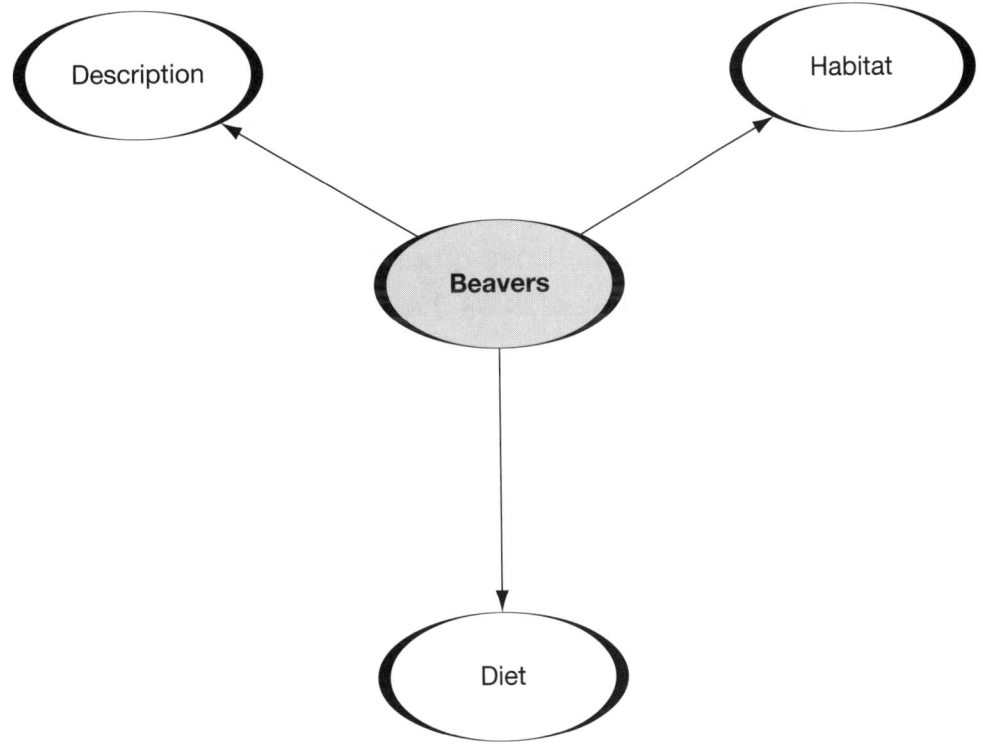

Name: _____ Date: _____

Read each paragraph. Underline the topic and clincher sentences, and circle the signal words. Identify the text structure (or structures) used in this mini-essay.

Types of Rocks

Rocks are classified into three different groups according to the way in which they were formed. They are igneous, sedimentary, and metamorphic rocks. These rocks are all related to each other through the rock cycle.

The first group is the igneous rocks, often called "fire rocks." These rocks are usually very hard. They can be formed above or below ground. Below Earth's surface, igneous rocks are formed when magma enters an underground chamber, cools very slowly, and turns into rocks full of large crystals. Above ground they are formed by the cooling of melted material such as the lava from a volcano. Some of these "fire-formed" rocks are granite, feldspar, and mica.

The next group of rocks is called sedimentary rocks. For millions of years, pieces of earth have been broken down and worn away by wind and water. These small pieces settle at the bottom of rivers, lakes, and oceans along with dead plants and tiny animal skeletons. Many layers form on top of the previous ones, pressing down and creating pressure on the lower layers. As they are compressed and hardened, these layers become rock. This action requires a very long period of time. Sedimentary rocks are soft and easily broken. Sandstone, shale, and limestone are some common types.

The last group into which rocks are classified is the metamorphic group. These rocks are "changed rocks." They once belonged to one of the other two groups but were under tremendous pressure. These forces built up heat that caused the rocks to change their composition. Metamorphic rocks are usually shiny and smooth. Slate, quartzite, and marble are examples of "changed" rocks.

All of these groups of rocks have played an important role in the development of Earth's crust. Over time, each type of rock changes to another as part of the never-ending rock cycle.

Name: _____ Date: _____

Share and Discuss

Types of Rocks

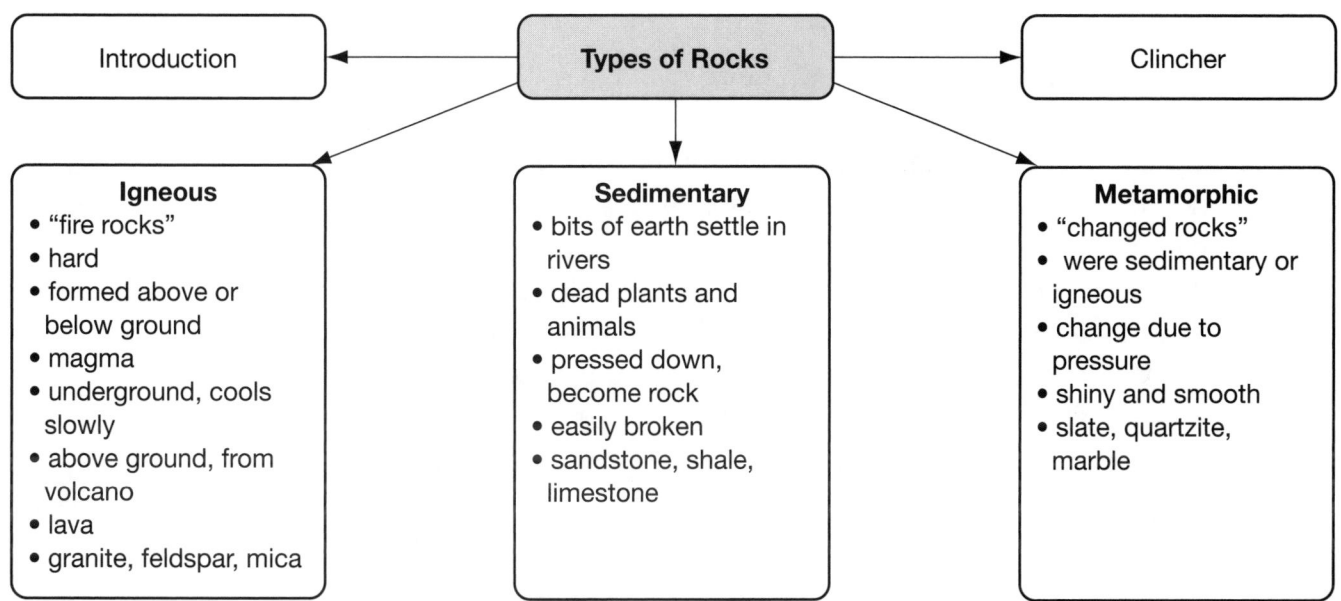

Introduction	Types of Rocks	Clincher

Igneous
- "fire rocks"
- hard
- formed above or below ground
- magma
- underground, cools slowly
- above ground, from volcano
- lava
- granite, feldspar, mica

Sedimentary
- bits of earth settle in rivers
- dead plants and animals
- pressed down, become rock
- easily broken
- sandstone, shale, limestone

Metamorphic
- "changed rocks"
- were sedimentary or igneous
- change due to pressure
- shiny and smooth
- slate, quartzite, marble

Name: _____ Date: _____

Read each paragraph. Underline the topic sentences, double-underline the clincher sentences, and circle the signal words for each structure. Identify the text structure (or structures) used in this mini-essay.

Hurricanes

Hurricanes are large, powerful storms that begin over the ocean. They leave destruction and death in their wake. Many people are studying methods to decrease the problems hurricanes cause.

A hurricane forms over warm ocean water. Air that has been warmed by the ocean begins to rise in an upward spiral and this causes areas of low pressure underneath it. Then, cooler air from a high-pressure area rushes in to fill the space left by the warm air. Soon after, this cooler air warms and also begins to rise and spin. This cycle continues until gradually it builds up to form a hurricane.

The effects of hurricanes are among the most extreme examples of natural disasters. High winds, heavy rains, storm surges, and sliding mud all cause extensive damage. Heavy rain and storm surges often result in a great deal of flooding. The winds of a hurricane can tear up trees, wreck houses, crush vehicles, and snap power lines. People are forced to evacuate their homes and find temporary shelter. Mudslides often result in washed out roads, railroads, and bridges so it is difficult for help to arrive. Hurricanes cause incredible amounts of damage.

Hurricanes cannot be prevented, but many things are being attempted to decrease the problems they cause such as severe damage to property and loss of life. One solution is to continue to improve the weather tracking systems. Radar and satellites in space are used to track and understand hurricanes better and to enable meteorologists to forecast them more accurately. Also, computers are being used to help create better warning systems. If people get enough warning, they can leave the risk areas in time and without panic, thereby saving lives. Another solution being used in Jamaica and Australia is to have stricter building codes so buildings can withstand much stronger winds. It is hoped that all attempts to decrease the devastating damage and loss of life caused by hurricanes will be successful.

Hurricanes are among the most dangerous storms in the world. They cause major damage and death whenever they occur. People will continue to look for ways to prevent these storms from creating the havoc that they do now.

Name: _____ Date: _____

This simple organizer shows jot notes of what will be covered in each paragraph.

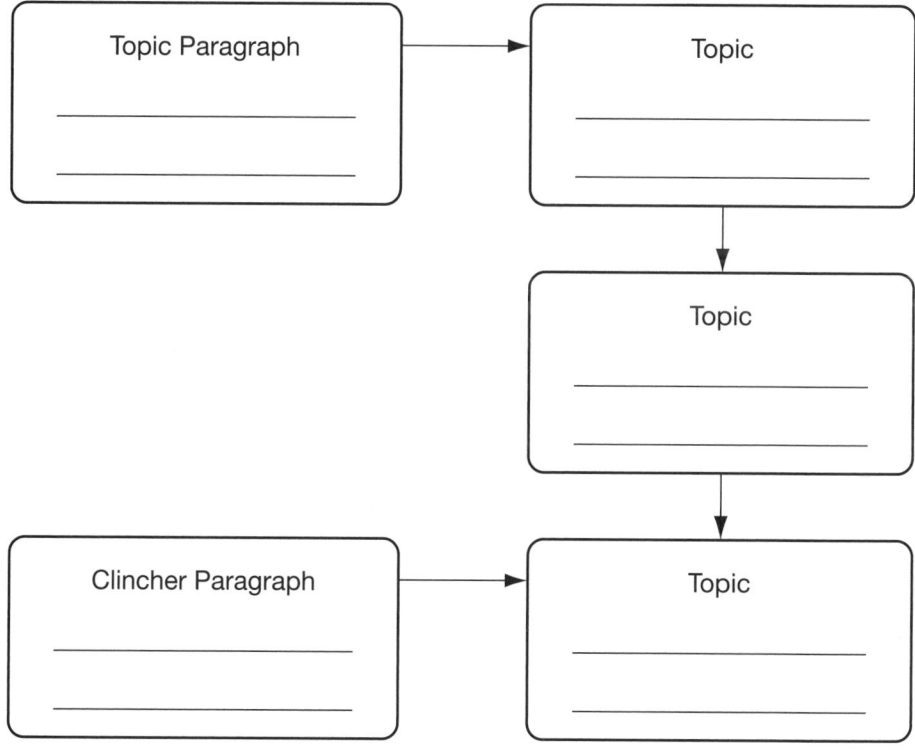

Name: _____ Date: _____

This organizer shows the different text structures that will be used in each paragraph.

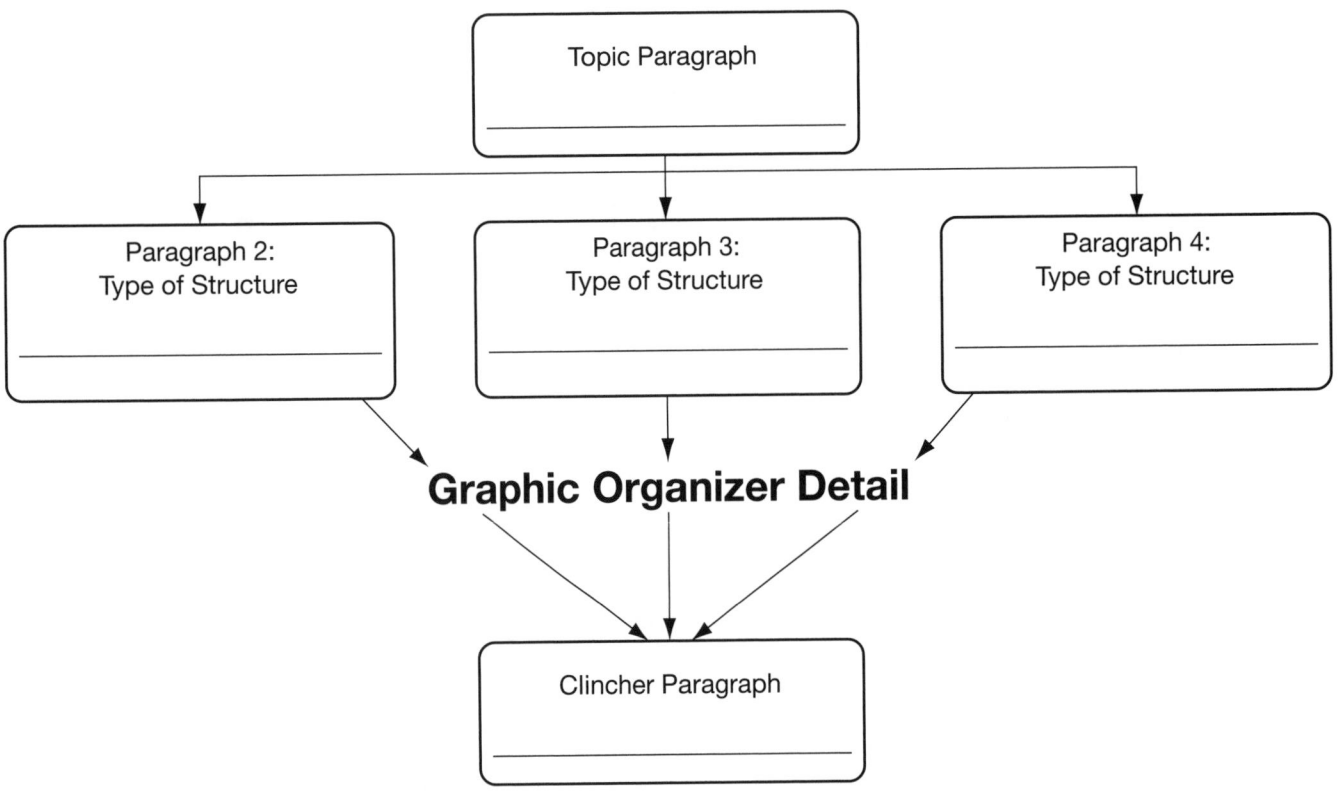

Name: _____ Date: _____

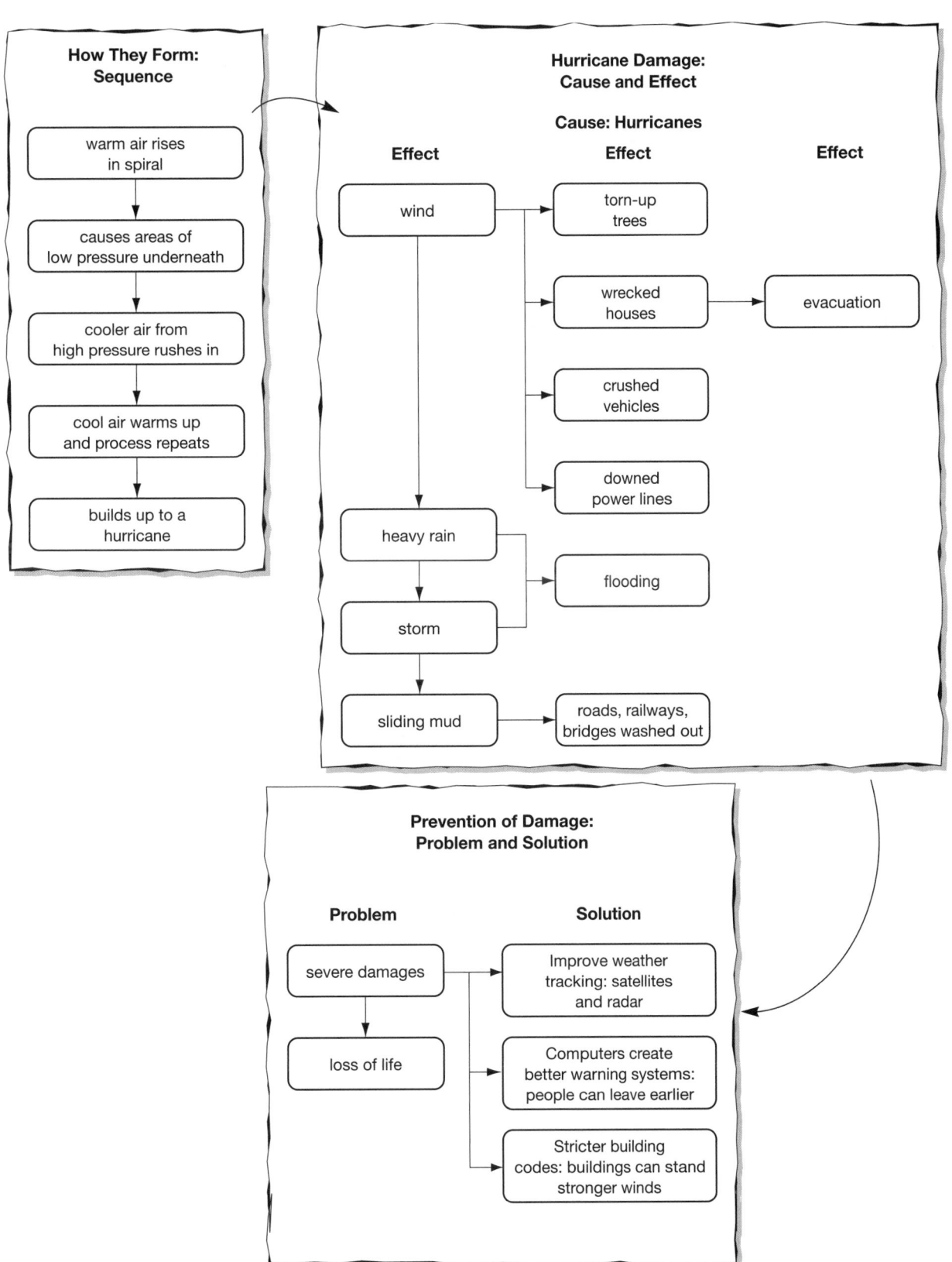

How They Form: Sequence

- warm air rises in spiral
- causes areas of low pressure underneath
- cooler air from high pressure rushes in
- cool air warms up and process repeats
- builds up to a hurricane

Hurricane Damage: Cause and Effect

Cause: Hurricanes

Effect	Effect	Effect
wind	torn-up trees	
	wrecked houses	evacuation
	crushed vehicles	
	downed power lines	
heavy rain	flooding	
storm		
sliding mud	roads, railways, bridges washed out	

Prevention of Damage: Problem and Solution

Problem	Solution
severe damages	Improve weather tracking: satellites and radar
loss of life	Computers create better warning systems: people can leave earlier
	Stricter building codes: buildings can stand stronger winds

Name: _____ Date: _____

A Creeping Tide of Oil

Canada's West Coast is a wild, rugged, and entirely beautiful place, but a silently creeping tide of oil can prove quite easily how fragile a coastline really is. On December 22, 1988, a tug boat collided with the barge it was towing through heavy seas off the coast of Washington State. Soon, 120 km of coastline, stretching as far north as Cape Scott on Vancouver Island, were fouled with 875 000 L of oil and littered with dead wildlife. The pristine beaches of Pacific Rim National Park were black with thick deposits of tar. The corpses of wildlife poisoned or drowned by the spill contaminated the food chain, threatening other creatures who would unknowingly ingest the oil with the small fish and animals they ate.

G. Sorestad, C. McClymont, and C. Graves, *In Context, Anthology Three,* (Toronto: Nelson Canada), 1990, 54.

Name: _____ Date: _____

Louis-Joseph Papineau (1786–1871)

Louis-Joseph Papineau was a wealthy seigneur in Lower Canada. He served as an officer in the militia, defending British North America from the Americans during the War of 1812.

He was elected to the Legislative Assembly of Lower Canada in 1809. He served as the Speaker of the Assembly almost continuously from 1815 to 1837. Papineau was a strong supporter of the Roman Catholic Church and many of the traditional Canadian ways. However, he also advocated changes to government.

As Speaker, Papineau became the leader of the Parti Canadien, which, after 1826, was called the Parti Patriote. In the 1830s, Papineau promoted an American-style, democratic system of government. Papineau and the Parti Patriote wanted political reform that would benefit the French in Lower Canada, since they were the vast majority of the population.

P. Clark, P. Arnold, R. McKay, and L. Soetaert, Canada Revisited (7th ed.) (Edmonton: Arnold Publishing), 1999, 192.

Name: _____ Date: _____

Dinosaurs

Dinosaurs lived 225 million to 66 million years ago. Today there are no dinosaurs. We know dinosaurs existed because scientists have found dinosaur bones and footprints. These bones and footprints are called fossils. Fossils have been found on every continent in the world. These fossils tell us that some dinosaurs were as small as chickens. Others weighed more than 72 tonnes, which is the same as 40 elephants.

The word "dinosaur" comes from two Greek words that mean terrible lizard. Dinosaurs are divided into two groups: carnivores (meat eaters) and herbivores (plant eaters). The best-known carnivorous dinosaur is the Tyrannosaurus rex. This dinosaur could be 12 metres long and weigh up to 8 tonnes. That is more than four elephants weigh all together! The most well-known small carnivorous dinosaur is the Velociraptor. This dinosaur was only about 2 metres long. This is the height of the average person.

The Brontosaurus is the probably the best-known plant-eating dinosaur. This dinosaur is now called Apatosaurus. It is one of the largest animals to ever walk Earth. The Apatosaurus could grow to be 20 metres long and weigh up to 27 tonnes. It walked on all four legs. It had a small head, but a long neck to reach leaves in the tops of trees.

Scientists do not know for sure what killed the dinosaurs. Some think they died of disease. Others believe they could not survive the change in the weather. The most widely accepted theory is that a huge comet or meteoroid struck Earth 65 million years ago. Such an event would have blocked out sunlight for a long period of time. This would have killed plants and resulted in the death of all living things, including the dinosaurs.

These "terrible lizards" may have disappeared, but they continue to fascinate us. Think of all the movies and books devoted to them. Each year, new dinosaur fossils are found, answering more questions about their puzzling history.

Adapted from "Dinosaurs," Kids InfoBits, Thomson Gale, 2005.

MONITORING AND ASSESSING STUDENT WORK

8

Assessment is the beginning, middle, and end of classroom instruction. Its *analytical* function informs the teacher of a student's prior knowledge, skills, and subject understanding (*diagnostic assessment*). This is "the starting point of each student's learning journey" (Cooper, 2007, 23). As well, assessment is ongoing and cumulative, providing descriptive feedback to the student and assessment data to the teacher (*formative assessment*). It includes evaluations of a student's completed assignments compared to a standard (*summative assessment*). This evaluation ends in a final judgment, often in the form of a mark for a task, term, or the school year. Today educators distinguish between "coaching" students, described as Assessment **for** Learning, and "judging" them, or Assessment **of** Learning. (See Figure 8.1 for a summary of the types of assessment for and of learning.) Assessment is viewed as a partnership where teachers and students work together to help set expectations. This was not always the case.

Classroom assessment was once solely the prerogative of the classroom teacher. It was more summative than formative ("of" rather than "for"). Students received marks based on teacher-made or commercially produced standards. Often students would not have a clear sense of the criteria before they did an assignment. Getting a good mark was like trying to hit a moving target blindfolded. Now classroom assessment has become a powerful tool for teachers *and* students. Many teachers share assessment criteria with their students before the students do assignments, sometimes also involving them in creating the criteria. Teachers are still responsible, of course, for the final evaluation of their students. However, through ongoing classroom assessments, along with assessments made by students and peer editors, teachers can provide ample opportunities for students to understand the various levels of performance before the final evaluation takes place.

> "... Assessment plays an essential role in helping students learn and improve their work. Evaluation informs students about the quality of a given task or piece of work, relative to a known standard." (Cooper, 2007, 12)

Assessment	What	When	Purpose
Assessment for Learning			
Diagnostic Assessment	• Determines appropriate starting points for instruction • Analyzes student strengths and weaknesses • Indicates areas of concern: what knowledge and skills students bring to a topic • Students can use self-assessments and peer feedback to help them understand what they know and what skills they still need to learn for any given task	• Beginning of the school year • Start of new units of study	• To help you plan instruction • To help you decide who will need enrichment, intervention, and extra support. • To encourage students to examine a task's criteria and determine whether they have met it • To determine whole-group, small-group, and individual instructional needs
Formative Assessment	• Gathers data during the learning process and provides descriptive feedback to both students and teachers to help improve learning • Indicates which students are able to transfer their learning to other areas of study • Assesses using observation, conferences, samples of student work, teacher created assessments, and student self-assessment ***This is the assessment focus throughout this book.***	• At planned points throughout the school year • When working individually, in pairs, or in groups • When reading or writing	• To help students be aware of gaps in their knowledge • To improve student performance on summative tasks • To encourage student goal setting • To reflect on effectiveness of instruction • To help you to further plan instruction
Assessment of Learning			
Summative Assessment	• Collects marks to indicate student progress and growth over time • Indicates the measure of success in teaching a task, skill, or unit of study	• Throughout the school year • For specific tasks and assignments	• To collate marks for report card assessment • To determine if a student needs individualized help and/or instruction • To communicate achievement to stakeholders (parents, administrators, teachers)

FIGURE 8.1

SELF-ASSESSMENT AND PEER FEEDBACK

Student self-assessment can help you get an accurate picture of whether students really understand the criteria that will be assessed. It provides you with information on whether they understand the basic concepts and whether they are able to edit or revise their work to reflect this understanding. I have found that students who are able to reflect on their own learning and assess their skills take a much greater interest in learning. They provide valuable information about the efficacy of your teaching and what changes in instruction might be necessary to improve it. Self-assessment and peer feedback allow students an opportunity to sort through their misunderstandings, and make changes before a final assessment is done.

Peer feedback is another excellent way for you to monitor your students' grasp of important concepts and learning criteria. When students assess someone else's work, they become more adept at assessing their own work as it gives them an opportunity to become more familiar with the criteria. It also provides students with the opportunity to observe and examine successful demonstrations of target knowledge and skills. The discussion that occurs between two students as they assess each other's writing is an invaluable part of the assessment process. However, it's important to note that students do not have a thorough enough understanding of the criteria on an assessment rubric to critically evaluate their peers' work.

> "Understanding what students know and are able to do enables teachers to plan for future learning, group students effectively, and provide specific, effective, and timely intervention." (Trehearne, et. al., 2006, 447).

> Self-assessment and peer feedback are essential to the foundation of meaningful personal growth setting.

ASSESSMENT CHECKLISTS AND RUBRICS

Performing an examination of a piece of work using a checklist is a way in which to track what the piece is or is not, whereas using a rubric results in qualitative judgements. Together, these tools are key to providing descriptive feedback during teacher/student conferencing.

Eliciting Student Criteria

One way to increase student motivation is to have students take part in developing class rubrics and assessment checklists. This encourages them to take responsibility for their learning and gives them a more thorough understanding of what they need to know and what is expected of them.

The criteria that **grades 4 to 8** students are first likely to suggest will be language conventions: having neat writing, using capitals and periods correctly, and making no spelling mistakes. Although conventions are important, it is equally important that we encourage students to look at traits of writing such as organization, ideas and content, and word choice. When students suggest only language conventions, encourage them to "dig deeper" by asking them leading questions. These questions will help them think of more specific criteria (e.g., whether the ideas in a structure are given in detail and fit with the main idea, whether or not the work has an organization to it, etc.). Introduce criteria one or two at a time after students have studied a few text structure paragraphs.

> Traits "are the characteristics or qualities that define good writing" (Trehearne, 2006, 230). These include
> - ideas presented
> - word choice
> - voice (the personality of the writer)
> - language conventions (grammar, spelling, etc.)
> - sentence fluency (using sentences that make sense and vary in length and structure)

Assessment Checklists

Let's look at how a teacher can guide students to develop the criteria for self-assessment or peer feedback checklists such as the ones used in this book.

> The strengths in my (the) enumerative paragraph include:
> or
>
> The areas that need improvement in my (the) enumerative paragraph include:
>
> (Self-assessment) My goal for future writing is:
> or
>
> (Peer assessment) My suggested goal for this writer is:

FIGURE 8.2

> **Checklists can be generated from the provincial standard column of a rubric.**

1. First ask students to suggest some organizational criteria for one of the text structures. (Since I usually do the sequence structure first, I'll use that as an example.) Students will usually suggest that they need a topic sentence, clincher sentence, and signal words. However, encourage them to be more specific by asking a leading question, such as, "What is important about the topic sentence?" For example, the criterion that you write on the board might be "My topic sentence should tell what the paragraph will be about."

2. Ask, "How many different signal words do you think we should use?" Since three or more is a great start, the second criterion might be "I need to have at least three different signal words in my paragraph."

3. To confirm the importance of the clincher sentence, ask, "Why is a clincher sentence important?" The answer would lead to the third criterion "My clincher sentence should sum up the ideas of my paragraph."

> **Sequence Criteria**
> 1. The topic sentence tells the subject of the paragraph.
> 2. I need to have three signal words.
> 3. The clincher sentence sums up the paragraph.
> 4. The paragraph tells the order of something.

4. Now ask students to think about their ideas. For a sequence paragraph, ask, "What is important in a sequence paragraph?" Students usually come up with the idea that "the instructions or ideas are in an order." Then the criterion might be "My paragraph tells the order of something that will happen."

5. When students are making up their first self-assessment checklist, I try to keep the number of criteria down to four or five. Once they are familiar with those, others can be added. However, do not overwhelm students by trying to assess *all* the criteria in one piece of writing.

6. The final step is to create a self-assessment checklist using the criteria developed by the students. They can then use the sheet to assess the paragraphs they write (working in pairs or individually). If you have used pre-made generic assessment tools to this point, you may notice

> **See pages 232–255 for examples of a pre-made assessment checklists/rubrics.**

Text Structures: Teaching Patterns in Reading and Writing

that students understand the criteria they develop themselves better than they do the criteria on the generic checklists. The student-developed criteria makes more sense to them because students understand where the criteria come from.

Assessment Rubrics

Students should also be involved in deciding on criteria for the assessment rubric. This takes a bit more time, but the peer feedback and self-assessment checklists you developed provide a good starting point.

In developing the criteria for the rubric, I find it easier if the class starts with the provincial standard. Ask students to look at the first criterion on their checklist (e.g., "My topic sentence should tell what the paragraph will be about."). Challenge them to think about what that topic sentence should be for each level of the rubric. For example, ask students what they think a provincial standard topic sentence would look like. (*This is the level we want all our students to reach.*) They might suggest "The topic sentence explains clearly what the paragraph is about." The word choice for the rubric will differ according to the grade of the students. For example, a **grade 8** class designing a rubric will possibly use much more sophisticated vocabulary than a **grade 4** class. Depending on the ability of the class, I either work with students to complete the other levels of the rubric or give them the criteria. I don't tend to spend a lot of time focusing on levels below the standard. I spend more time on what is needed to achieve the standard and beyond.

Once students have a criterion descriptor for each level for topic sentences, they can repeat the steps for the other criteria on their checklists. By helping you create their rubrics, students will have more ownership of them, hopefully realizing that teachers do not just pick criteria out of the air—that assessment criteria are based on the skills required to complete the task.

> Rubrics can be used for assessment for learning as long as students have had a great deal of practical experience reading and writing the structure. It is also important to note that students should always have access to assessment rubrics (whether they develop them or not).

IDENTIFYING TEXT STRUCTURES: READING LIKE A WRITER

After students have learned to write the various structures and have spent some time identifying instructional models in their basic form, it is important to check that students (in small groups and individually) can identify the structures they have seen before. Here is an activity I have found that gives you accurate and quick descriptive feedback as to whether or not the students are able to recognize each text structure:

1. Give students a paragraph for each structure they have studied. Any of the additional paragraphs in the blackline master section of each chapter could be used for this purpose. Identify the paragraphs with numbers, letters, etc.

2. Have them name the structures and give the reasons for their responses, using a chart similar to the one in Figure 8.3.

3. Encourage students to look at the signal words and topic sentences for proof to help them identify each structure.

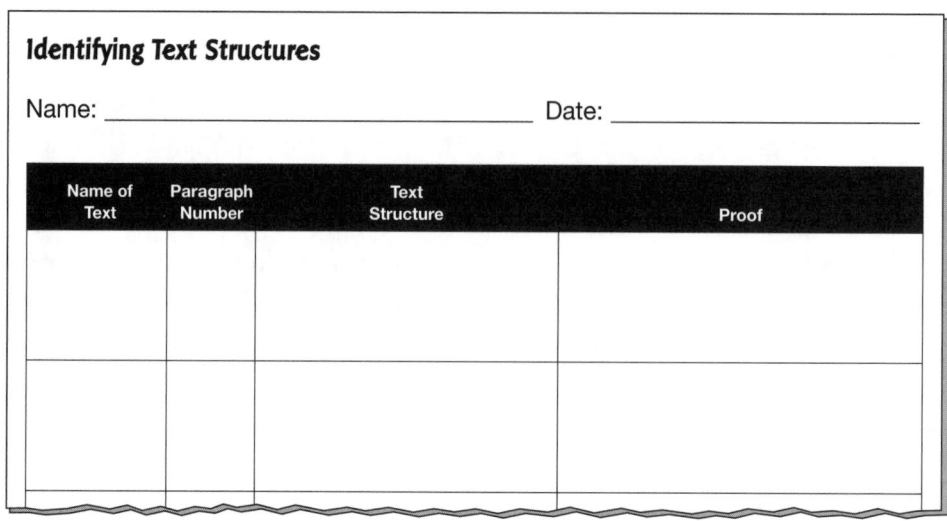

Identifying Text Structures

Name: _____ Date: _____

Name of Text	Paragraph Number	Text Structure	Proof

FIGURE 8.3   BLM 8.24

Any of the paragraphs in the blackline master section of each chapter could be used for this purpose.

Another important area to check for student understanding is the identification of text structures in textbooks and trade books.

Class Checklist for Identifying Text Structures in Reading Material

Names of Students	Sequence	Enumerative	Compare and Contrast	Cause and Effect	Problem and Solution	Question and Answer	Description

FIGURE 8.4   BLM 8.22

Checklist for Identifying Text Structure Criteria

Name: _____ Date: _____

	Sequence	Enumerative	Compare and Contrast	Cause and Effect	Problem and Solution	Question and Answer	Description
Is able to identify the structure when it is in its basic form in an individual paragraph.							
Is able to identify the characteristics of the structures when reading textbooks and trade books (signal words, topic sentence, clincher sentence, etc.).							
Is able to identify the structure when reading textbooks or trade books even though it is not in its basic form (bullets used instead of signal words, no clincher sentence, etc.).							

Comments

FIGURE 8.5   BLM 8.23

Figure 8.4, BLM 8.22, Class Checklist for Identifying Text Structures in Reading Material, and Figure 8.5, BLM 8.23, Checklist for Identifying Text Structure Criteria, enable you to track students' ability to identify a text structure in the material they are reading. Put a check mark in each box once it is evident that the student can identify that structure.

Assessment Blackline Masters

Student Self-Assessment Checklist for Sequence Structures

Name: _____ Date: _____

Organization		
My graphic organizer fits with my sequence paragraph.	Yes	No
I have a topic sentence.	Yes	No
I have a clincher sentence.	Yes	No
Word Choice		
I used sequence signal words.	Yes	No
I used _____ different sequence signal words. (number)		
Ideas and Content		
My topic sentence: • tells the reader that the topic will be discussed in a specific order. • catches the reader's attention.	Yes Yes	No No
My clincher sentence ties the ideas of my paragraph together.	Yes	No
The supporting sentences in my paragraph describe the steps involved in the sequence.	Yes	No

The strengths in my sequence paragraph include:

The areas that need improvement in my sequence paragraph include:

My goal for future writing is:

Peer Feedback Checklist for Sequence Structures

Author: _____ Peer Editor: _____ Date: _____

Organization		
The graphic organizer fits with the sequence paragraph.	Yes	No
There is a topic sentence.	Yes	No
There is a clincher sentence.	Yes	No
Word Choice		
Sequence signal words were used.	Yes	No
_____ different sequence signal words were used. (number)		
Ideas and Content		
The topic sentence: • tells the reader that the topic will be discussed in a specific order. • catches the reader's attention.	Yes Yes	No No
The clincher sentence ties the ideas of the paragraph together.	Yes	No
The supporting sentences in the paragraph describe the steps involved in the sequence.	Yes	No

The strengths in the sequence paragraph include:

The areas that need improvement in the sequence paragraph include:

My suggested goal for the writer is:

Assessment Rubric for Sequence Structures

Name: _____ Date: _____

	Level 1	Level 2	Level 3	Level 4
Graphic Organizer	Organizer is incomplete and/or does not fit the sequence structure.	Organizer is fairly complete, may have minor errors; indicates a sequence structure is being used.	Organizer is complete; clearly indicates a sequence structure is being used.	Organizer is complete; clearly indicates a sequence structure is being used and is of original design.
Topic Sentence	Weak topic sentence; doesn't indicate that a sequence will be given.	Topic sentence evident, a basic format is used; some indication that a sequence will be given.	Topic sentence indicates that a sequence will be given; captures the reader's attention.	Topic sentence clearly states that a sequence will be given; captures the imagination of the reader.
Signal Words	Sequence signal words are used improperly.	Some sequence signal words used; not always used correctly.	Effective use of sequence signal words.	Effective use of advanced sequence signal words.
Clincher	Weak clincher sentence; no connecting of ideas.	Clincher sentence evident, basic format.	Good clincher sentence, sums up ideas in paragraph.	Strong clincher sentence, ties ideas together well.
Body Sentences	Few points link to the main idea; no supporting details describe the sequence.	Some points link to the main idea; a few supporting details describe the sequence.	All points link to the main idea; supporting details describe the sequence.	All points link to the main idea and have supporting details that clearly describe the sequence.
Understanding of Structure	Shows little understanding of the sequence structure.	Shows some understanding of the sequence structure.	Shows a considerable understanding of the sequence structure.	Shows a thorough understanding of the sequence structure.

To move to the next level, I must …

Student Self-Assessment Checklist for Enumerative Structures

Name: _____   Date: _____

Organization		
My graphic organizer fits with my enumerative paragraph.	Yes	No
I have a topic sentence.	Yes	No
I have a clincher sentence.	Yes	No
Word Choice		
I used enumerative signal words.	Yes	No
I used _____ different enumerative signal words. (number)		
Ideas and Content		
My topic sentence: • tells the reader that the list of some characteristics or attributes of the topic will be given. • catches the reader's attention.	Yes Yes	No No
My clincher sentence ties the ideas of my paragraph together.	Yes	No
The supporting sentences in my paragraph provide details for each item in the list.	Yes	No

The strengths in my enumerative paragraph include:

The areas that need improvement in my enumerative paragraph include:

My goal for future writing is:

Peer Feedback Checklist for Enumerative Structures

Author: _____ Peer Editor: _____ Date: _____

Organization		
The graphic organizer fits with the enumerative paragraph.	Yes	No
There is a topic sentence.	Yes	No
There is a clincher sentence.	Yes	No
Word Choice		
Enumerative signal words were used.	Yes	No
_____ different enumerative signal words were used. (number)		
Ideas and Content		
The topic sentence: • tells the reader that a list will be given about a topic. • catches the reader's attention.	Yes Yes	No No
The clincher sentence ties the ideas of the paragraph together.	Yes	No
The supporting sentences in the paragraph provide details about each item in the list.	Yes	No

The strengths in the enumerative paragraph include:

The areas that need improvement in the enumerative paragraph include:

My suggested goal for this writer is:

Assessment Rubric for Enumerative Structures

Name: _____ Date: _____

	Level 1	Level 2	Level 3	Level 4
Graphic Organizer	Organizer is incomplete and/or does not fit enumerative structure.	Organizer is fairly complete, may have minor errors; indicates an enumerative structure is being used.	Organizer is complete; clearly indicates an enumerative structure is being used.	Organizer is complete; clearly indicates an enumerative structure is being used and is of original design.
Topic Sentence	Weak topic sentence, doesn't indicate that a list will be given.	Topic sentence evident, a basic format is used; some indication that a list will be given.	Topic sentence indicates that a list will be given; captures the reader's attention.	Topic sentence clearly states that a list will be given; captures the imagination of the reader.
Signal Words	Enumerative signal words are used improperly.	Some enumerative signal words used, not always used correctly.	Effective use of enumerative signal words.	Effective use of advanced enumerative signal words.
Clincher	Weak clincher sentence; no connecting of ideas.	Clincher sentence evident, basic format.	Good clincher sentence, sums up ideas in paragraph.	Strong clincher sentence, ties ideas together well.
Body Sentences	Few points link to the main idea; no supporting details that describe the items in the list.	Some points link to the main idea; a few supporting details describe the items in the list.	All points link to the main idea; supporting details describe the items in the list.	All points link to the main idea; supporting details clearly describe the items in the list.
Understanding of Structure	Shows little understanding of the enumerative structure.	Shows some understanding of the enumerative structure.	Shows a considerable understanding of the enumerative structure.	Shows a thorough understanding of the enumerative structure.

To move to the next level, I must …

Student Self-Assessment Checklist for Compare and Contrast Structures

Name: _____ Date: _____

Organization		
My graphic organizer fits with my compare and contrast paragraph.	Yes	No
I have a topic sentence.	Yes	No
I have a clincher sentence.	Yes	No
Word Choice		
I used compare and contrast signal words.	Yes	No
I used _____ different compare and contrast signal words. (number)		
Ideas and Content		
My topic sentence: • tells the reader what will be compared and contrasted. • catches the reader's attention.	Yes Yes	No No
I compared and contrasted using the same criteria.	Yes	No
My clincher sentence ties the ideas of my paragraph together.	Yes	No
The supporting sentences in my paragraph give details about what is being compared and contrasted.	Yes	No

The strengths in my compare and contrast paragraph include:

The areas that need improvement in my compare and contrast paragraph include:

My goal for future writing is:

Peer Feedback Checklist for Compare and Contrast Structures

Author: _____ Peer Editor: _____ Date: _____

Organization		
The graphic organizer fits with the compare and contrast paragraph.	Yes	No
There is a topic sentence.	Yes	No
There is a clincher sentence.	Yes	No
Word Choice		
Compare and contrast signal words were used.	Yes	No
_____ different compare and contrast signal words were used. (number)		
Ideas and Content		
The topic sentence: • tells the reader what will be compared and contrasted. • catches the reader's attention.	Yes Yes	No No
The same criteria was used to compare and contrast.	Yes	No
The clincher sentence ties the ideas of the paragraph together.	Yes	No
The supporting sentences in the paragraph give details about what is being compared and contrasted.	Yes	No

The strengths in the compare and contrast paragraph include:

The areas that need improvement in the compare and contrast paragraph include:

My suggested goal for this writer is:

Assessment Rubric for Compare and Contrast Structures

Name: _____ Date: _____

	Level 1	Level 2	Level 3	Level 4
Graphic Organizer	Organizer is incomplete and/or does not fit the compare and contrast structure.	Organizer is fairly complete, may have minor errors; indicates a compare and contrast structure is being used.	Organizer is complete; clearly indicates a compare and contrast structure is being used.	Organizer is complete; clearly indicates a compare and contrast structure is being used and is of original design.
Topic Sentence	Weak topic sentence, doesn't indicate that a compare and/or contrast will take place.	Topic sentence evident, a basic format is used; some indication that a compare and/or contrast will take place.	Topic sentence indicates that a compare and/or contrast will take place; captures the reader's attention.	Topic sentence clearly states that a compare and/or contrast will take place; captures the imagination of the reader.
Signal Words	Compare and contrast signal words are used improperly.	Some compare and contrast signal words used, not always used correctly.	Effective use of compare and contrast signal words.	Effective use of advanced compare and contrast signal words.
Clincher	Weak clincher sentence; no connecting of ideas.	Clincher sentence evident, basic format.	Good clincher sentence, sums up ideas in paragraph.	Strong clincher sentence, ties ideas together well.
Body Sentences	Few points link to the main idea; no supporting details describe the comparison and/or contrast.	Some points link to the main idea; a few supporting details describe the comparison and/or contrast.	All points link to the main idea; supporting details describe the comparison and/or contrast.	All points link to the main idea and have supporting details that clearly describe the comparison and/or contrast.
Understanding of Structure	Shows little understanding of the compare and contrast structure.	Shows some understanding of the compare and contrast structure.	Shows a considerable understanding of the compare and contrast structure.	Shows a thorough understanding of the compare and contrast structure; uses the same criteria to compare and contrast.

To move to the next level, I must...

Student Self-Assessment Checklist for Cause and Effect Structures

Name: _____ Date: _____

Organization		
My graphic organizer fits with my cause and effect paragraph.	Yes	No
I have a topic sentence.	Yes	No
I have a clincher sentence.	Yes	No
Word Choice		
I used cause and effect signal words.	Yes	No
I used _____ different cause and effect signal words. (number)		
Ideas and Content		
My topic sentence: • tells the reader what cause and/or effect will be discussed. • catches the reader's attention.	Yes Yes	No No
My clincher sentence ties the ideas of my paragraph together.	Yes	No
The supporting sentences in my paragraph give details about the causes and effects being discussed.	Yes	No

The strengths in my cause and effect paragraph include:

The areas that need improvement in my cause and effect paragraph include:

My goal for future writing is:

Peer Feedback Checklist for Cause and Effect Structures

Author: _____ Peer Editor: _____ Date: _____

Organization		
The graphic organizer fits with the cause and effect paragraph.	Yes	No
There is a topic sentence.	Yes	No
There is a clincher sentence.	Yes	No
Word Choice		
Cause and effect signal words were used.	Yes	No
_____ different cause and effect signal words were used. (number)		
Ideas and Content		
The topic sentence: • tells the reader what cause and/or effect will be discussed. • catches the reader's attention.	Yes Yes	No No
The clincher sentence ties the ideas of the paragraph together.	Yes	No
The supporting sentences in the paragraph give details about the causes and effects being discussed.	Yes	No

The strengths in the cause and effect paragraph include:

The areas that need improvement in the cause and effect paragraph include:

My suggested goal for this writer is:

Assessment Rubric for Cause and Effect Structures

Name: _____ Date: _____

	Level 1	Level 2	Level 3	Level 4
Graphic Organizer	Organizer is incomplete and/or does not fit the cause and effect structure.	Organizer is fairly complete, may have minor errors; indicates a cause and effect structure is being used.	Organizer is complete; clearly indicates a cause and effect structure is being used.	Organizer is complete; clearly indicates a cause and effect structure is being used and is of original design.
Topic Sentence	Weak topic sentence, doesn't indicate that a cause and/or effect will be given.	Topic sentence evident, a basic format is used; some indication that a cause and/or effect will be given.	Topic sentence indicates that a cause and/or effect will be given; captures the reader's attention.	Topic sentence clearly states that a cause and/or effect will be given; captures the imagination of the reader.
Signal Words	Cause and effect signal words are used improperly.	Some cause and effect signal words used, not always used correctly.	Effective use of cause and effect signal words.	Effective use of advanced cause and effect signal words.
Clincher	Weak clincher sentence; no connecting of ideas.	Clincher sentence evident, basic format.	Good clincher sentence, sums up ideas in paragraph.	Strong clincher sentence, ties ideas together well.
Body Sentences	Few points link to the main idea; no supporting details describe the cause and/or effect.	Some points link to the main idea; a few supporting details describe the cause and/or effect.	All points link to the main idea; supporting details describe the cause and/or effect.	All points link to the main idea and have supporting details that clearly describe the cause and/or effect.
Understanding of Structure	Shows little understanding of the cause and effect structure.	Shows some understanding of the cause and effect structure.	Shows a considerable understanding of the cause and effect structure.	Shows a thorough understanding of the cause and effect structure.

To move to the next level, I must …

Student Self-Assessment Checklist for Problem and Solution Structures

Name: _____ Date: _____

Organization		
My graphic organizer fits with my problem and solution paragraph.	Yes	No
I have a topic sentence.	Yes	No
I have a clincher sentence.	Yes	No
Word Choice		
I used problem and solution signal words.	Yes	No
I used _____ different problem and solution signal words. (number)		
Ideas and Content		
My topic sentence: • tells the reader what problem and solution will be discussed. • catches the reader's attention.	Yes Yes	No No
My clincher sentence ties the ideas of my paragraph together.	Yes	No
The supporting sentences in my paragraph give details about the problem and the possible solutions.	Yes	No

The strengths in my problem and solution paragraph include:

The areas that need improvement in my problem and solution paragraph include:

My goal for future writing is:

Peer Feedback Checklist for Problem and Solution Structures

Author: _____   Peer Editor: _____   Date: _____

Organization		
The graphic organizer fits with the problem and solution paragraph.	Yes	No
There is a topic sentence.	Yes	No
There is a clincher sentence.	Yes	No
Word Choice		
Problem and solution signal words were used.	Yes	No
_____ different problem and solution signal words were used. (number)		
Ideas and Content		
The topic sentence: • tells the reader what problem and solution will be discussed. • catches the reader's attention.	Yes Yes	No No
The clincher sentence ties the ideas of the paragraph together.	Yes	No
The supporting sentences in the paragraph give details about the problem and the possible solutions.	Yes	No

The strengths in the problem and solution paragraph include:

The areas that need improvement in the problem and solution paragraph include:

My suggested goal for this writer is:

Assessment Rubric for Problem and Solution Structures

Name: _____ Date: _____

	Level 1	Level 2	Level 3	Level 4
Graphic Organizer	Organizer is incomplete and/or does not fit the problem and solution structure.	Organizer is fairly complete, may have minor errors; indicates a problem and solution structure is being used.	Organizer is complete; clearly indicates a problem and solution structure is being used.	Organizer is complete; clearly indicates a problem and solution structure is being used and is of original design.
Topic Sentence	Weak topic sentence, doesn't indicate that a problem and solution will be given.	Topic sentence evident, a basic format is used; some indication that a problem and solution will be given.	Topic sentence indicates that a problem and solution will be given; captures the reader's attention.	Topic sentence clearly states that a problem and solution will be given; captures the imagination of the reader.
Signal Words	Problem and solution signal words are used improperly.	Some problem and solution signal words used, not always used correctly.	Effective use of problem and solution signal words.	Effective use of advanced problem and solution signal words.
Clincher	Weak clincher sentence; no connecting of ideas.	Clincher sentence evident, basic format.	Good clincher sentence, sums up ideas in paragraph.	Strong clincher sentence, ties ideas together well.
Body Sentences	Few points link to the main idea; no supporting details describe the problem and solution.	Some points link to the main idea; a few supporting details describe the problem and solution.	All points link to the main idea; supporting details describe the problem and solution.	All points link to the main idea and have supporting details that clearly describe the problem and solution.
Understanding of Structure	Shows little understanding of the problem and solution structure.	Shows some understanding of the problem and solution structure.	Shows a considerable understanding of the problem and solution structure.	Shows a thorough understanding of the problem and solution structure.

To move to the next level, I must …

Self-Assessment Checklist for Question and Answer Structures

Name: _____ Date: _____

Organization		
My graphic organizer fits the structure I used to answer the question.	Yes	No
My answer begins with a topic sentence.	Yes	No
My answer ends with a clincher sentence.	Yes	No
Word Choice		
I used appropriate signal words for the text structure I used to answer the question.	Yes	No
Ideas and Content		
The paragraph clearly answers the question and provides supporting details.	Yes	No
My question requires a detailed answer. It cannot be answered in one or two words.	Yes	No

The strengths in my question and answer paragraph include:

The areas that need improvement in my question and answer paragraph include:

My goal for future writing is:

Peer Feedback Checklist for Question and Answer Structures

Author: _____ Peer Editor: _____ Date: _____

Organization		
The graphic organizer fits the structure used to answer the question.	Yes	No
The answer begins with a topic sentence.	Yes	No
The graphic organizer fits the structure used to answer the question.	Yes	No
Word Choice		
The author used appropriate signal words for the text structure he/she used to answer the question.	Yes	No
The answer ends with a clincher sentence.	Yes	No
Ideas and Content		
The question requires a detailed answer. It cannot be answered in one or two words.	Yes	No
The paragraph clearly answers the question and provides supporting details.	Yes	No

The strengths in the question and answer paragraph include:

The areas that need improvement in the question and answer paragraph include:

My suggested goal for this writer is:

Assessment Rubric for Question and Answer Structures

Name: _____ Date: _____

	Level 1	Level 2	Level 3	Level 4
Graphic Organizer	Organizer is incomplete and/or does not fit the structure used.	Organizer is fairly complete, may have minor errors.	Organizer is complete; clearly shows understanding of structure used.	Organizer is complete; clearly shows understanding of structure used and is original in design.
Topic Sentence	Weak topic sentence, not necesarily related to the question asked.	Topic sentence evident; basic format.	Topic sentence is linked with the question; catches the reader's attention.	Topic sentence is clearly and effectively linked with the question; catches the reader's imagination.
Signal Words (when appropriate)	Question and answer signal words are used improperly.	Some signal words used; not always used correctly.	Good use of signal words appropriate to the structure.	Excellent use of signal words appropriate to the structure.
Clincher Sentence	Weak clincher sentence; no connecting of ideas	Clincher sentence evident, basic format.	Good clincher sentence; sums up ideas in paragraph.	Strong clincher sentence; ties ideas together well.
Body Sentences	Question not answered, no supporting details.	Question partially answered; a few supporting details are evident.	Question answered; good supporting details are evident.	Question clearly answered; strong supporting details are evident.
Understanding of Structure	Shows little understanding of the structure.	Shows some understanding of the structure.	Shows a considerable understanding of the question and answer structures.	Shows a thorough understanding of question and answer structures.

To move to the next level, I must ...

Student Self-Assessment Checklist for Description Report/Mini-Essay Structures

Name: _____ Date: _____

Organization		
My graphic organizer is complete and shows clear understanding of the structure(s) I have used.	Yes	No
Report/Mini-Essay		
I have a topic sentence for each paragraph.	Yes	No
I have a clincher sentence for each paragraph (report) or a clincher paragraph (mini-essay).	Yes	No
I have the same number of sections in my organizer as paragraphs in my mini-essay.	Yes	No
Word Choice		
I used _____ different signal words appropriate for structure(s) I have used. (number)		
Ideas and Content		
My topic sentence: • tells the reader the topic of the paragraph. • catches the reader's attention.	Yes Yes	No No
My clincher sentence ties the ideas of my paragraphs together.	Yes	No
The points in my paragraphs all link to the main idea, and there are supporting details.	Yes	No

The strengths in my description report/mini-essay include:

The areas that need improvement in my description report/mini-essay include:

My goal for future writing is:

Peer Feedback Checklist for Description Report/Mini-Essay Structures

Author: _____   Peer Editor: _____   Date: _____

Organization		
The graphic organizer is complete and shows clear understanding of the structure(s) used by the author.	Yes	No
Report/Mini-Essay		
There is a topic sentence for each paragraph.	Yes	No
There are clincher sentences for each paragraph (report) or a clincher paragraph (mini-essay).	Yes	No
There are the same number of sections in the organizer as paragraphs in the mini-essay.	Yes	No
Word Choice		
_____ different signal words were used (appropriate for structure(s) used). (number)		
Ideas and Content		
The topic sentence: • tells the reader the topic of the paragraph. • catches the reader's attention.	Yes Yes	No No
The clincher sentences tie the ideas of the paragraph together.	Yes	No
The points in the paragraphs all link to the main idea, and there are supporting details.	Yes	No

The strengths in the description report/mini-essay include:

The areas that need improvement in the description report/mini-essay include:

My suggested goal for this writer is:

Assessment Rubric for Description Report/Mini-Essay Structures

Name: _____ Date: _____

	Level 1	Level 2	Level 3	Level 4
Graphic Organizer	Organizer is incomplete and/or does not fit the structure.	Organizer is fairly complete, may have minor errors.	Organizer is complete; clearly shows understanding of structure.	Organizer is complete; clearly shows understanding of structure, and is original in design.
Alignment of Organizer to Paragraphs	No understandable divisions have been used.	Number of paragraphs is not equal to the number of sections in the organizer.	Number of paragraphs is equal to the number of sections in the organizer.	A topic paragraph and clincher paragraph are included in the organizer.
Text Structure Format Used	Proper use of topic and clincher sentences rarely evident.	Proper use of topic and clincher sentences evident in some of the paragraphs; signal words used if there is another structure involved.	Use of topic and clincher sentences and signal words evident in most of the paragraphs.	Use of topic and clincher sentences and signal words evident throughout the description report/mini-essay.
Body Sentences	Few points link to the main idea; there are no supporting details.	Some points link to the main idea; there are few supporting details.	All points link to the main idea; there are some supporting details.	All points link to the main idea and have supporting details.
Understanding of Description Format	Shows little understanding of description format.	Shows some understanding of description format.	Shows a considerable understanding of description format.	Shows a thorough understanding of the description format.

To move to the next level, I must …

Class Checklist for Identifying Text Structures in Reading Material

BLM 8.22

Names of Students	Sequence	Enumerative	Compare and Contrast	Cause and Effect	Problem and Solution	Question and Answer	Description

Checklist for Identifying Text Structure Criteria

Name: _____ Date: _____

	Sequence	Enumerative	Compare and Contrast	Cause and Effect	Problem and Solution	Question and Answer	Description
Is able to identify the structure when it is in its basic form in an individual paragraph.							
Is able to identify the characteristics of the structures when reading textbooks and trade books (signal words, topic sentence, clincher sentence, etc.).							
Is able to identify the structure when reading textbooks or trade books even though it is not in its basic form (bullets used instead of signal words, no clincher sentence, etc.).							

Comments

Identifying Text Structures

Name: _____ Date: _____

Name of Text	Paragraph Number	Text Structure	Proof

BIBLIOGRAPHY

Anders, G. and Beech, L. *Reading: Mapping for meaning book 3, grades 5–6* (New York, NY: Sniffen Court Books) 1990.

Berger, M. H., and Berger, G. *Why do volcanoes blow their tops? Questions and answers about volcanoes and earthquakes.* (New York, NY: Scholastic) 1999.

Berger, M. H., and Berger, G. *Do stars have points? Questions and answers about stars and planets.* (New York, NY: Scholastic) 1998.

Biancarosa, G. After third grade. *Association for Supervision and Curriculum Development* 63(2), October 2005.

Booth, D. *Even hockey players read: Boys and reading* (Markham, ON: Pembrooke Publishers) 2002.

Bourgeois, P. *The moon* (Toronto, ON: Kids Can Press) 1995.

Bruno, S. *The human body* (Milwaukee, WI: Gareth Stevens Publishing) 2002.

Chall, J. *Stages of reading development* (New York, NY: McGraw-Hill) 1983.

Chall, J., Jacobs, V., and Baldwin, L. *The reading crisis: Why poor children fall behind* (Cambridge, MA: Harvard University Press) 1990.

Charman, A. *I wonder why trees have leaves and other questions about plants.* (New York, NY: Larousse Kingfisher Chambers) 1997.

Clark, P., Arnold, P., McKay, R., and Soetaert, L. *Canada revisited 7* (Calgary, AB: Arnold Publishing) 1999.

Cooper, D. *Talk about assessment: Strategies and tools to improve learning* (Toronto, ON: Thomson Nelson) 2007, 12.

Culham, R. *6 +1 traits of writing, the complete guide grades 3 and up* (New York, NY: Scholastic Professional Books) 2003.

Diehl, J., and Plumb, D. *What's the difference? 10 animal look-alikes* (Toronto, ON: Annick Press) 2000.

Dillabough, D. Effect of instruction in expository text structure on 6th grade research skills (unpublished research paper) 1996.

Donovan, H., and Ellis, M. Paired reading—more than an evening of entertainment. *Reading Teacher* 59(2), 2005, 174–177.

Doyle, S., Bowman, J., Martin, S., and Stannard, H. *B.C. science probe 5* (Toronto, ON: Thomson Nelson) 2006.

Draper, G. A., French L., and Craig, A. *Human geography 8* (Vancouver, BC: Gage Educational) 2000.

Duke, N. K., and Kays, J. Can I say "once upon a time?" Kindergarten children developing knowledge of informational book language. *Early Childhood Research Quarterly* 13(2), 1998, 295–318.

Duke, N. K. The case for informational text: Younger students need to expand their repertoire and build literacy skills with informational text. *Educational Leadership* 61(6), March 2004, 40–44.

Dymock, S. J., and Nicholson, T. *Reading comprehension: What is it? How do you teach it?* (Wellington, NZ: New Zealand Council for Educational Research) 1999.

Dymock, S. Teaching expository text structure awareness. *The Reading Teacher* 59(2), 2005.

Englert, C. S., and Hiebert, E. Children's developing awareness of text structure in expository materials. *Journal of Educational Psychology* 76(1), 1984, 65–74.

Gibb, T., Hirsch, A. J., White, D., White, S., Wiese, J., and Ritter, B. *Science technology 7* (Toronto, ON: Nelson) 2000.

Graves, M. F., and Graves, B. B. *Scaffolding reading experiences: Designs for student success* 2nd ed. (Norwood, MA: Christopher-Gordon) 2003.

Griffin, C. C., and Tulbert, B. L. The effects of graphic organizers on students' comprehension and recall of expository text: A review of the research and implications for practice. *Reading and Writing Quarterly* 11(1), 1995, 73–89.

Hickman, P. *The kids Canadian tree book* (Toronto, ON: Kids Can Press) 1995.

Kamil, M., and Lane, D. *A classroom study of the efficacy of using information text for first grade reading instruction* (San Diego, CA: American Educational Research Association) 1997.

Kristo, J. V., and Bamford, R. A. *Nonfiction in focus: A comprehensive framework for helping students become independent readers and writers of nonfiction, K–6* (New York, NY: Scholastic) 2004.

Mathieu, W. L. *Manitoba* (Toronto, ON: Thomson Nelson) 2004.

Maxim, D. Nonfiction literature as the "text" of my intermediate classroom: That's a fact. In Bamford, R. A., and Kristo, J. V. (Eds.) *Making facts come alive: Choosing quality nonfiction literature K–8*, (Norwood, MA: Christopher-Gordon) 1998.

McCormick Calkins, L. *The art of teaching reading* (New York, NY: Addison-Wesley Educational Publishers) 2001.

Miller, K., and George, J. Expository passage organizers: Models for reading and writing. In *Journal of Reading* 35(5), 1992, 372–377. Quoted in Robb, L. *Teaching reading in social studies, science and math* (New York, NY: Scholastic) 2003, 295.

Mixon, K. Three learning styles… four steps to reach them. *Teaching Music* 11(4), February 2004, 48–52.

Moss, B. Teaching expository text structures through information trade book retelling. *The Reading Teacher* 57(8), 2004, 710–718.

Ontario Ministry of Education. *Me read--? No way! A practical guide to improving boys' literacy skills* (Toronto, ON: Ontario Ministry of Education, Queen's Printer for Ontario) 2004.

Pearson, P. D., and Duke, N. K. Comprehension instruction in the primary grades. In Block, C. C., and Pressley, M. (Eds.). *Comprehension instruction: Research-based best practices* (New York, NY: Guilford) 2002, 247–258.

Porterfield, J. *Looking at the human impact on the environment with graphic organizers: Using graphic organizers to study the living environment* (New York, NY: The Rosen Publishing Group) 2006.

Pressley, M. What should comprehension be the instruction of? In Kamil, M., Mosenthal, P. B., Pearson, P. D., and Barr, R. (Eds.) *Handbook of reading research*, Vol. 111 (New York, NY: Longman) 1984–1991, 545–561.

Ritter, B., et al. *Nelson Science & Technology 7* (Toronto, ON: Thomson Nelson) 2000.

Romanek, T. *Achoo, the most interesting book you'll ever read about germs* (Toronto, ON: Kids Can Press) 2003.

Shields, P. N., and Ramsay, D. *Our world, grade 3* (Toronto, ON: Thomson Nelson) 2005.

Shields, P. N., and Ramsay, D. *World communities* (Toronto, ON: Thomson Nelson) 2005.

Sorestad, G., McClymont, C., and Graves, C. *Anthology three* (Toronto, ON: Thomson Nelson) 1990.

Spandel, V. *Creating writers through 6 trait writing assessment and instruction* 4th ed. (Boston, MA: Pearson, Allyn & Bacon) 2004.

Spence, C. *Creating a literacy environment for boys: Ideas for teachers, administrators, and parents* (Toronto, ON: Thomson Nelson) 2006.

Sweet, A. P., and Snow, C. E., (Eds.). *Rethinking reading comprehension* (New York, NY: Guilford Press) 2003.

Teele, S. Overcoming barricades to reading: A multiple intelligences approach. (Thousand Oaks, CA: Corwin Press) 2004, 110.

Trehearne, M. P. *Comprehensive literacy resource for grades 3–6 teachers* (Toronto, ON: Thomson Nelson) 2006.

West, P. Those damned boys again! How to get boys achieving. Available at: www.icponline.org/feature_articles/f11_01.htm. Accessed December 2000.

Wilson, G. *Using the national healthy school standard to raise boys' achievement* (London, UK: Department for Education and Skills) 2003.

Yopp, R. H., Yopp, H. K. Sharing informational text with young children. *The Reading Teacher*, 53(5), 2000.

INDEX